USING CONFLICT
in
ORGANIZATIONS

Edited by
Carsten K.W. De Dreu & Evert Van de Vliert

SAGE Publications
London • Thousand Oaks • New Delhi

SAGE Publications Ltd
6 Bonhill Street
London EC2A 4PU

SAGE Publications Inc
2455 Teller Road
Thousand Oaks, California 91320

SAGE Publications India Pvt Ltd
32, M-Block Market
Greater Kailash – I
New Delhi 110 048

British Library Cataloguing in Publication data

A catalogue record for this book is
available from the British Library

   ISBN 0 7619 5090 7
   ISBN 0 7619 5091 5 (pbk)

Library of Congress catalog card number 97–065722

Typeset by M Rules
Printed in Great Britain by The Cromwell Press Ltd,
Broughton Gifford, Melksham, Wiltshire

Contents

Acknowledgements

The fourteen chapters in this book demonstrate the positive value of conflict for groups and organizations. Although the majority of the chapters in this volume are new, three chapters were published previously. We thank Afzal Rahim, editor of *International Journal of Conflict Management*, for allowing us to reprint the 1994 journal articles by Bornstein and Erev, and by Putnam. We also thank the editorial board of *Journal of Social Issues* for allowing us to reprint the 1994 Donnellon and Kolb article.

A number of people provided critical help at various stages of this project. An excellent team of reviewers was made up of: Andre Bussing, Richard Cosier, Paul 't Hart, Boris Kabanoff, Paul Kirkbride, Ad van Knippenberg, Marceline Kroon, Chris McCusker, Linda Putnam, Stephen Robbins, Kjell Rognes, Dean Tjosvold, Charles Vlek, Nanne de Vries, Arjaan Wit and Vincent Yzerbyt. We also express our thanks to Judith Sauvé at the University of Amsterdam, and to Sandra Peper and Fop Coolsma at the University of Groningen for their administrative support. Hans Lock at Sage has been a wonderful editor to work with, and we thank him for his patience, trust and constructive help throughout.

Notes on contributors

Allen C. Amason is an assistant professor of management at the University of Georgia. He holds a PhD from the University of South Carolina. His research focuses on top management team interaction and strategic decision making and has been published in such journals as the *Academy of Management Journal*, the *Journal of Management* and *Organizational Dynamics*.

Robert A. Baron is professor of management and professor of psychology at Rensselaer Polytechnic Institute. He received his PhD from the University of Iowa in 1968. Professor Baron has held faculty appointments at Purdue University, the University of Minnesota, the University of Texas, the University of South Carolina and Princeton University. In 1982 he was a visiting fellow at Oxford University. From 1979 to 1981 he served as a program director at the National Science Foundation (Washington, DC). He has been a fellow of the American Psychological Association since 1978. He is the author or co-author of thirty books, including *Behavior in organizations* (now in its 6th edn), *Social psychology* (8th edn), *Human aggression* (2nd edn) and *Understanding human relations* (3rd edn). Professor Baron's research and consulting activities focus primarily on the following topics: (1) impact of the physical environment (e.g. lighting, air quality, temperature) on productivity, (2) organizational conflict and (3) workplace aggression and violence.

Gary Bornstein received his PhD in psychology from the University of North Carolina at Chapel Hill in 1983. He is now the director of the social psychology programme at the Hebrew University of Jerusalem. He is interested in behavioural game theory, particularly as it applies to social dilemmas and intergroup conflicts. His research has been published in such journals as *Psychological Review, Journal of Experimental Social Psychology, Journal of Personality and Social Psychology* and *Journal of Conflict Resolution*.

Peter J. Carnevale is a professor of psychology at the University of Illinois at Urbana-Champaign. He is co-author of *Negotiation in social conflict* (1993, Brooks/Cole) and *International negotiation: the structure and process of resolving international conflicts* (1998, Lynne Rienner). He was the recipient of the Erik H. Erikson Early Career Award from the International Society of Political Psychology as well as the Edwin E. Ghiselli Award for Research Design from the Society for Industrial and Organizational Psychology. He is president of the International Association for Conflict Management and chair of the Conflict Management Division of the Academy of Management.

Carsten K. W. De Dreu is associate professor of organizational psychology at the University of Amsterdam. His research focuses on social judgment and information processing in negotiation and conflict management, and on minority influence on attitude change and thought processes. His research has been published in such journals as *Journal of Conflict Resolution, Journal of Experimental Social Psychology, Journal of Personality and Social Psychology* and *Organizational Behavior and Human Decision Processes.*

Nanne K. De Vries is associate professor of social psychology at the University of Amsterdam. He received his PhD from the University of Groningen and has worked for the Department of Health Education at the University of Maastricht and for the Department of Social Psychology at the University of Groningen. His research focuses on attitudes and attitude change, with special emphases on minority influence, the role of affect and intergroup attitudes. His research has been published in such journals as *British Journal of Social Psychology, Organizational Behavior and Human Decision Processes, Journal of Behavioral Decision Making* and *European Review of Social Psychology.*

Anne Donnellon is associate professor in the management division of Babson College in Wellesley, MA. Her research focuses on the process and performance of decision making groups. Donnellon is author of *Team talk: the power of language in team dynamics* (1996, Harvard Business Press), and she has produced a CD-ROM, also with Harvard Business Press, called *teams that work.* Her research has been published in such journals as *Administrative Science Quarterly, Journal of Management, Organizational Studies* and *Organizational Dynamics.* Anne Donnellon received her PhD from Pennsylvania State University, her MA from Columbia University and her BA from the University of Cincinnati.

Ido Erev received his PhD in psychology from the University of North Carolina at Chapel Hill in 1990. He is now at the faculty of Industrial Engineering and Management at the Technion–Israel Institute of Technology. His main research interest is the two-sided relation between human cognitive abilities and the implications of decision theory. His research has been published in such journals as *Psychological Review, Journal of Conflict Resolution, Journal of Experimental Social Psychology* and *Organizational Behavior and Human Decision Processes.*

Martin C. Euwema is an assistant professor of organizational psychology at the University of Utrecht, The Netherlands. He received his PhD at the Free University of Amsterdam. His research and consulting interests are in the areas of conflict management and organization development, especially team building, network relations and strategy implementation. Martin Euwema served as a board member of the International Association for Conflict Management between 1994 and 1996.

Ronald J. Fisher is professor of psychology and founding coordinator of the Applied Social Psychology Graduate Program at the University of Saskatchewan, Saskatoon, Canada. He holds a BA and an MA in psychology from the University of Saskatchewan and received his PhD in social psychology from the University of Michigan in 1972. His writings include *Social psychology: an applied approach* (1982, St Martin's Press) and *The social psychology of intergroup and international conflict resolution* (1990, Springer-Verlag). His primary interests are in the study of protracted social conflict and in developing the scholar-practitioner field of interactive conflict resolution.

Onne Janssen is an assistant professor of organizational psychology at the University of Groningen, The Netherlands. He holds a PhD from the University of Groningen. His research interests include social conflict, decision making and innovative behaviour in organizations. Some of his recent research has appeared in the *International Journal of Conflict Management*.

Karen E. Jehn is an assistant professor of management at the Wharton School of the University of Pennsylvania. Her current research is in the areas of intragroup and intergroup conflict, strategic decision making, deception in organizations, and multinational organizational teams in US–foreign joint business ventures. Her research has been published in such journals as *Academy of Management Journal, International Journal of Conflict Management* and *Administrative Science Quarterly*.

Deborah M. Kolb is professor of management at Simmons College Graduate School of Management and Executive Director of the Program on Negotiation at Harvard Law School. She is the author of *Mediators* (1983, MIT Press), co-editor of *Hidden conflict in organizations* (1992, Sage) and editor of *Making talk work: Profiles of mediators at work* (1995, Jossey-Bass). Professor Kolb is currently carrying out field research on gender issues in negotiations, dispute resolution and diversity, and on work/family practices and their gender equity in corporations. Deborah Kolb received an MBA from the University of Colorado and her PhD from MIT's Sloan School of Management.

Aukje Nauta is a post doctoral researcher at the School of Management at the University of Groningen, The Netherlands. She has just finished her doctoral dissertation on interpersonal conflict in organizations. Some of her research has been published in the *Journal of Applied Social Psychology*.

Anthony R. Pratkanis is professor of psychology at the University of California, Santa Cruz. He is co-author of *Age of Propaganda* and co-editor of *Attitude and Function* and of *Social Psychology* (Vols 1–3). His research interests include social influence, persuasion and attitudes.

Tahira M. Probst is a graduate student at the University of Illinois at Urbana-Champaign. She received her MA in industrial/organizational psychology from the University of Illinois in 1995 and is currently pursuing her PhD in I-O psychology. Her research interests include social value orientation, intergroup competition and cross-cultural negotiation.

Linda L. Putnam (PhD, University of Minnesota) is professor and head of the Department of Speech Communication at Texas A&M University. Her current research interests include negotiation and organizational conflict and language analysis in organizations. She has published over 70 articles and book chapters in management and communication journals and books. She is the co-editor of *The new handbook of organizational communication* (in press); *Communication and negotiation* (1992), *The handbook of organizational communication* (1987) and *Communication and organization: an interpretative approach* (1983). Linda Putnam is the 1993 recipient of the Charles H. Woolbert Award for a seminal article in the communication field and is a fellow of the International Communication Association.

David M. Schweiger is a professor of management at the University of South Carolina and visiting professor of strategic management at Groupe ESC, Lyon, France. He holds a DBA from the University of Maryland. His research, teaching and consulting interests include top management teams, mergers and acquisitions, and strategy implementation. Dr Schweiger has published extensively in and is on the editorial boards of a number of academic and practitioner journals.

Dean Tjosvold is professor of organizational behavior at Simon Fraser University (British Columbia) and at Lingham College (Hong Kong). After graduating from Princeton University he earned his master's degree in history and his PhD in the social psychology of organizations at the University of Minnesota, both in 1972. He has taught at the Pennsylvania State University, and was a visiting professor at the University of Groningen, The Netherlands, 1991–1992, and at Hong Kong University of Science and Technology, 1994–1995. In 1992, Simon Fraser University awarded him a university professorship for research contributions. Dean Tjosvold is the author of over 100 articles on managing conflict, cooperation and competition, decision making, and other management issues. His books include *The conflict-positive organization* (1991), *Learning to manage conflict: Getting people to work together productively* (1993) and *Psychology for leaders: Using motivation, power and conflict to manage more effectively* (1996).

Marlene E. Turner is a professor of organization and management at San José State University. Her research interests include group and organizational responses to threat and recipient reactions to affirmative action. She is co-editor of 'Social Psychological Perspectives on Affirmative Action', a special issue of *Basic and Applied Social Psychology*, and of a forthcoming special issue of *Organizational Behavior and Human Decision Processes* on groupthink.

Evert Van de Vliert is professor of organizational and applied social psychology at the University of Groningen, The Netherlands. He worked for several years as an organizational consultant before he received his PhD from the Free University of Amsterdam. Professor Van de Vliert is co-editor (with Vernon Allen) of *Role transitions: Explorations and explanations* (1984, Plenum Press) and author of the forthcoming monograph *Complex interpersonal conflict behaviour: Theoretical Frontiers* (Taylor & Francis). He is past president of the International Association for Conflict Management, and is interested in all aspects of social conflict, negotiation and mediation. His research has appeared in such journals as *Journal of Personality and Social Psychology, Journal of Applied Psychology* and *Academy of Management Journal.*

Introduction: Using Conflict in Organizations

Carsten K. W. De Dreu and Evert Van de Vliert

Is conflict helpful? To whom? Why would the stimulation of conflict be beneficial to group performance? How do organizations profit from conflict, and what should we do to make conflict productive? What kind of conflict is helpful, and what kind is to be avoided? What are the underlying processes and principles that make conflict fruitful? This book gives answers to these questions. It brings together fourteen chapters on the beneficial effects of conflict in groups and organizations.

Conflict is studied in the political sciences, in business administration, in economics, in sociology and in psychology. Within each of these disciplines we often witness a tendency to treat conflict as a pathological state and to seek its causes and treatment; others take conflict for granted and study the behaviour and behavioural consequences associated with it (Blake & Mouton, 1964; Schelling, 1960). With some exceptions (e.g. Robbins, 1974; Tjosvold, 1991), scholars and practitioners view conflict as something negative, an enemy to effective group functioning and organizational performance. For example, organizational psychologist Edgar Schein notes that 'they [groups] are likely to become competitive with one another and seek to undermine their rivals' activities, thereby becoming a liability to the organization as a whole' (1988, p. 172).

The chapters in this book, each in its distinct way, take up the challenge to demonstrate the flip side of this negative picture. Using a psychological, organizational behaviour, communications or game-theoretical perspective, the authors show when, how and why conflict in groups and organizations becomes productive, and thus enhances rather than decreases performance. Their descriptions, empirical foundations and explanations may shift the predominant focus from conflict prevention and resolution to conflict elicitation and control. There is still a long way to go before our leaders and managers wake up to the fact that they need conflict as well as harmony.

Conflict occurs when an individual or group feels negatively affected by another individual or group (Thomas, 1992; Wall & Callister, 1995), for example because of a perceived divergence of interests (Rubin, Pruitt & Kim, 1994), or because of another's incompatible behaviour (Deutsch, 1973). In groups and organizations, conflict may be related to power differentials, to competition over scarce resources, to tendencies to differentiate rather than converge, to negative interdependence between work units, to ambiguity over

responsibility or jurisdiction, or to a denial of one's self-image or characteristic identifications including values and sensitivities (see Deutsch, 1973;
Greenberg & Baron, 1993).

Organizational conflict may occur between two individuals, within small
groups and work teams, or between groups and (temporary) coalitions.
Accordingly, the chapters in this book cover a variety of small and larger conflicts and disputes that occur in groups and organizations. Some chapters
examine conflict at a micro level, between two individuals sharing an office,
or between two small groups competing for scarce resources (e.g. Tjosvold,
Chapter 2; Bornstein & Erev, Chapter 8; Carnevale & Probst, Chapter 9).
Others treat the causes and management of conflict between existing groups
such as in diversity disputes (Donnellon & Kolb, Chapter 11), labour–management disputes and teacher–board negotiations (Putnam, Chapter 10;
Fisher, Chapter 13). In addition, several chapters closely study conflict in
teams. For example, Turner and Pratkanis (Chapter 4) and Amason and
Schweiger (Chapter 7) look at decision making teams, while Jehn (Chapter 6)
studies conflict in production teams.

The book is divided into four parts that approach the issue of conflict and
performance in different ways. Part I deals with the relationship between conflict management and performance, and treats the conditions under which
conflict management may help groups and organizations to be more productive rather than hinder them in their goals. Part II examines conflict within
teams, and searches for the processes and principles that make conflict helpful
in decision making teams and production groups. Part III deals with between-
group conflict and competition. It addresses the complex interplay between
intergroup competition and within-group conflict and cooperation.
Specifically, it provides a reappraisal of the basic message that competition
between groups stimulates cooperation within teams, and offers new insights
into the conditions that foster and hinder this process. Part IV gives a first out-
line of how to design interventions based on the knowledge given in the first
three parts of the book. It contains theory-based advice for those who are in
conflict, and those who assist in conflict resolution, with the aim of making
conflict beneficial to groups and organizations.

Part I: conflict management and performance

Many scholars and practitioners do not recognize that conflict is inherent to
social interaction and common to organizational life (e.g. Katz & Kahn,
1978; March & Simon, 1958). They search for optimal ways of managing
conflict to prevent its destructive effects on interpersonal perceptions, the
social climate within teams, and the interaction between groups. However,
we also need to search for conflict management strategies that help conflict
to be productive. The first three chapters in this book attempt to do exactly
that.

In Chapter 1, De Dreu reviews various negative consequences of avoiding and suppressing conflict, and several positive effects of stimulating and promoting conflict. Departing from the accepted argument that for conflict to be productive, conflict management should be constructive and take the form of problem solving rather than contending, he shows how conflict management is contingent upon the type of conflict issue. Cognitive conflict involving disputes over scarce resources, over procedures or policies or over opinions enhance problem solving and reduce contending behaviours, whereas affective conflict involving one's personal or group identity, norms and values do the reverse. De Dreu concludes that constructive conflict management is a positive function of cognitive conflict, and a negative function of affective conflict.

Chapters 2 and 3 explicitly link the constructive management of conflict to performance. Tjosvold (Chapter 2) reviews an impressive body of research showing that when people view their goals to be positively rather than negatively linked, they are much more likely to trust each other, to discuss differences of opinion in an open-minded fashion, and to integrate interests and aspirations into settlements that yield high mutual satisfaction. Interestingly Tjosvold's research programme begins to show the value of this so-called 'constructive controversy' not only for American industry, but also for organizational conflict in Asian countries with their high level of collectivism, and within Northern European culture such as The Netherlands with its strong emphasis on egalitarian values. In Chapter 3, Van de Vliert, Nauta, Euwema and Janssen discuss some of their recent research findings which show that constructive conflict management is not always and without exception based on being pleasant, and being orientated towards the other party. A series of studies involving senior nurses, industrial managers, police officers and consultants showed that problem solving behaviours combined with contending behaviours proved to be more effective and performance-enhancing than problem solving behaviours alone. Specifically, problem solving preceded by 'forcing' produced better substantive and relational outcomes than other behavioural configurations. For conflict to be productive, constructive controversy involving a measure of firm, contentious behaviour appears to be fundamental.

Part II: within-group conflict and performance

People belong to groups that are part of larger social systems. In particular, organizations break down into many different groups and other subunits, each with its own tasks, challenges and social dynamics. We witness an increasing tendency in organizations to decentralize and to organize work in small, semi-autonomous work units. This process away from individual work and towards team-work implies an enhanced need for team coordination, increases group member interdependence and the possibility of influencing one another, and thus increases the likelihood of conflict. When and how is conflict in teams and other small groups beneficial to their performance?

Turner and Pratkanis (Chapter 4) take us back to the early work by Irving

Janis on groupthink – the extreme concurrence seeking within decision making groups. They review several instances in which concurrence seeking and the suppression of conflict led to low quality decisions with sometimes extremely negative consequences. Although previous work identified a series of remedies against groupthink such as implementing devil's advocacy, Turner and Pratkanis offer good arguments as to why these remedies may fail. As an alternative, they advance a model which argues that groupthink in part derives from the desire of individual group members to be part of a group with a positive social identity. Turner and Pratkanis argue that enhancing affective conflict reinforces the need for a positive social identity, and that only cognitive conflict counters groupthink.

In Chapter 5, De Dreu and De Vries take a closer look at the consequences of minority dissent for individual and group performance. Their review of the literature shows that minority dissent increases individual creativity and innovation, improves the decision quality in teams, and may enhance an organization's public image. Because minority arguments are often neglected and quickly rejected as invalid and inconceivable, De Dreu and De Vries argue that for a minority to be effective in influencing majority members, they should pursue a consistent and fairly rigid strategy, and provide extremely high quality arguments. But even then, the minority's impact will often only be on related levels and will influence public opinions only after a certain amount of time. Some strategies that speed up and facilitate the influence of minority dissent are discussed.

Chapter 6 (Jehn) and Chapter 7 (Amason & Schweiger) focus on the relationship between conflict issue – cognitive or affective – and performance in task groups, and on decision quality in top management teams. Each in its own way, these chapters provide compelling evidence for the proposition that conflict in groups is beneficial when the group engages in cognitive conflict while staying away from affective issues. Jehn analyses the antecedents of cognitive and affective conflict in terms of team composition. She argues that the extent to which group members' values correspond (value consensus) and match the ideal values (value fit) reduces the extent to which cognitive and affective conflict in teams emerges. While affective conflict negatively impacts team performance, cognitive conflict tends to enhance productivity. Interestingly, this effect appears to be especially true when teams perform nonroutine tasks; when the tasks become routine, conflict is shown to be bad irrespective of its specific nature.

Amason and Schweiger direct our attention to the fact that although cognitive conflict enhances performance while affective conflict reduces it, these two types of conflict are difficult to separate. As a consequence, managers should cultivate a team environment that is open to and tolerant of diverse and dissenting viewpoints, whereby a cooperative norm prevents those disagreements from being misinterpreted as personal attacks or political manoeuvring. In fact, the work on positive goal interdependence by Tjosvold in Chapter 2 provides a basic framework for accomplishing exactly this.

Part III: between-group conflict and competition

Organizational groups have incentives to cooperate in order to facilitate organizational prosperity, as well as incentives to compete with each other in order to obtain good outcomes for the ingroup. Sometimes, for example between concern divisions, intergroup competition is even built in to enhance within-group productivity and cooperation. But is this an effective strategy? And if so, why? And what are the precise conditions that make intergroup competition productive?

Chapter 8 by Bornstein and Erev draws attention to the fact that scholars and practitioners often treat groups that are in competition as unitary players, thus neglecting the within-group interdependencies that exist. In fact, as Bornstein and Erev convincingly argue, individuals within groups have both incentives to compete with the outgroup in order to 'win the game', as well as incentives to compete with members of the ingroup about who will take up the battle with the outgroup. A series of laboratory as well as field experiments showed that intergroup competition enhances within-group cooperation because it motivates employees to work harder, and to coordinate better.

Carnevale and Probst (Chapter 9) continue the work by Bornstein and Erev by examining other aspects of within-group performance during intergroup competition. In their research, Carnevale and Probst pre-tested subjects to classify them as competitive, individualistic or cooperative. These individuals then performed tasks either in the presence of or in the absence of intergroup competition. Results showed that competitive people – those who are the least likely to engage in constructive controversy – were the most creative and innovative in their proposals to their fellow ingroup members when intergroup competition was present. They were the least creative when intergroup competition was absent. Carnevale and Probst showed that intergroup competition enhances within-group coordination and creativity, especially when individual group members are inclined towards competition rather than cooperation.

Putnam (Chapter 10) uncovers the benefits of conflict through examining the functions, intergroup relationships and symbolic significance of negotiation. Drawing from survey and ethnographic data in two teacher–school board negotiations, the study reveals that bargaining serves a communication function of signalling potential problems, clarifying misunderstandings and exchanging information. These functions surface indirectly through interaction patterns and subtle cues implicit in arguments, proposal exchanges and examples. The productive nature of conflict in negotiation also hinges on developing ties among and between teams, constituents and publics.

Donnellon and Kolb (Chapter 11) address disputes that arise out of, or are complicated by, social diversity. As new social groups enter the workforce and move up in organizations, conflicts rooted in class, gender, race and ethnicity have become more prominent. Existing discourses of organizational conflict management mask such conflicts, dealing with them in ways that are not constructive for all the parties concerned. An ideology of meritocracy in organizations that grants privilege according to individual accounts of success, an absence of collective identity by groups and differential access to power and influence keep disputes that arise from diversity from being heard properly. Some approaches are suggested to help organizations deal constructively – for all involved – with conflicts that have their bases in social diversity.

Part IV: designing interventions: towards applications

The final part of the book provides a first step towards an application of the insights offered in the first three sections. Baron (Chapter 12) offers an analysis of the sociocognitive errors, including biased attributions, stereotypes, costs of thinking too much, and affect- and emotion-based cognitive deficits. He provides intelligent remedies that may help individuals in conflict to prevent conflict escalation, to avoid affective conflict, and to foster cognitive conflict. Then in Chapter 13, based on the relevant literature as well as on a wealth of his own intervention experience, Fisher provides an in-depth discussion of what third parties should do and what they should avoid doing when mediating a dispute. His analysis demonstrates the importance of enhancing controversy when there is too little conflict in a given situation, and of 'differentiation before integration'. His chapter offers a rich source of strategies and tactics for doing so.

Chapter 14 by Van de Vliert gives a concluding overview of the book, with a special emphasis on the possibilities for intervention. According to his analysis, conflict stimulation may have direct, indirect and conditional effects on performance. Van de Vliert offers four entry points for intervention, namely manipulating antecedent conditions, extending conflict issues, stimulating escalative behaviours and developing escalative consequences. In line with what many chapters demonstrate, his concluding advice is that stimulating escalative behaviours and developing escalative consequences may be better suited to piecemeal escalation than manipulating antecedent conditions and extending conflict issues.

References

Blake, R. and Mouton, J.S. (1964). *The managerial grid*. Houston, TX: Gulf.

Deutsch, M. (1973). *The resolution of conflict: Constructive and destructive processes*. New Haven: Yale University Press.

Greenberg, J. and Baron, R.A. (1993). *Behavior in organizations*. Boston: Allyn & Bacon.

Katz, D. and Kahn, R.L. (1978). *The social psychology of organizations*. New York: Wiley.

March, J. and Simon, H. (1958). *Organizations*. New York: Wiley.

Robbins, S.P. (1974). *Managing organizational conflict: a nontraditional approach*. Englewood Cliffs, NJ: Prentice-Hall.

Rubin, J.Z., Pruitt, D.G. and Kim, S.H. (1994). *Social conflict: Escalation, stalemate, and settlement*. New York: McGraw-Hill.

Schein, E.H. (1988). *Organizational psychology*. Englewood Cliffs, NJ: Prentice-Hall.

Schelling, T.C. (1960). *The strategy of conflict*. Cambridge, MA: Harvard University Press.

Thomas, K.W. (1992). Conflict and negotiation processes in organizations, in M.D. Dunnette and L.M. Hough (eds), *Handbook of industrial and organizational psychology* (2nd edn). Palo Alto, CA: Consulting Psychologists Press, pp. 651–717.

Tjosvold, D. (1991). *The conflict-positive organization*. Houston: Addison-Wesley.

Wall, J. and Callister, R. (1995). Conflict and its management. *Journal of Management, 21*, 515–58.

PART I

CONFLICT MANAGEMENT AND PERFORMANCE

1

Productive Conflict: The Importance of Conflict Management and Conflict Issue

Carsten K. W. De Dreu

Conflict is the process that begins when an individual or group feels nega-tively affected by another person or group (Thomas, 1992; Wall & Callister, 1995). It occurs in interpersonal encounters between two colleagues, in deci-sion making teams, between work groups, and in board meetings. Conflict involves stress and anxiety, it often produces negative interpersonal attitudes and perceptions, it causes the social climate within groups to deteriorate, and it sometimes causes physical injury. A good example is the conflict that emerged in a Dutch hospital. Due to ongoing tensions between the head of operations and the nursing staff, non-emergency surgery for fifty patients had to be postponed in one week. Or consider the large-scale conflict between union and management at the Canadian business unit of Paccar, a leading US trucking company. After eight months of non-stop strikes for better retire-ment arrangements, Paccar decided to shut down the entire factory, and to fire all employees.

Most people dislike conflict because of its negative consequences. Their natural reaction is to avoid conflict and get it over with as soon as possible. Yet avoiding and suppressing conflict is sometimes a mistake and not always in the best interests of the individuals and groups concerned. In fact, growing evidence suggests that conflict may be beneficial to performance in groups and organizations, and that avoiding and suppressing conflict reduces indi-vidual creativity, decision quality in teams, product development, and communication between work groups. Moreover, a case can be made that stimulating conflict sometimes enhances individual, group or organizational performance. Too much emphasis on the negative consequences may detract attention from the beneficial effects that conflict may have.

In this chapter I will first of all review some research findings to demon-strate the beneficial effects of conflict. Negative consequences of avoiding and suppressing conflict and positive effects of stimulating conflict will be highlighted. I will discuss conflict management strategies that help or hinder the productivity of conflict, and I will then take a closer look at the role of conflict issue in this process. The final section will conclude with some questions for further research.

Positive effects of conflict on performance

Performance may be operationalized in many different ways, such as productivity relative to one's most effective competitor, a supervisor's evaluation of his or her employees' commitment, the quality of group decisions, or the creativity in product development and individual thought processes (e.g. Pritchard, 1992). In case of social conflict, the issue of performance is complicated by the fact that multiple parties with sometimes opposite goals are involved, and that enhanced performance by one party may hinder the opposing party's goal achievement (Van de Vliert & De Dreu, 1994). We therefore need to consider effects of conflict on performance at the individual level (e.g. individual creativity, independent attitudes), at the group level (e.g. joint outcomes from negotiation, intragroup cooperation, decision quality), and at the organizational level (e.g. product development, employee commitment). Note that a conflict-related decrease in performance at one level may be accompanied by a smaller, an equal or an even larger increase in performance at another.

Thomas (1992) argued that the time horizon of short- versus longer-term goal achievement is a crucial factor for really understanding the benefits of social conflict. Conflict may increase or decrease the likelihood of short-term achievement of a shared goal such as making profit. In the longer run, the positive or negative effects may persist, become stronger, or disappear. For example, the conflict between the head of operations and the nursing staff in the Dutch hospital may, in the long run, result in better working conditions, participative decision making, and probably improved health care. The ongoing strike at Paccar may have resulted in an increase in managerial efficiency to cope with the slowed-down production process, and enhanced union commitment among employees, but in the long run this led to exceedingly negative outcomes for all – the shutdown of the entire factory. The point is that conflict may have positive effects on performance in the short run, in the long run, or both.

To further explore the value of conflict for performance, two complementary perspectives may be adopted. The first one is probably well known and assesses what we lose by (too much) suppressing and avoiding conflict (e.g. Rubin, Pruitt & Kim, 1994). Another, more provocative perspective is to assess what we gain by stimulating conflict and by promoting overt conflict management (Brown, 1983; Robbins, 1974).

Some negative consequences of suppressing conflict

Principal parties as well as third parties such as managers and mediators often suppress conflict. Kolb and Bartunek (1992) collected a variety of instances in which organizational members avoid dealing with their irritations and annoyances by means of overt interaction. Conflict parties often deny the existence of an issue, or reduce its importance in order to avoid dealing with it (Brown, 1983). In the realm of group decision making, we often witness a tendency in leaders to suppress conflict with and among subordinates through strong demands for compliance. And mediators sometimes feel an inclination to reduce active confrontation by both disputants and to induce a positive social climate (see Fisher, 1992). The tendency to suppress conflict. may be rooted in, for example, a lack of self-efficacy, fear of retaliation, an urge to reach decisions and to be productive, or a desire to maintain face.

Suppressing conflict by group leaders and fellow group members may lead to 'groupthink' – the extreme concurrence seeking by decision making groups (Janis, 1989). As many cases illustrate, suppressing conflict with concomitant groupthink may have disastrous consequences (Turner & Pratkanis, 1994; Turner, Pratkanis, Probasco & Leve, 1992). Decision making teams at NASA, for example, were so self-confident and concerned with their public image that they suppressed any dispute or conflicting ideas to maintain consensus. The disaster with the *Challenger* space shuttle illustrates where this one-sided focus on reaching consensus may lead (see Turner & Pratkanis, Chapter 4 in this book).

Managers often seek a homogeneous workforce and suppress minority dissent. Research demonstrated that doing so may reduce creativity and innovation, and may break down individuality and independence (De Dreu & De Vries, 1993; Nemeth & Staw, 1989). Cohen and Staw (1995) demonstrate the value of dissent. Their case analysis of fact checkers in the publishing industry shows that this institutionalized form of dissent reduces the number of libel suits, and may increase the public image of the publishing company (see also De Dreu & De Vries, this book, Chapter 5).

Research on the effectiveness of various conflict management styles revealed that avoidance has a robust negative impact on interpersonal relations and conflict resolution, sometimes even exceeding the negative impact of contending behaviours (e.g. Van de Vliert, Euwema & Huismans, 1995). Mounting evidence also suggests that suppressing conflict compared to more active confrontation leads to enhanced escalation of the conflict in the longer run (Hocker & Wilmot, 1991). One reason is that avoidance leaves the conflict issue intact, so that it necessarily returns to the stage sooner or later. Another reason derives from theories of mental control that propose that avoiding and suppressing a particular thought may lead to increased presence of this and related thoughts when suppression is alleviated. In the domain of stereotyping, for example, research showed that when subjects were asked to write an essay about soccer hooligans without using their prejudices and stereotypes regarding these people, they later reacted in a much more stereotypic fashion than did control subjects (Macrae, Milne & Bodenhausen, 1994). Avoiding conflict and suppressing conflict-related thoughts may lead to more conflictful behaviours and escalation of the dispute after time has passed.

Some positive consequences of stimulating conflict

People often hesitate to actively stimulate conflict because they fear uncontrollable consequences, because it goes against a more general norm of behaving peacefully, and because they lack the skills required to stimulate social conflict in a controllable way. Still, the fact that conflict may have beneficial consequences is sometimes recognized and built into organizational structures. For example, the political and judicial system within many societies has built-in opposition intended to guarantee high quality decision making and fair trial.

Conflict may be stimulated by creating or expanding conflict issues, and by engaging oneself or another conflict party in more contentious conflict behaviour (Van de Vliert & De Dreu, 1994). For example, the awareness of disagreement and affective tension may be increased by a principal party through strategic conflict behaviour, or by a third party through conflict intervention. Negotiators sometimes deliberately mobilize their constituents to sharpen the issues and to publicly convey their frustrations (Friedman, 1994). Likewise, mediators sometimes knowingly expand the conflict issues by giving up impartiality and by siding with the weaker party to counterbalance ineffective power differences (Ippolito & Pruitt, 1990). One may draw attention to differences in opinion one's opponent seems unaware of, one may exploit another's tendency to make hostile attributions (see Baron, Chapter 12, this book), or one may increase the opposing party's concession aversion by communicating a loss rather than gain perspective on the dispute (De Dreu, Carnevale, Emans & Van de Vliert, 1994).

There is increasing evidence that stimulating conflict enhances group functioning and organizational performance. Putnam (1994; Chapter 10, this book) analyses teacher–board negotiations and concludes that active confrontation through negotiation promotes intergroup communication, increases mutual understanding and results in a greater acceptance of agreements and decisions than more tacit coordination. Walton, Cutcher-Gershenfeld and McKersie (1994, pp. 72–3) report both the negative and the positive consequences of union–management negotiations in the auto-supply, the pulp and paper, and the railroad industry. Inspection of their data reveals that within the pulp and paper industry 20% of the negotiations resulted in negative consequences only, such as costly strikes, while 20% of the negotiations had primarily positive consequences such as improved performance. For the auto-supply, and the railroad industries, these percentages were 30 and 60, and 25 and 50, respectively. Apparently, active confrontation between union and management has positive consequences for employee performance. Bornstein and Erev (1994; Chapter 8, this book) demonstrate that explicit competition between groups may enhance intragroup cooperation and reduces free-riding. Carnevale and Probst (Chapter 9, this book) show that competitive people become exceedingly creative and flexible with their ingroup members during intergroup competition.

Worchel, Coutant-Sassic and Wong (1993) suggest that intragroup conflict and between-group competition play a prominent role at various stages of group life. They argue that conflict plays a catalyst role in group development and pushes groups from one stage into another. First, conflict is often invited with relevant 'outgroups' which fosters a sense of group identity. Once identity is established, groups turn their attention to the issue of productivity and conflict re-enters the field when success is attributed to own personal characteristics and failure is attributed to fellow group members' faults and shortcomings. In this second stage, conflict thus catalyzes decay and pushes the group towards segregation and the formation of new (sub)groups. Worchel et al. (1993) argue that conflict is responsible for destroying the integrity of the group, but also plays a crucial role in helping define the boundaries of the new group and giving it an identity. In organizations this issue of group development may translate into organizational citizenship behaviour (e.g. Organ, 1988): Stimulating (inter)group conflict may enhance compliance with organizational goals and promote altruistic attitudes towards fellow ingroup members.

Fisher (this book, Chapter 13) is even more explicit in employing the idea that stimulating conflict may have positive effects. His analysis indicates that third party stimulation of open confrontation between disputants brings underlying issues out into the open, sharpens one's own insights in interests and goals, and paves the way for more optimal integration of seemingly opposing interests. Thus, third party stimulation of conflict increases differentiation between disputants, which in turn allows for improved integration (see also Walton, 1987).

An optimal level of conflict

The above showed that the suppression and avoidance of conflict leads to groupthink, reduces individual creativity and increases the likelihood of uncontrolled escalation of the conflict in the long run. Stimulating intergroup conflict promotes mutual understanding, enhances employee performance, reduces free-riding, and enhances creativity. Stimulating conflict within groups produces higher quality of decisions, helps groups to define their boundaries, and leads parties to integrate seemingly opposed interests.

That suppressing conflict may reduce performance and that stimulating conflict may promote it suggests that there is an optimal level of conflict within groups and organizations. Too much conflict is certainly to be avoided, but the absence of conflict seems undesirable as well. This is consistent with Walton (1969) who argues that very high levels of stress due to intense conflict results in consideration of fewer alternatives, rigidity, reduction in dimensionality of thinking, and in increased tendencies to perceive threat and to use power. If on the other hand the stress level is very low (because of the absence of conflict), there is 'no sense of urgency, no necessity to look for alternative ways of behaving, and no incentive for conciliatory overtures' (Walton, 1969, p. 111). When conflict is absent, stimulating it may increase cognitive flexibility and the ability to handle complex information. In situations

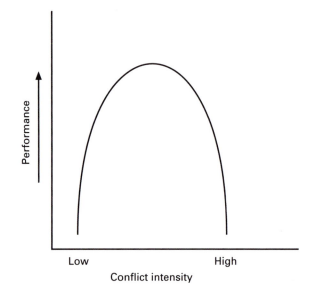

Figure 1.1   *Relation between conflict intensity and performance*

characterized by intense conflict, cognitive flexibility benefits from reduction in and resolution of the dispute. This general idea, for which Walton provided empirical evidence, is depicted in Figure 1.1.

The importance of conflict management and conflict issues

Conflict involves antecedent conditions such as policy differences and scarce resources, affective states such as stress, cognitive states such as awareness of conflictful situations, and conflict behaviours such as threatening the opponent or making concessions (Pondy, 1967; Schmidt & Kogan, 1972; Thomas, 1992). Figure 1.2 is a graphic display of this conflict process, which also shows that a focal party's conflict management strategy may influence conflict issues via the opposing party's conflict management reactions. To understand productive conflict we should consider (a) conflict management strategies because they strongly influence subsequent interaction and outcomes, and (b) conflict issues because they impact on conflict management strategies through thoughts and feelings.

Conflict management and productive conflict

Theory and research identified four main strategies for dealing with conflict.
1. *Contending*: Parties remain committed to their position and try to persuade the other party to yield to this position. Contending involves dominant,

Figure 1.2   *Conflict process*

assertive behaviours including the use of verbal and perhaps physical force, threats, a search for outside help to form a winning coalition, and manipulation of information. 2. *Yielding*: Being the opposite of contending, parties give in to their opponent's demands – they make unilateral concessions and unconditional promises. 3. *Problem solving*: Parties seek to integrate their own and the other's interests to achieve mutually satisfying outcomes. Pruitt and Carnevale (1993) discuss a variety of problem solving behaviours in the context of negotiation and mediation. Examples are exchanging information about priorities and preferences, looking for mutually promising alternatives, and focusing on underlying interests rather than superficial goals and aspirations. 4. *Avoidance*: Parties remain inactive or withdraw from dealing with the conflict issues through social interaction (e.g. Kolb & Bartunek, 1992; Rubin et al., 1994). Avoidance is the least overt way of enacting conflict and it may take quite a while before other members realize that there is conflict, or properly attribute another member's behaviour to a conflict experience.[1]

Problem solving behaviours produce more constructive interaction, greater mutual satisfaction and better outcomes than contending and avoiding, with yielding taking an intermediate position (Rubin et al., 1994; Thomas, 1992; Tjosvold, Chapter 2, this book). Table 1.1 shows the preferences for each of the four conflict management strategies among various groups of Dutch employees. Each strategy was measured reliably with three or four questions, with the same questions being asked in each group. As can be seen, both contending and problem solving obtain high ratings, indicating strong preferences for these conflict management strategies. This points to the potential for constructive interaction with its sometimes positive effects on performance as well as for destructive interaction with its generally negative consequences for performance.

Critical in the decision to engage in problem solving or contending behaviour is the extent to which the focal party wishes to take his or her opponent's goals, interests, desires and personal integrity into consideration. When this 'concern for other' is low, contending is more likely than problem solving. But if concern for other is high, problem solving is a much more likely strategy (e.g. Ben-Yoav & Pruitt, 1984; Carnevale & Lawler, 1986; De Dreu & Van Lange, 1995).

Table 1.1   *Preferences for conflict management strategies in several Dutch samples*

Groups	Strategy			
	Avoiding	Contending	Yielding	Problem solving
1. Managers ad interim (N = 55)	1.30[a]	5.06[b]	1.69[a]	5.06[b]
2. Project managers (N = 127)	2.53[a]	3.09[b]	2.90[ab]	3.51[bc]
3. Persons in work teams (N = 86)	1.69[a]	2.52[b]	1.81[ab]	4.03[c]

Note: Within each row, means not sharing a similar superscript differ at $p < 0.05$.
Higher numbers indicate stronger preference to use the strategy (in row 1, range is
1 = not at all, to 7 = very much; in row 2 and 3, range is 1 = not at all, to 5 = very much).

Parties have a high rather than low concern for their opponent for either genuine reasons (one really likes the other and wishes him well), or for instrumental reasons (it serves one or more egoistic goals) (Pruitt & Carnevale, 1993). Deutsch (1973; see also Tjosvold, Chapter 2, this book) argues that when parties perceive their goals to be positively linked concern for other is higher and problem solving more likely than when parties perceive their goals to be independent, or negatively linked. Van de Vliert, De Dreu, De Boer, Jorritsma and Kluwer (1992) found that concern for other was a positive function of other's problem solving, and a negative function of other's contending and avoiding behaviour. As we will see below, conflict management and concern for other may also be a function of conflict issue.

Conflict issues and productive conflict

Conflict may arise over many different issues such as the division of scarce resources, policies, what to consider in the decision making process, how to approach the task, what humour is funny, what norms and values are valid and appreciated, and which beliefs are to be respected. In analogy to the classic distinction that social interaction focuses on either task-related or social-emotional issues (Bales, 1954; Cosier & Rose, 1977; Guetzkow & Gyr, 1954), one may categorize conflict issues in terms of task-related, *cognitive* issues (e.g. scarce resources, policies, procedures, and roles), and social-emotional, *affective* issues (e.g. norms, values, one's personal or group identity). Indeed, growing evidence suggests that outsiders as well as disputants themselves are able to detect whether conflict is characterized by strong emphasis on ongoing relationships rather than aspects of the task, and whether it contains a certain degree of attention to affective states such as hatred and jealousy rather than a more intellective analysis of actions and situations (Pinkley, 1990; Pinkley & Northcraft, 1994).

The distinction between cognitive and affective issues is key to understanding productive conflict. Jehn (1994, 1995) conducted several studies on the influence of cognitive versus affective conflict in teams, and found that cognitive conflict enhances group performance, while affective conflict reduces performance and satisfaction. Amason (1996) investigated the influence of cognitive versus affective conflict in strategic decision making groups. He reached a similar conclusion: While affective conflict lowers decision quality by top management teams, cognitive conflict actually enhances decision quality as well as commitment to the decision itself. Turner and Pratkanis (1994; Chapter 4, this book) developed their social identity maintenance model of groupthink, and they argue persuasively that stimulating cognitive conflict mitigates groupthink, while affective conflict may actually promote social identity maintenance and concomitant groupthink. Conflict over cognitive issues is more likely to enhance individual and group performance than conflict over affective issues.

Conflict issue and conflict management

The previous section may have suggested that performance benefits from high levels of cognitive conflict. The problem with maintaining or promoting cognitive conflict is that cognitive debates easily evoke affective issues (Van de Vliert & De Dreu, 1994; Walton, 1987). Baron (Chapter 12, this book) discusses several social cognition mechanisms, including reliance on stereotypes and negative emotions, that contribute to this process. He shows, for example, how people in conflict may be subject to a 'hostile attribution bias', which is the tendency to perceive hostile intentions or motives behind the other disputant's actions and behaviours when these are ambiguous. The hostile attribution bias often leads disputants into an escalatory conflict spiral, in which cognitive conflict may be overruled by intense negative emotions.

Different conflict issues may, however, trigger different reactions. Affective issues are more threatening and involve more negative emotions than cognitive issues. Negative emotions produce aggressive behaviours (Berkowitz, 1989). Affective issues also implicate the self and concomitant identity to a greater extent than cognitive issues, and implicating the self reduces the cognitive resources that are needed to engage in constructive forms of conflict management such as problem solving. Affective issues may produce less constructive interaction than cognitive issues.

Some evidence for this proposition is available. Druckman, Broome and Korper (1988) engaged subjects in a multi-issue negotiation related to the national identity of Cygnus, an imaginary island. One group of subjects learned to have good and deep understanding of other's values and traditions (facilitation condition), one group was told to separate values from statements and positions on issues (delinked condition), and in a third group an attempt was made to establish a close link between values and positions on issues (embedded condition). Results revealed that in the embedded condition values were perceived as more salient, the climate was perceived as less tolerant and the opponent was seen as more hostile and less fair. In addition, fewer issues were settled through negotiation in the embedded condition than in the other two.

The Druckman et al. (1988) experiment showed that when affective issues such as values are at stake, interaction becomes less constructive. To obtain further evidence, we asked MBA students with some work experience to respond to a short scenario which described a conflict between them and a colleague either over work-related matters (cognitive issue) or over person-related matters (affective issue). After subjects finished reading the scenario, we asked them to report in their own words how they would proceed in this situation. These responses were then reliably content-coded by two independent judges in terms of the four conflict management strategies described above. To cover all responses, two categories were added, namely 'going to one's supervisor' and 'talk it over with others'. Analyses revealed a significant association between conflict issue and respondents' conflict management strategy: Cognitive issues produced more problem solving and less contending reactions than affective issues did (see Table 1.2).

Table 1.2   *Conflict management strategies as a function of conflict issue*

	Conflict issue	
Conflict management strategy	Affective	Cognitive
Problem solving	28%	37%
Contending	33%	15%
Avoiding	9%	12%
Yielding	0%	4%
Going to superior	21%	29%
Talk to others	9%	3%

Note: Numbers reflect the percentage of subjects per column choosing this strategy.
Overall $X^2(5) = 12.95, p < 0.05$.

Figure 1.2 indicated that conflict management strategies may feed back on conflict issues. One may indeed hypothesize that more constructive conflict management strategies such as problem solving are less likely to evoke affective issues than destructive strategies such as contending and avoiding. To test this, we asked managers in two organizations to what degree conflict in their work team in the past was usually dealt with through contending, to what degree through problem solving, to what degree through avoiding, and to what degree through unconditional yielding (always: 1 = not at all, to 5 = very much). Another part of the questionnaire assessed the amount of cognitive issue and the amount of affective issue currently present with a scale developed by Jehn (1994). As can be seen in Table 1.3, past avoiding and past contending correlated positively, and past problem solving correlated negatively, with the amount of affective conflict currently experienced. Cognitive conflict was unrelated to past conflict management strategies.

The data in Tables 1.2 and 1.3 provide some first indication that conflict issue and conflict management interact: Cognitive issues produce more problem

Table 1.3   *Association between past conflict management strategy and current*
amount of affective and cognitive issue

	2.	3.	4.	5.	6.
1. Past avoiding	0.56**	–0.15	–0.08	0.18	0.41**
2. Past contending		–0.25*	0.05	0.17	0.43**
3. Past yielding			0.18	–0.15	–0.14
4. Past problem solving				–0.18	–0.40**
5. Current amount of cognitive issue					0.34**
6. Current amount of affective issue					

*Note:*** $p < 0.001$, * $p < 0.01$ ($N = 116$). Data are based on self-report by managers from two
different Dutch organizations.

solving and less contending behaviours than affective issues do, and contending behaviours produce more, while problem solving behaviours produce less,
affective issues. Other studies found that cognitive issues sometimes lead to
enhanced performance, while affective issues generally reduce performance
(Amason, 1996; Jehn, 1994, 1995). Current data suggest that this may be due to
the fact that affective issues produce more destructive conflict management,
which produce more affective issues, and so on. Cognitive conflict produces
constructive conflict management, and thus creates the potential for enhanced
performance (Tjosvold, this book, Chapter 2). Figure 1.3 is a graphic display of
this process.

Time 1   Time 2

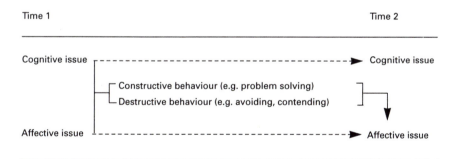

Figure 1.3   *Interplay between conflict issue and conflict management strategy*

Conclusions and avenues for further research

This chapter introduced conflict from the perspective that conflict is inherent
to all social life but that avoiding and suppressing it is neglecting its positive
value for individuals, groups and organizations. It was argued that suppressing conflict may have undesirable consequences such as reduced innovation

and groupthink. In addition, examples were given of situations in which stimulating conflict has desirable consequences, such as better quality of decision making and improved mutual understanding.

To understand productive conflict better, the relationship between conflict issue and conflict management strategies was explored. Two types of issues were identified, namely cognitive issues and affective issues. It was hypothesized that affective conflict reduces performance because it triggers negative, destructive conflict management strategies such as avoiding and contending, and that cognitive conflict enhances performance because it triggers positive, constructive behaviours such as problem solving. Some preliminary data were presented that support this hypothesis. In addition, data were presented that indicate that conflict management in turn impacts the amount and nature of conflict issue. That is, destructive behaviours such as avoiding and contending were found to produce and bolster affective issue, whereas constructive behaviours such as problem solving were found to reduce affective issue. Cognitive issue appeared unrelated to past conflict management strategy.

Further research is needed to examine additional reasons why affective issue reduces and cognitive issue enhances performance. As mentioned, affective issue implicates the self, and evokes more negative emotions, which distracts from the task to a greater extent than cognitive issue. Research should test the prediction that affective issue reduces performance because it absorbs more cognitive resources than cognitive conflict. In addition, further research is needed to test current findings on the relation between issue and behaviour in behavioural experiments, and to examine the generalizability from the scenario studies with self-report data used in the current chapter to field settings and real conflict interaction. Finally, research is needed to test the idea that issue influences performance through conflict management. In the current chapter, performance was not addressed.

Conflict in groups and organizations is often avoided and suppressed because we fear its negative consequences. Yet avoiding and suppressing conflict may have negative consequences as well, and sometimes stimulating conflict leads to better performance than does no conflict at all. The interplay between cognitive or affective issues and constructive or destructive ways of conflict management appears fundamental for conflict to be productive and beneficial to individuals, groups and organizations.

Notes

Financial support for this chapter was provided by a grant from the Royal Netherlands Academy of Sciences. I thank Chiara Andreatta, Hanneke Franssen, Chris McCusker and Rud Kuiper for their help with some of the data reported in this chapter. This chapter also benefited from comments by Ellen Giebels, Onne Janssen and Evert Van de Vliert.

1. Some authors identify a fifth strategy, named *compromising*: Parties try to find middle-of-the-road solutions by mere giving and taking (Blake & Mouton, 1964; Thomas, 1992). In the present context, compromising is seen as suboptimal problem solving (cf. Rubin et al., 1994).

References

Amason, A.C. (1996). Distinguishing the effects of functional and dysfunctional conflict on strategic decision making: Resolving a paradox for top management teams. *Academy of Management Journal, 39*, 1.

Bales, R. (1954). How people interact in conferences. *Scientific American, 192*, 31–5.

Ben-Yoav, O. and Pruitt, D.G. (1984). Resistance to yielding and the expectation of cooperative future interaction. *Journal of Experimental Social Psychology, 20*, 323–35.

Berkowitz, L. (1989). Frustration-aggression hypothesis: Examination and reformulation. *Psychological Bulletin, 106*, 59–73.

Blake, R. and Mouton, J.S. (1964). *The managerial grid*. Houston, TX: Gulf.

Bornstein, G. and Erev, I. (1994). The enhancing effect of intergroup competition on group performance. *International Journal of Conflict Management, 5*, 207–304.

Brown, D. (1983). *Managing conflict at organizational interfaces*. Reading, MA: Addison-Wesley.

Carnevale, P.J. and Lawler, E.J. (1986). Time pressure and the development of integrative agreements in bilateral negotiations. *Journal of Conflict Resolution, 30*, 636–59.

Cohen, L. and Staw, B.M. (1995). *'Fun's over, fact-finders are here'. A case study of institutionalized dissent*. Paper presented at the Academy of Management meetings, Vancouver, BC, August 11–14.

Cosier, R. and Rose, G. (1977). Cognitive conflict and goal conflict effects on task performance. *Organizational Behavior and Human Performance, 19*, 378–91.

De Dreu, C.K.W., Carnevale, P.J., Emans, B.J.M. and Van de Vliert, E. (1994). Effects of gain-loss frames in negotiation: Loss aversion, mismatching, and frame adoption. *Organizational Behavior and Human Decision Processes, 60*, 90–107.

De Dreu, C.K.W. and De Vries, N.K. (1993). Numerical support, information processing, and attitude change. *European Journal of Social Psychology, 23*, 647–62.

De Dreu, C.K.W. and McCusker, C. (1997). Gain-loss frames and cooperation in two-person social dilemmas. *Journal of Personality and Social Psychology*, 47.

De Dreu, C.K.W. and Van Lange, P.A.M. (1995). Impact of social value orientation on negotiator cognition and behavior. *Personality and Social Psychology Bulletin, 21*, 1178–88.

Deutsch, M. (1973). *The resolution of conflict: Constructive and destructive processes*. New Haven: Yale University Press.

Druckman, D., Broome, B.J. and Korper, S.H. (1988). Value differences and conflict resolution: Facilitation or delinking? *Journal of Conflict Resolution, 32*, 489–510.

Fisher, R.J. (1992). Generic principles for resolving intergroup conflict. *Journal of Social Issues, 50*, 47–66.

Friedman, R. (1994). *Front-stage back-stage*. Cambridge, MA: The MIT Press.

Guetzkow, H. and Gyr, J. (1954). An analysis of conflict in decision making groups. *Human Relations, 7*, 367–81.

Hocker, J.L. and Wilmot, W.W. (1991). *Interpersonal conflict*. Dubuque, IA: Brown Publishers.

Ippolito, C.A. and Pruitt, D.G. (1990). Power balancing in mediation: Outcomes and implications of mediator intervention. *International Journal of Conflict Management, 1*, 341–56.

Janis, I.L. (1989). *Crucial decisions: Leadership in policymaking and crisis management*. New York: Free Press.

Jehn, K.A. (1994). Enhancing effectiveness: An investigation of advantages and disadvantages of value-based intragroup conflict. *International Journal of Conflict Management, 5*, 223–38.

Jehn, K.A. (1995). A multimethod examination of the benefits and detriments of intragroup conflict. *Adminstrative Science Quarterly, 40*, 256–82.

Kolb, D.M. and Bartunek, J.M. (eds, 1992). *Hidden conflict in organizations: Uncovering behind-the-scenes disputes*. London: Sage.

Macrae, C.N., Milne, A.B. and Bodenhausen, G.V. (1994). Stereotypes as energy-saving devices: A peek inside the cognitive toolbox. *Journal of Personality and Social Psychology, 66*, 37–47.

Nemeth, C.J. and Staw, B.M. (1989). The tradeoffs of social control and innovation in groups and organizations, in L. Berkowitz (ed.), *Advances in experimental social psychology, 22*, 175–210.

Organ, D.W. (1988). *Organizational citizenship behavior*. Lexington, MA: Lexington Books.

Pinkley, R. (1990). Dimensions of conflict frame: Disputant interpretations of conflict. *Journal of Applied Psychology*, *75*, 117–26.

Pinkley, R. and Northcraft, G. (1994). Conflict frames of reference: Implications for dispute processes and outcomes. *Academy of Management Journal*, *37*, 193–205.

Pondy, L. (1967). Organizational conflict: Concepts and models. *Administrative Science Quarterly*, *17*, 296–320.

Pritchard, D. (1992). Organizational productivity, in M.D. Dunnette & L.M. Hough (eds), *Handbook of industrial and organizational psychology* (2nd edn). Palo Alto, CA: Consulting Psychologists Press, Vol. 3, pp. 443–71.

Pruitt, D.G. and Carnevale, P.J. (1993). *Negotiation in social conflict*. London: Open University Press.

Putnam, L.L. (1994). Productive conflict: Negotiation as implicit coordination. *International Journal of Conflict Management*, *5*, 207–304.

Robbins, S.P. (1974). *Managing organizational conflict: a nontraditional approach*. Englewood Cliffs, NJ: Prentice-Hall.

Rubin, J.Z., Pruitt, D.G. and Kim, S.H. (1994). *Social conflict: Escalation, stalemate, and settlement*. New York: McGraw-Hill.

Schmidt, S.M. and Kogan, T.A. (1972). Conflict: Toward conceptual clarity. *Administrative Science Quarterly*, *17*, 359–70.

Thomas, K.W. (1992). Conflict and negotiation processes in organizations, in M.D. Dunnette and L.M. Hough (eds), *Handbook of industrial and organizational psychology* (2nd edn). Palo Alto, CA: Consulting Psychologists Press, Vol. 3, pp. 651–717.

Turner, M.E. and Pratkanis, A.R. (1994). Social identity maintenance prescriptions for preventing Groupthink: Reducing identity protection and enhancing intellectual conflict. *International Journal of Conflict Management*, *5*, 207–304.

Turner, M.E., Pratkanis, A.R., Probasco, P. and Leve, C. (1992). Threat, cohesion, and group effectiveness: Testing a social identity maintenance perspective on groupthink. *Journal of Personality and Social Psychology*, *63*, 781–96.

Van de Vliert, E. and De Dreu, C.K.W. (1994). Optimizing performance by stimulating conflict. *International Journal of Conflict Management*, *5*, 211–22.

Van de Vliert, E., De Dreu, C.K.W., De Boer, A., Jorritsma, R. and Kluwer, E. (1992). De invloed van voorafgaand gedrag en werkervaring op conflicthantering (Influence of prior behaviour and work experience on conflict management), in R.W. Meertens, A.P. Buunk, P.A.M. van Lange and B. Verplanken (eds), *Sociale psychologie & beinvloeding van intermenselijke en gezondheidsproblemen*. The Hague: Vuga, pp. 37–48.

Van de Vliert, E., Euwema, M.C. and Huismans, S.E. (1995). Managing conflict with a subordinate or superior: the effectiveness of conglomerated behavior. *Journal of Applied Psychology, 80*, 271–81.

Wall, J. and Callister, R. (1995). Conflict and its management. *Journal of Management, 21*, 515–58.

Walton, R.E. (1969). *Interpersonal peacemaking: Confrontations and third party consultation*. Reading, MA: Addison-Wesley.

Walton, R.E. (1987). *Innovating to compete*. San Francisco: Jossey-Bass.

Walton, R.E., Cutcher-Gershenfeld, J.E. and McKersie, R. (1994). *Strategic negotiations: a theory of change in labor-management relations*. Cambridge: Harvard Business School Press.

Worchel, S., Coutant-Sassic, D. and Wong, F. (1993). Toward a more balanced view of conflict: There is a positive side, in S. Worchel and J.A. Simpson (eds), *Conflict between people and groups: Causes, processes, and resolutions*. Chicago: Nelson Hall, pp. 76–89.

2

Conflict within Interdependence: Its Value for Productivity and Individuality

Dean Tjosvold

For neurosis is after all only a sign that the ego has not succeeded in making a synthesis, that in attempting to do so it has forfeited its unity.

Sigmund Freud

When two [persons] in business always agree, one of them is unnecessary.

William Wrigley

No person, group or nation is an island. Interdependence, though often ignored and sometimes derogated and denied, is the basic reality of our lives. The global marketplace has made the scale of this reality more apparent. Conflict is a central reason for our mixed attitudes towards interdependence. Independence is thought to be a means of eluding conflict and its assumed costs and pain. But conflict, as this book indicates, is not necessarily destructive.

Research reviewed in this chapter shows that conflict is a way of confronting reality and creating new solutions to tough problems. Conflict, when well managed, breathes life and energy into our relationships and strengthens our interdependence and makes us much more innovative and productive. Conflict is necessary for true involvement, empowerment and democracy. Through debating their different perspectives, people voice their concerns and create solutions responsive to several points of view. They can then become united and committed.

This chapter also argues that positive conflict develops our individuality so that we feel more fulfilled and capable. Conflict provides an opportunity to form and express our needs, opinions and positions. At the same time we try to understand the perspectives of others and we become less egocentric. Resolving issues leaves people feeling more integrated, adjusted and competent. Through conflict, people feel unique and independent as well as connected to others.

Well-managed conflict is an investment in the future. People trust each other more, feel more powerful and efficacious, and believe their joint efforts will pay off. Feeling more able and united, people are more prepared to contribute to their groups and organizations. Success in turn further strengthens relationships and individuality.

But the power of conflict can be channelled destructively. Conflicts that are avoided and poorly managed can wreak havoc on us and our organizations. Problems fester and obsolete ideas are implemented. People remain aloof, sceptical and angry; they become rigid, fixated and ambivalent. Both individuals and their organizations lose.

The potential value of conflict also points to the challenges to manage it well. The consequences of positive conflict – strong relationships, productivity and individuality – have to be managed. The more open and united the relationship, the more self-aware and empathetic the individuals, and the greater the progress in solving problems, the more successful the conflict management. There are no simple techniques that transform all frustrations into positive conflict. Managing conflict gives more but requires more.

This chapter argues that positive conflict results in strong relationships, high performance, and mature and competent individuals, which in turn foster more effective conflict in a beneficial, reinforcing cycle. I use Deutsch's (1973, 1990) theory of cooperation and competition which has proved valuable for understanding the nature of positive conflict and when it occurs. There will then be a summary of experimental findings on the impact of conflict on problem solving and field studies demonstrating the value of open-minded discussion of different points of view for organizational effectiveness. I will propose that positive conflict aids individual development, competence and well-being. Learning to manage conflict is a wise investment for individuals and organizations to prepare for an uncertain future.

Theoretical approach

Conflict has traditionally been defined in terms of opposing, divergent interests. Conflict is thought to occur in mixed-motive situations where the contrient (competitive) interests require distributive bargaining and the promotive (cooperative) goals allow for an integrative resolution leaving both parties better off than no agreement (Bacharach & Lawler, 1981; Deutsch & Krauss, 1962; Rubin, Pruitt & Kim, 1994; Walton & McKersie, 1965). Yet assuming that conflict inevitably involves opposing interests, goals and aspirations makes documenting the positive role of conflict very difficult, as research has showed.

Morton Deutsch (1973) proposed an approach to understanding conflict that has proved fruitful. Although highly respected, his specific contributions to defining and understanding conflict are not as well understood or appreciated as they should be. Deutsch clearly distinguished conflict from cooperative and competitive interdependence.

Conflict involves incompatible activities. People are in conflict when the actions of one person are interfering, obstructing or in some other way making another's behaviour less effective. Team members' arguing for different positions gets in the way, at least temporarily, of their making a decision. Asking a question during a speech frustrates the presenter's attempts to present his or her findings.

What is crucial about defining conflict as incompatible activities is that it does not equate action with goals, a confusion often made in the writing and practice of conflict management. Team members argue for different solutions to a problem as a means to reach their goal of the best solution possible. Just because people's actions are incompatible does not mean that their desired end-states are. Their goals and aspirations can still be compatible. They can still get where they want to go. Team members arguing different positions both want the solution that will make their team successful, but make contrasting proposals of how to accomplish this compatible goal. The person interrupting and the presenter may still have the compatible goal of understanding the material accurately; they have different conclusions of how this goal can be accomplished. Of course, sometimes conflict is such that there are incompatible goals that make mutual benefit unlikely or even impossible. However, this incompatibility should be discovered, not assumed in the definition of conflict.

Based on his previous theorizing and research on group processes, Deutsch proposed that people's beliefs about how they depend upon each other drastically affects their expectations, communication and problem solving, core activities of conflict management. Deutsch identified three kinds of interdependence: promotive (cooperation), contrient (competition), and independence. Pure forms of these rarely occur in the real world. What is critical is how people believe their goals are predominantly linked; these perceptions affect their expectations and actions, and thereby their success in managing conflict. This chapter uses promotive and contrient interdependence to describe how people believe their goals are predominately related.

Deutsch's approach powerfully examines conflict within its interdependence. Conflicts occur in relationships. The prior relationship impacts conflict management; conflict management impacts the future relationship. Hundreds of studies have developed the theory of promotive and contrient interdependence and showed it to be an elegant, powerful way to understand interaction and conflict (Johnson & Johnson, 1989; Tjosvold, 1991, 1993).

Promotive interdependence creates the expectations and interactions that facilitate positive conflict. People believe their goals are positively linked so that as one person moves towards goal attainment, others move towards reaching their goals. They understand that the others' goal attainment helps them; they can be successful together. They want each other to succeed so that they can both succeed. Task force members, committed to the cooperative goal of presenting the best recommendation possible to management, encourage each other to investigate solutions and develop proposals so that they can all succeed and enhance their reputations. Within this context, they express their various ideas directly, open-mindedly consider them, and integrate them to solve problems.

With incompatible, competitive goals, people believe that one's successful goal attainment makes others less likely to reach their goals. If one 'wins', others 'lose'. In contrient interdependence, people conclude that they are better off when others act ineffectively; when others are productive, they are less likely to be successful themselves. Task force members, committed to the competitive goal of appearing to be the most important and influential person on the task force to management, are frustrated when another investigates and proposes a useful solution because they believe they may not reach their goal. Within this context, they find it difficult to manage conflict. They are tempted to avoid because they do want a tough discussion but, once engaged, they press their solutions and try to impose them.

Independence occurs when people believe their goals are unrelated. The goal attainment of one neither helps nor hinders the goal attainment of others. Success by one brings neither failure nor success for others. People who work independently conclude that it means little to them if others act effectively or ineffectively. Independent team members care little whether others develop useful ideas or work hard. Independent work creates disinterest and indifference.

Constructive controversy

A great many experiments and field studies – a recent review identified 500 studies – support the basic propositions that promotive, compared to contrient, interdependence fosters open communication, resource exchange, perspective-taking and mutual influence that result in productivity on most tasks and social support (Johnson & Johnson, 1989). This section reviews research that directly investigates the impact of promotive and contrient interdependence on the discussion of opposing views and the success of problem solving. Findings show that through open conflict people combine and integrate their ideas to solve problems and strengthen their relationship. Conflict is essential to realize the benefits of collaborative work.

The dynamics induced by promotive interdependence and contributing to effective joint work has been characterized as constructive controversy (Johnson, Johnson, Smith & Tjosvold, 1990; Tjosvold, 1985). Contrary to the popular view that cooperative goals promote harmony and conflict avoidance, constructive controversy proposes that the open-minded discussion of opposing views is critical for making cooperative situations productive and enhancing. It is under competitive and individualistic conditions that people are more likely to avoid conflict, try to win the fight, or even dissolve the relationship.

With compatible goals, protagonists welcome open discussion and realize it is important to work out settlements so that they can continue to assist each other. Recognizing that it is in everyone's self-interest to promote each other's effectiveness, they freely speak their minds and are willing to engage in conflictful discussions (Van Berklom & Tjosvold, 1981). Direct controversy in turn has been shown to contribute to full exchange of perspectives and understanding of issues. When confronted with an opposing view, people feel uncertain about the most adequate solution; they doubt that their own position is correct (Tjosvold, 1982; Tjosvold & Deemer, 1980, 1981; Tjosvold & Johnson, 1977,

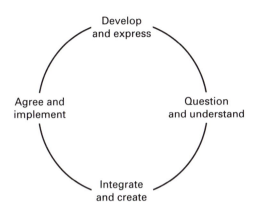

Figure 2.1 *Constructive controversy dynamics*

1978; Tjosvold, Johnson & Fabrey, 1980; Tjosvold, Johnson & Lerner, 1981). Given this uncertainty about the adequacy of their own positions, they are curious and seek to understand opposing views. For example, people in controversy, compared to those in agreeable discussions, asked their protagonists more questions and demonstrated greater interest in understanding the opposing perspective. They recalled more opposing arguments, identified the reasoning others were using, and predicted the reasoning others would use on new issues more accurately than people with similar views. (See Figure 2.1.)

Compatible goals have created a willingness to consider and incorporate opposing views (Tjosvold, 1982; Tjosvold & Deemer, 1980; Tjosvold & Johnson, 1978; Tjosvold et al., 1980; Tjosvold et al., 1981). Knowing that people are trying to use the controversy for mutually beneficial ends and showing mutual respect help people use their discussion of opposing views to integrate several points of view. They combine the most reliable information and the best ideas to make a high quality decision they are willing to implement (Tjosvold, 1982; Tjosvold & Deemer, 1980). Maintaining mutual respect while disagreeing is necessary in order to maintain open-mindedness and integration of opposing views (Tjosvold, 1983).

With competitive goals, people in their determination to win and outdo each other are closed-minded. Although they often prefer to avoid conflict, especially with their bosses and others with authority and power, the underlying problems continue to frustrate them. If they do decide to confront their protagonists, they often do so in a tough, dominating manner that escalates the conflict. They have been found to reject the opposing position and the person arguing it, to refuse to incorporate other ideas into their own decision making, and to fail to reach an agreement. These patterns in turn frustrate productivity, intensify stress and disrupt relationships.

Conflict for organizational effectiveness

To what extent do these dynamics and outcomes of constructive controversy generalize to organizations? The high internal validity of the experiments reviewed above come at the cost of questions regarding the extent that their findings occur in actual organizations. Field studies have documented that cooperative, constructive controversy dynamics generalize to decision making in organizations (Tjosvold & Tsao, 1989). For example, effective project managers both engage in open discussion of conflict and discuss issues in cooperative ways; ineffective project managers both avoid conflict and try to win (Barker, Tjosvold & Andrews, 1988). Studies have extended research to show the vital role of the dynamics and outcomes of promotive interdependence and constructive controversy on a wide range of issues critical for organizational success. This section reviews research on positive conflict in making decisions and the practical requirement to serve customers.

Decision making in organizations

Managers answered questions to indicate whom they involved in making an important successful and unsuccessful decision and answered a fifteen-item questionnaire measuring the extent that they discussed their opposing views openly for mutual benefit (Tjosvold, Wedley & Field, 1986). Whereas involving people was modestly related to success, using constructive controversy accounted for more than 40% of the variance on effective decision making.

Self-managing teams are expected to make their own decisions rather than rely on their supervisors. These groups must then be able to use their conflicts to resolve issues. Compatible goals and constructive controversy were found to contribute greatly to effective self-managing teams (Alper & Tjosvold, 1993). A midwestern manufacturing plant had implemented a self-managing team structure for five years and was interested in using cooperation theory to analyze their self-managing teams. The 544 employees involved in the 59 teams completed a questionnaire based on cooperation theory. Teams were responsible for scheduling, housekeeping, safety, expense purchases, accident investigation and quality.

The structural equation analysis indicated that teams relying on promotive interdependent conflict management, compared to teams with contrient, win–lose conflict, felt confident that they could deal with their many differences. This conflict efficacy resulted in productive and innovative work as rated by themselves and their managers. This success in turn led team members to be personally committed to working as a team. Managing conflict can substantially impact organizational problem-solving and individual attitudes towards team-work.

Organizations need innovative solutions to cope with rapid changes. Faculty members and employees of a large post-secondary educational institution were interviewed about when they were able to solve problems in new and creative ways, and when they were frustrated, or unable to develop a new approach (Tjosvold & McNeely, 1988). When they discussed their opposing views openly and forthrightly and considered all views, they were able to develop innovative solutions. When they discussed issues competitively from only one point of view and were unable to incorporate different views, they failed to make progress and developed solutions low on quality and creativity.

Managers have long complained that employees resist new technological innovations and, as a consequence, investments do not pay off in the expected productivity increases. Less recognized is that employees must identify problems and discuss solutions to use the technology. Employees of a retail chain in promotive interdependence were able to use new scanning technology efficiently because they exchanged information and hammered out ideas about how to solve the many problems the technology created (Tjosvold, 1990).

Customer service

All organizations have the practical challenge of serving their customers or face the prospect of reduced support. Serving customers is not accomplished by the skill and flair of individual salespersons. To market high technology effectively, for example, service, training, engineering and technical personnel must coordinate with each other and with salespersons (Tjosvold & Wong, 1992). Cooperative goals promote the open, lively discussions that result in integrated, creative solutions that solve problems and create value for customers (Tjosvold, Dann & Wong, 1992).

Coordinated action is needed to respond to customer problems successfully. Compatible goals and controversy were found to help employees from a customer service division of a large telecommunications company combine their ideas and actions to deal successfully with customer complaints. When employees from different departments had compatible goals and discussed their opposing views constructively, customers were well served, the company's image was enhanced, time and materials were efficiently used, and employees felt more confident about themselves and their work relationships. In contrast, competitive interactions wasted time and materials, damaged the company's reputation, and undermined future work. Discussing views openly and cooperatively helped managers from diverse departments win engineering contracts and improve productivity in a large consulting firm (Tjosvold, 1988).

Successful salespersons are often thought to be smooth and competitive, but a recent study documents that they develop strong compatible goals and deal with conflicts directly (Wong & Tjosvold, 1992). Twenty-five salespersons of a large international airline and forty travel agents and managers in charge of corporate travel described specific interactions. When the sales representatives and their customers believed their goals were compatible, they felt that they could rely on each other, felt accepted and avoided trying to dominate. They went out of their way to assist each other, give information and explain issues. They explored their different views to solve problems and used their conflicts to strengthen their relationships.

In promotive interdependence, salespersons and clients felt good about their interaction, made progress solving the problem and getting the task accomplished, worked efficiently, formed a stronger work relationship, and had confidence that they could work successfully in the future. These interactions enhanced sales and reputations. In contrast, salespersons and clients with incompatible and independent goals tended to be suspicious, avoided open and constructive discussion of ideas and differences, and attempted to dominate the other; they had negative feelings, failed to make much progress on the task, worked inefficiently, weakened their relationships, and had doubts about future collaboration. They refused to listen and accommodate, lost sales, and felt disappointed and embarrassed.

In summary, experiments have developed internally valid findings on the impact of interdependence and constructive controversy on problem solving discussion and effectiveness. Field studies have shown that these dynamics occur and affect the essence of organizational effectiveness. Together they are powerful support for the value of well-managed conflict. They also specify that promotive interdependence underlies this positive conflict and that open discussion, understanding others, integrating views and reaching agreement are critical skills for positive conflict.

Conflict for individuality

Being organized has been considered incompatible with being human (Argyris, 1970). Traditionally structured and managed organizations are thought to be inimical to the needs for individuals for ongoing growth and development. Individuals strive for self-expression, self-esteem and psychological health whereas organizations want compliance and conformity. Organizations sometimes lose out because they alienate employees and fail to capture their ideas and energy. This section argues that positive conflict can help identify how organizations can be managed to foster individual growth and development. Conflict and developmental psychology research, when considered together, suggests that the contribution of positive conflict for individuality is deep and broad.

Developmental conflicts

Conflicts within people have been considered central dynamics impacting development and psychological health. Psychoanalytic psychologists have emphasized the conflict between moral ideals, internal sexual and aggression drives, and rational thought. Cognitive developmental and even behavioural psychologists have also employed the idea of internal conflicts. The emphasis has been that the failure to resolve these internal conflicts leaves people anxious and ineffective. Cognitive developmentalists, for example, have theorized an internal debate where different ways of thinking, sometimes called cognitive or moral stage reasoning, compete with each other to be dominant (Kohlberg, 1969; Piaget, 1948). Arrested development occurs when more concrete, undeveloped ways of thinking are unchallenged or rigidly defended.

Interpersonal conflicts would seem to have a great impact on the resolution of intrapersonal conflicts. The demands and arguments of peers and authority figures impact the resolution of the struggle between moral ideals, needs and reasoning. Cognitive developmentalists have proposed that interpersonal debate among people of different stages promotes the adoption of more adequate ways of reasoning (Kohlberg, 1969; Piaget, 1948).

It is hypothesized that to the extent that people manage their interpersonal conflicts positively they are able to resolve their internal conflicts. With promotive interdependence with colleagues and managers, employees are more prepared to listen and incorporate new ideas into their thinking. Similarly, the open-mindedness of positive conflict can facilitate the effects of cognitive and moral controversial discussions on adoption of higher stages of reasoning (Tjosvold & Johnson, 1977).

In a masterful synthesis of behavioural, cognitive and psychoanalytic approaches, Breger (1974) identified core conflicts that run throughout the developmental process. Major ones include conflict between gratification and denial, between independence and dependence, and between anxiety and security. Typically, immature persons move from one extreme to another. They unrealistically demand independence but later become highly dependent. At one stage they try to do every new activity; later they become anxious and unwilling to experiment.

Successful development depends on the integration of the opposing tendencies of gratification and denial, independence and dependence, and anxiety and security. Competent adults are able to resolve these internal conflicts. They seek long-term goals but enjoy their present activities. They recognize both their independence and dependence and are skilful at managing their interdependence. They neither completely accept nor reject the status quo nor everything new, but build upon the present by incorporating emerging ideas and procedures.

Although biological and intellectual changes impact their prevalence and forms, the usefulness of these developmental conflicts depend upon how their interpersonal manifestations are handled. Managers and other authority figures cannot ignore the unrealistic independence demands of employees and must demonstrate and argue with them as to why limits are imposed. Otherwise employees might continue to be unrealistic and hold immature attitudes about need gratification, and how to relate to authority and others, and may be overly anxious and conforming. However, tough, win–lose conflict can leave people feeling that either they dare not risk asserting their independence and must remain passive or they must continually fight for independence or risk intolerable, permanent dependence. Positive conflict is needed to resolve internal conflicts so that individuals continue to mature into persons who are fulfilled, independent and innovative, yet respectful and responsive to others.

Conflict management may have a great impact on the development of self-identity (Breger, 1974). Throughout development and adult years, people are formulating their sense of self in part by identifying with parents, peers and larger social groups. Identifying the self after admired others is easily incorporated, leaving people feeling self-accepted and united. However, rage, fear, anxiety and helplessness – which result from destructive, escalated conflict – also provoke identification; incorporating these relationships leaves people feeling anxious and divided.

Developmental conflicts pose the important stakes of managing interpersonal conflict. Potentially, conflict between people can have significant, long-lasting impact on their individual competence. Impressive field experiments indicate that the conflict within a promotive interdependence context facilitates their openness to new, opposing views, incorporation of new ideas and actions, and learning (Johnson, Johnson, Pierson & Lyons, 1985; Smith, Johnson & Johnson, 1981, 1984). Evidence also suggests that this positive conflict strengthens commitment to their interdependence (Alper & Tjosvold, 1993).

Conflict dynamics

Research on conflict in problem solving indicates that in promotive interdependence, protagonists express their views and needs. Such self-expression can be expected to increase self-exploration and awareness. Telling others what is important may also foster self-acceptance; protagonists are announcing that their needs and opinions are valuable and should be considered. As they espouse their positions and respond to questions, they clarify their thinking and make their arguments more logical and evidence-based. Self-awareness and acceptance are fundamental to individual development.

Conflict provides the opportunity and incentives to listen carefully to the arguments, feelings and needs of others in addition to voicing one's own. As research reviewed demonstrates, engaging in constructive controversy results in knowing the other's arguments and predicting how the other would argue on a new contentious issue. The absence of conflict leaves the false impression that people understand each other. Through the give-and-take of conflict, people shed their illusions and assumptions of each other to know their actual positions and needs. Perspective-taking is essential for emotional, social, cognitive and moral development (Rogers, 1965). Empathy helps people experience their own emotional depth and complexity. Demonstrating this understanding credibly communicates interest in others and provokes social support in return. Understanding the more complex thinking of others leads to higher cognitive and moral reasoning.

Creativity identifies original and better ways to accomplish a purpose and often occurs because ideas previously considered independent are combined (Shalley, 1995). Conflict, when well managed, provides a forum for integrating ideas that originally are thought incompatible. As they argue their positions, people come to see the inadequacy of their ideas and the value of opposing ones. Then they combine them in ways neither person had considered previously. Well-managed conflict leads to resolution and agreement. People give up their grievances, accept apologies, and agree to new, less frustrating ways of proceeding. They use their anger to solve problems rather than plan revenge. Innovation replaces self-righteous closed-mindedness; people create new ideas rather than convince themselves they are right and others wrong. They feel successful and powerful for they have confronted difficult issues and created solutions that make them more productive and satisfied. They accept imperfect solutions to their problems because they realize that resources are scarce and others' demands and interests must be accommodated. Well-managed conflict helps individuals confront reality and accept limitations, yet still feel they can influence their situation, conditions critical for psychological health.

Disciplinary boundaries among personality, developmental, individual differences, social psychology and applied conflict researchers have interfered with developing more direct empirical documentation of the value of positive conflict for individual development. Investigating the role of conflict on individuality requires a combined perspective. These studies will probably also require innovative methods that combine the best of social developmental psychology.

Preparing for the future

The autocratic, command and control, tell and sell ways of organizing are being replaced by more participative, democratic, empowered ways to manage organizations, societies and international relations. Even if this trend does not continue, it is clear that we need to become more skilled to make these new forms effective. A recent study reinforces that positive conflict is central to these new forms (Tjosvold, Hui & Law, in press). Democratic leaders were found to be successful in getting the job done, strengthening relationships, and leaving themselves and employees feeling powerful. But to be perceived as democratic they had to foster open-minded discussion of various points of view which in turn depended upon promotive interdependence. For employees to participate in decision making fully and contribute to organizational productivity requires that they express and integrate their divergent views (Tjosvold, 1987).

One reason for the emergence of these new forms is that today's complex problems require a multi-disciplinary approach. For example, psychologists, physicians, venture capitalists, computer specialists, and bio-mechanic experts join forces to create a new medical procedure; this group must also form partnerships to test their procedures in Europe and to collaborate with regulators. A boss dictating what everyone should do is impractical and counterproductive. Realizing that the great potential of this diversity requires effective conflict management, leaders develop forums and teach skills for positive conflict (Tjosvold & Tjosvold, 1993).

The global village imposes the challenge to manage conflict across cultures where people may have their own notions and procedures about how conflicts should be resolved. Chinese people do not have the same style and manner when dealing with conflict as North Americans. Culturally diverse people have conflict over how they manage conflict.

Although a theory cannot be assumed to apply to different cultures, a conflict theory that cannot be is increasingly irrelevant. Recent studies indicate that the promotive and contrient interdependence approach can analyse conflict among Europeans and Asians and between Asians and North Americans (Kluwer, De Dreu, Dijkstra, Van der Glas, Kuiper and Tjosvold, 1993; Tjosvold & Chia, 1989; Tjosvold et al., in press; Tjosvold, Lee & Wong, 1992; Tjosvold, Moy & Sasaki, in press; Tjosvold, Sasaki & Moy, 1995; Tjosvold & Tsao, 1989).

This knowledge offers the possibility of forming negotiation methods that avoid imposing the style of one culture on another. After reviewing the evidence, diverse people can agree that they want to manage their conflicts productively, and that they should develop strong promotive interdependence and the constructive controversy skills to do so. They use interdependence theory to create conflict positive norms and procedures appropriate and effective for them (Tjosvold, 1993).

Despite the move towards more participation, diversity and material prosperity, individuality is in poor health. It is the age of alienation and anger. Rates of depression within the United States, for example, appear to be growing at a disturbing high rate (Seligman, 1988). There are no easy answers. However, it is unlikely that papering over people's frustrations and irritations can be effective. Dealing with their grievances directly can reduce their anger and, as we have hypothesized, help them feel more unique and powerful and act more competently. Moving away from projecting inadequacies and blaming others to discussing their frustrations constructively and developing strong relationships can help people become more open to and resolved about their internal conflicts, fears and rages. Developing conflict-positive organizations and families can be a powerful approach to dealing with today's malaise (Tjosvold, 1991; Tjosvold, Tjosvold & Tjosvold, 1991).

Changing our organizations to be conflict-positive is a tough, long-term solution, requiring informed, persistent action and ongoing research and development. This does not suit today's proclivity for the quick-fix. Yet trying to hang on to the status quo is risky. The failure to strengthen our relationships and conflict skills is disinvesting in the future. We face greater stagnation and anomie. The choice is clear; our ability to act is not.

The theme of this chapter, to paraphrase Albert Einstein, is that 'God would not be so mean to make us so interdependent if we could not put conflict to work for us.' Conflict, when managed within a promotive interdependent context and with constructive controversy skills, can help us confront our pervasive interdependence. Positive conflict also provides the stimulating give-and-take to create innovative solutions. Individuals express and accept their uniqueness and become more mature, skilful and competent.

Research reviewed identifies to the power of positive conflict for solving organizational problems and building individual competence and well-being. Positive conflict offers considerable hope but it also poses significant challenges. Researchers must break away from conflict-negative notions to further substantiate the nature of positive conflict and the conditions under which it occurs. Conflict is so pervasive and complex that developing elegant theories has proved difficult. More fully documenting the impact of interpersonal conflict on individual development will require breaking out of disciplinary boundaries.

The challenges for people of action are also substantial. Traditional ideas of leadership and teamwork are conflict-negative. But the reality is that people must deal with conflicts directly and constructively to make organizations effective. Developing more realistic, viable conflict-positive values, styles and procedures will require ongoing learning and experimentation.

Conflict is a common challenge. Employees and managers, European and Asian, artisan and artist all have conflicts and are more effective if they manage them constructively. It is indicated by theory and research that cooperative goals and the open-minded discussion of opposing views can serve as a common approach for diverse people. Their unity is based on a common desire and method to deal with their differences, not on unrealistic notions of harmony and agreement. Conflict also unites practitioners and researchers in a common pursuit of valid, useful knowledge to manage the differences that threaten to divide us.

References

Alper, S. and Tjosvold, D. (1993). *Cooperation theory and self-managing teams on the manufacturing floor.* Paper, International Association for Conflict Management, Eugene, OR.

Argyris, C. (1970). *Intervention theory and method: a behavioral science view.* Reading, MA: Addison-Wesley.

Bacharach, S.B. and Lawler, E.J. (1981). *Bargaining: Power, tactics, and outcomes.* San Francisco: Jossey-Bass.

Barker, J., Tjosvold, D. and Andrews, I.R. (1988). Conflict approaches of effective and ineffective managers: a field study in a matrix organization. *Journal of Management Studies, 25,* 167–78.

Breger, L. (1974). *From instinct to identity: the development of personality.* Englewood Cliffs, NJ: Prentice-Hall.

Deutsch, M. (1973). *The resolution of conflict.* New Haven, CT: Yale University Press.

Deutsch, M. (1990). Sixty years of conflict. *The International Journal of Conflict Management, 1,* 237–63.

Deutsch, M. and Krauss, R.M. (1962). Studies of interpersonal bargaining. *Journal of Conflict Resolution, 6,* 52–72.

Johnson, D.W. and Johnson, R.T. (1989). *Cooperation and competition: Theory and research.* Edina, MN: Interaction Books.

Johnson, D.W., Johnson, R., Pierson, W. and Lyons, V. (1985). Controversy versus concurrence seeking in multi-grade and single-grade learning groups. *Journal of Research in Science Teaching, 22,* 835–48.

Johnson, D.W., Johnson, R.T., Smith, K. and Tjosvold, D. (1990). Pro, con, and synthesis: Training managers to engage in constructive controversy, in B. Sheppard, M. Bazerman and R. Lewicki (eds), *Research in negotiations in organization.* Greenwich, CT: JAI Press, Vol. 2, pp. 139–74.

Kluwer, E., De Dreu, C.K.W., Dijkstra, S., Van der Glas, F., Kuiper, A. and Tjosvold, D. (1993). Doelinterdependentie en conflicthantering in profit-en non-profit-organisaties (Goal inter-dependence and conflict management in profit and nonprofit organizations). *Toegepaste sociale psychologie (Applied social psychology)*. Delft, The Netherlands: Euburon, pp. 208–18.

Kohlberg, L. (1969). Stage and sequence: the cognitive-development approach to socialization, in D.A. Goslin (ed.), *Handbook of socialization theory and research*. Skokie, IL: Rand McNally, pp. 347–480.

Piaget, J. (1948). *The moral judgment of the child*. New York: Free Press.

Rogers, C. (1965). Dealing with psychological tensions. *Journal of Applied Behavioral Science, 1*, 6–25.

Rubin, J.Z., Pruitt, D.G. and Kim, S. H. (1994). *Social conflict: Escalation, stalemate, and set-tlement*. New York: McGraw-Hill.

Seligman, M. (1988). Boomer blues. *Psychology Today, 22*, October, 50–5.

Shalley, C.E. (1995). Effects of coation, expected evaluation, and goal setting on creativity and productivity. *Academy of Management Journal, 38*, 483–503.

Smith, K., Johnson, D.W. and Johnson, R. (1981). Can conflict be constructive? Controversy versus concurrence seeking in learning groups. *Journal of Educational Psychology, 73*, 651–63.

Smith, K., Johnson, D.W. and Johnson, R. (1984). Effects of controversy on learning in cooper-ative groups. *Journal of Social Psychology, 122*, 199–209.

Tjosvold, D. (1982). Effects of the approach to controversy on superiors' incorporation of sub-ordinates' information in decision making. *Journal of Applied Psychology, 67*, 189–93.

Tjosvold, D. (1983). Social face in conflict: a critique. *International Journal of Group Tensions, 13*, 49–64.

Tjosvold, D. (1985). Implications of controversy research for management. *Journal of Management, 11*, 21–37.

Tjosvold, D. (1987). Participation: a close look at its dynamics. *Journal of Management, 13*, 739–50.

Tjosvold, D. (1988). Cooperative and competitive interdependence: Collaboration between departments to serve customers. *Group & Organization Studies, 13*, 274–89.

Tjosvold, D. (1990). Making a technological innovation work: Collaboration to solve problems. *Human Relations, 43*, 1117–31.

Tjosvold, D. (1991). *Conflict-positive organization: Stimulate diversity and create unity*. Reading, MA: Addison-Wesley.

Tjosvold, D. (1993). *Learning to manage conflict: Getting people to work together productively*. New York: Lexington Books.

Tjosvold, D. and Chia, L.C. (1989). Conflict between managers and employees: the role of coop-eration and competition. *Journal of Social Psychology, 129*, 235–47.

Tjosvold, D., Dann, V. and Wong, C.L. (1992). Managing conflict between departments to serve customers. *Human Relations, 45*, 1035–54.

Tjosvold, D. and Deemer, D.K. (1980). Effects of controversy within a cooperative or competi-tive context on organizational decision-making. *Journal of Applied Psychology, 65*, 590–5.

Tjosvold, D. and Deemer, D.K. (1981). Effects of control or collaborative orientation on partic-ipation in decision-making. *Canadian Journal of Behavioral Science, 13*, 33–43.

Tjosvold, D., Hui, C. and Law, K. (in press). Empowerment in the leadership relationship in Hong Kong: Interdependence and controversy. *Journal of Social Psychology*.

Tjosvold, D. and Johnson, D.W. (1977). The effects of controversy on cognitive perspective taking. *Journal of Educational Psychology, 69*, 679–85.

Tjosvold, D. and Johnson, D.W. (1978). Controversy within a cooperative or competitive context and cognitive perspective taking. *Contemporary Educational Psychology, 3*, 376–86.

Tjosvold, D., Johnson, D.W. and Fabrey, L. (1980). The effects of affirmation and acceptance on incorporation of an opposing opinion in problem solving. *Psychological Reports, 47*, 1043–53.

Tjosvold, D., Johnson, D.W. and Lerner, J. (1981). The effects of affirmation and acceptance on incorporation of an opposing opinion in problem-solving. *Journal of Social Psychology, 114*, 103–10.

Tjosvold, D., Lee, F. and Wong, C.L. (1992). Managing conflict in a diverse workforce: a Chinese perspective in North America. *Small Group Research, 23*, 302–32.

Tjosvold, D. and McNeely, L.T. (1988). Innovation through communication in an educational bureaucracy. *Communication Research, 15*, 568–81.

Tjosvold, D., Moy, J. and Sasaki, S. (in press). Managing for customers and employees in Hong Kong: The quality and teamwork challenges. *Journal of Market -Focused Management.*

Tjosvold, D., Sasaki, S. and Moy, J. (1995). *Developing commitment in Japanese organizations in Hong Kong: Cooperative teamwork and constructive controversy.* Paper, City University of Hong Kong.

Tjosvold, D. and Tjosvold, M.M. (1993). *The emerging leader: Ways to a stronger team.* New York: Lexington.

Tjosvold, D. and Tjosvold, M.M. (in press). *The diverse positive organization: How to work across organizational and cultural boundaries.* San Francisco: Jossey-Bass.

Tjosvold, D., Tjosvold, M.M. and Tjosvold, J. (1995). *Love and anger: Managing family conflict.* Minneapolis: Team Media.

Tjosvold, D. and Tsao, Y. (1989). Productive organizational collaboration: the role of values and cooperative goals. *Journal of Organizational Behavior*, 10, 189–95.

Tjosvold, D., Wedley, W.C., Field, R.H.G. (1986). Constructive controversy, the Vroom-Yetton model, and managerial decision making. *Journal of Occupational Behaviour*, 7, 125–38.

Tjosvold, D. and Wong, C.L. (1992). *Cooperative conflict and coordination to market technology.* Paper, International Association of Conflict Management conference, Minneapolis, June .

Van Berklom, M. and Tjosvold, D. (1981). The effects of social context on engaging in controversy. *Journal of Psychology, 107*, 141–5.

Walton, R. and McKersie, R.B. (1965). *A behavioral theory of labor negotiations.* New York: McGraw-Hill.

Wong, C. and Tjosvold, D. (1994). Goal interdependence and quality in services marketing. *Psychology & Marketing, 12*, 189–205.

3

The Effectiveness of Mixing Problem Solving and Forcing

Evert Van de Vliert, Aukje Nauta, Martin C. Euwema and Onne Janssen

Social conflict is a phenomenon so omnipresent in organizational life that we can all too easily take it for granted. Members of the organization react by choosing from well-trodden paths: they avoid a reproach, they accommodate a poor plan, they negotiate on a price or solve a problem, and sometimes they fight an opponent on principle. This chapter addresses the question of how these categories of daily conflict behaviours relate to organizational effectiveness. It focuses on the effectiveness of the principal parties' behavioural components of problem solving and 'forcing' in dyadic interpersonal conflict. A first section provides definitions of the concepts used, an overview of four perspectives on dyadic effectiveness and a discussion of the theoretical rationale of the studies. This is followed by reports of three field studies, which demonstrate the usefulness of a 'complexity perspective' by examining the dyadic effectiveness of simultaneous and sequential combinations of problem solving and forcing.

Theoretical background

Definitions

Individuals are in *conflict* when they are obstructed or irritated by another individual or a group; they subsequently react in a beneficial or costly way. Two important and very different modes of outward reaction to the inner conflict issue experienced are problem solving and forcing. *Problem solving* is reconciling the parties' basic interests. *Forcing* is contending the adversary in a direct way.

Conflict behaviour is viewed as personally effective to the extent that an individual succeeds in realizing the benefits or costs desired for oneself. Personal effectiveness may or may not be in accord with the *dyadic effectiveness* that we studied: the extent to which components of conflict behaviour are producing better outcomes for the organizational dyad by mitigating the conflict issues, improving the relationship between the parties, or both (see Thomas, 1992; Tjosvold, 1991; see also Chapter 1, this book).

Perspectives on dyadic effectiveness

The *one-best-way perspective* states that, compared to avoiding, accommo-dating, compromising and forcing, problem solving is the most constructive mode of conflict management because it always serves the joint welfare best (e.g. Blake & Mouton, 1964, 1970; Pneuman & Bruehl, 1982; Tjosvold, 1991; see also Chapter 2 in this book). In contrast, the *contingency perspective* contends that the answer regarding what is effective can only be given in the light of situational realities, and that each mode of conflict management, even forcing, is appropriate under some circumstances (e.g. Axelrod, 1984; Hocker & Wilmot, 1991; Rahim, 1992). Thomas's (1992) *time perspective* combines the preceding perspectives. It asserts that the contingency approach provides answers to the short-term question of how best to cope with the here and now, while the 'one-best-way' approach deals with the longer term task of creating desirable future circumstances for the organization.

Though the one-best-way, contingency and time perspectives on dyadic effectiveness are theoretically different, they implicitly have two assumptions in common. First, modes of handling conflict are pure and mutually inde-pendent variables. That is, avoiding, accommodating, compromising, problem solving and forcing do not overlap each other. Second, modes of handling conflict have pure and mutually independent relations with effectiveness. That is, avoiding, accommodating, compromising, problem solving and forc-ing do not influence each other's impact on the consequences for the dyad members and their organization.

Breaking away from the prevailing three perspectives, we propose the addi-tion of a *complexity perspective* that makes the following alternative assumptions (for details, see Van de Vliert, in press). The first assumption holds that a reaction to a conflict issue consists of multiple behavioural com-ponents rather than a single and pure mode of behaviour. Indeed, mixtures of avoiding, accommodating, compromising, problem solving and forcing are the rule rather than the exception (Falbe & Yukl, 1992; Knapp, Putnam & Davis, 1988; Rubin, Pruitt & Kim, 1994; Yukl, Falbe & Young Youn, 1993). For example, 'tacit coordination' is a merger of reactions in which one sticks to one's guns and withholds relevant information while revealing obligingness and real interests through nonverbal cues (e.g. Borisoff & Victor, 1989; Pruitt, 1981; Putnam, 1990). For the simultaneous or sequential aggregation of var-ious degrees of several modes of conflict behaviour, we have coined the term 'conglomerated conflict behaviour' (Van de Vliert, in press; Van de Vliert, Euwema & Huismans, 1995). The second novel assumption holds that com-ponents of conglomerated conflict behaviour intermediate or moderate each other's impact on the substantive and relational outcomes of the conflict. For example, 'logrolling' as the juxtaposition or alternation of being exacting about a benefit or cost that is important to oneself but unimportant to the opponent, while being obliging about a benefit or cost that is unimportant to oneself but important to the opponent, is an effective form of conglomerated conflict behaviour (Lax & Sebenius, 1986; Rubin et al., 1994).

Rationale of the studies

In agreement with the above line of reasoning, a previous study showed that problem solving by police sergeants *vis-à-vis* police constables is especially effective at high levels of forcing (Van de Vliert et al., 1995). Dyadic effectiveness of such conglomerations of problem solving and forcing makes sense for at least three reasons.

First of all, most conflict issues are so complex that problem solving might be more appropriate for some aspects of the discord, while forcing might be more appropriate for other aspects. For example, problem solving is especially appropriate for merging pieces of insight as well as working through a negative feeling, whereas forcing is especially appropriate for responding to an emergency element as well as implementing an important but unpopular decision (Rahim, 1992; Thomas, 1992). As a consequence, the effectiveness might well increase if problem solving is competently interspersed with forcing, or vice versa.

In the second place, the fact that conflict is rooted in concern for one's own rather than the other party's goals might also help explain why conglomerations of problem solving and forcing are so effective. One of the main differences between the two modes of behaviour is that problem solving does whereas forcing does not communicate concern for the realization of the other party's goals (Janssen & Van de Vliert, 1996; Van de Vliert, in press). It implies that the existence of a conflict issue as such is less consistent with problem solving than with forcing. Especially in escalated conflicts, this might give problem solving a glimpse of unnaturalness that needs more causal explanation, whereas it might give forcing a glimpse of obviousness that is taken for granted. Therefore, compared to problem solving, a conglomeration of problem solving and forcing might not infrequently be perceived by the opponent as more genuine and understandable, which then makes itself felt in more constructive responses and better joint outcomes.

Last but not least, according to the contingency perspective, each component of conglomerated conflict behaviour may undermine effectiveness. The juxtaposition or alternation of problem solving and forcing might therefore dampen the risks of effectiveness reduction. The risks of problem solving include that so-called win–win outcomes are out of the question, that the parties' mutual relationship blocks such outcomes, and that the ultimate solution is not worth the necessary time and energy investments (Hocker & Wilmot, 1991). The risks of forcing include escalation beyond acceptable cost limits, a deteriorating relationship and stalemate following failure of contentious tactics (Rubin et al., 1994). Indeed, a sophisticated mixture of problem solving and forcing might reduce both types of risks (for a similar argument and qualitative empirical evidence, see Walton, Cutcher-Gershenfeld & McKersie, 1994).

Taken together, we felt confident to hypothesize that the dyadic effectiveness of conglomerated conflict behaviour is a positive function of problem solving in combination with forcing.

Study 1

Overview

The first investigation was executed in a hospital setting. We selected a realistic and incendiary conflict issue, defined and operationalized escalating reactions to that conflict, and trained confederates to perform these standardized behaviours. We then recruited senior nurses as subjects and videotaped their interaction with a confederate. Finally, we had neutral observers assess the effectiveness of the conglomerated conflict behaviour; the same observers later scored each tape for the occurrence of problem solving and forcing.

Method

Fifty-four male and forty-three female senior nurses from Dutch hospitals were chosen as subjects because, as first-line supervisors, they occupied a conflict-prone position in their organization.

Conflict simulation. Pilot studies yielded the following conflict issue. A senior nurse finds an elderly patient highly upset, complaining about someone who has treated her in a rude manner. The patient says she has asked for more medicine but did not get it. She was told to accept the pain and stop nagging. When she started to cry, the other just left the room. To control for the potentially confounding impact of gender and power, differences in sex composition and hierarchical position were randomly varied. The accused other, either female or male, was a superior physician or a subordinate nurse. Confederates were trained to role play the accused other by confronting the subject with the conflict issue in an intensifying way. The confederate had to start with trivialization of the incident, continue with disagreement about the underlying organizational policy, and end with a personal attack on the behaviour of the senior nurse in this matter.

The subjects attended regular curricula for nurses in lower management functions. On arrival in the training centre, the experimenter explained the crucial function that the individual role plays would fulfil during the training. He had the subject read the conflict scenario, answered any questions, and brought the subject into a room in which a camera was situated in one corner. The experimenter waited outside for the end of the confrontation with the confederate, which took about fifteen minutes on average.

Measurements. In order to assess the dyadic effectiveness of the total conflict interaction, each videotape was independently rated by four trained observers, who were unaware of the goals of the study. They used multiple rating scales for substantive and relational outcomes (1 = very ineffective; 7 = very effective; see for details Van de Vliert et al., 1995). The substantive outcomes concerned the ultimate number of conflict issues, the severeness of these issues, proximity to a solution, the chances of recidivism, and the quality of concerted task performance. The relational outcomes concerned the attention given to communalities, the ultimate amount of mutual distrust and mutual understanding, as well as the ultimate atmosphere, and personal relationship. Averaged across coders, these criteria of dyadic effectiveness constituted one homogeneous measure.

We subsequently trained the same observers to rate the conflict behaviour. In additional runs, they independently assessed the occurrence of the components of problem solving and forcing. The following operationalizations were included: *Problem solving*: exchanges accurate information; works through differences; deals with each party's concerns. *Forcing*: makes effort to get one's way; uses power to win; makes authority decision. For each behaviour each coder completed a rating scale (1 = occurred not at all; 5 = occurred to a great extent), after which the ratings were combined into one measure for problem solving and one for forcing.

Results

Table 3.1 provides the means, standard deviations, intercorrelations and reliability estimates of problem solving, forcing and effectiveness. Note that problem solving and forcing are negatively interrelated and have opposite relations with effectiveness.

Table 3.1   *Means, standard deviations, reliabilities and intercorrelations of problem solving, forcing and effectiveness for Study 1 and Study 2*

	Study 1[a]			Study 2[b]					
	M	*SD*	Rel.[c]	*M*	*SD*	Rel.	1	2	3
1. Problem solving	1.43	0.27	0.79	2.95	0.94	0.73	–	–0.43*	0.65*
2. Forcing	3.29	0.64	0.90	3.06	1.00	0.92	–0.59*	–	–0.46*
3. Effectiveness	2.90	0.38	0.95	3.05	1.15	0.93	0.66*	–0.82*	–

Note: The correlations on the right of the table above the diagonal relate to Study 1; those below the diagonal relate to Study 2.
[a] $N = 97$; scales range from 1 to 5 for problem solving and forcing, and from 1 to 7 for effectiveness.
[b] $N = 39$; scales range from 1 to 7.
[c]   Cronbach's alpha.
* $p \leq 0.01$.

We used multiple regression analysis to test our hypothesis. Problem solving and forcing together account for 46% of the variance in the substantive and relational outcomes for the dyad. More importantly, their interaction effect is also significant ($p < 0.05$). In agreement with the hypothesis, effectiveness is a positive function of problem solving in combination with forcing. As represented in Figure 3.1, the most effective mixture of conflict behaviour is the combination of much problem solving and much forcing.

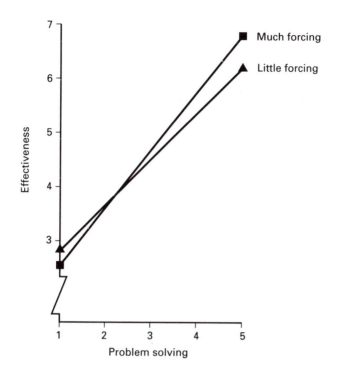

Figure 3.1   *Joint effectiveness of problem solving and forcing: Study 1*

Discussion

In order to really produce good substantive and relational outcomes for the hospital, senior nurses have to manifest conglomerated conflict behaviour. They have to pepper their problem solving moves with moves of forcing. Specifically, the most effectively operating senior nurses attempted to solve the problem while they also made efforts to get their way, used power to win, and even made authoritarian decisions. This finding does not unconditionally support the one-best-way view that problem solving, and not forcing, serves the organization best. Nor does it support the contingency view that either problem solving or forcing will be most appropriate under the simulated circumstances. The complexity perspective fares better instead. The senior nurses handle the conflict more effectively to the extent that they combine much problem solving and much forcing into a behavioural compound that might be seen as a form of 'constructive controversy' (see Johnson, Johnson & Smith, 1989; Tjosvold, 1985).

Study 1 evoked a number of questions that incited us to undertake Study 2. First of all, the confederate was a professional actor; do conflict interactions with real members of one's own organization have similar effects? Second, the confederate simulated only one specific escalatory process: trivializing the incident, attacking the underlying policy, and attacking the person. Also, as problem solving is a more dyadic mode of behaviour than forcing, this escalatory process might have influenced the senior nurse's reactions of problem solving and forcing differently. Do the findings also hold when the conflict interaction is a more natural event, occurring between two subjects instead of one subject and one confederate? Third, is effective conflict management between hospital employees with a naturally caring profession also effective between employees in other organizations? Taken together, the optimal pattern of responses may be quite different between 'colleagues' in a different type of organization, who manifest different sequences of reactions to the conflict issue and to each other's behaviour.

Study 2

Overview

The research project was continued in a national management development centre of the police force. As part of regular training activities, dyads of unit managers, who were not close colleagues, handled an easily recognizable standardized conflict of interest. As before, the role play was videotaped for both feedback and research purposes. Neutral observers later appraised the occurrence of problem solving and forcing, as well as the effectiveness of the conglomerated conflict behaviour.

Method

Sixty-three male and fifteen female unit managers from Dutch police organizations participated. No members of the thirty-nine dyads were co-workers in daily life.

Conflict simulation. Pilot studies resulted in the following conflict scenario. The subject is a manager of a police unit in a large city. The chief of the police district has 'created' a budget to appoint a clerical member of staff who will take work off a unit manager's shoulders. The subject and another unit manager, A and B, are badly in need of this assistant, albeit for different reasons (the scenario then specified these reasons for both A and B). In order to obtain the extra staff position, the chief of the district leaves A and B the joint option to either both hand in a written request for an assistant, or both orally motivate their request in a meeting with the board of the district. This choice complicates the conflict of interest. A, who is a good writer, prefers a written proposal, whereas B, who is good at oral presentations, prefers it the other way. A and B have made an appointment to confront the issue and to decide in favour of either the written proposal or the oral presentation.

The conflict simulation formed part of a number of training sessions for managers of police units. The subjects were randomly assigned, first to dyads, and then to the roles of A and B. On arrival in the simulation room, the experimenter had them read the conflict scenario, and identify themselves with their respective roles of A and B. The dyad then had about ten minutes to enact the conflict. Each interaction was videotaped and later coded.

Measurements. We trained four observers, who were unaware of the goals of the study, to assess the individual use of the behavioural components of problem solving and forcing (for details, see Study 1). This was done for A and B separately, after which each observer's average scores were calculated. The coders' average ratings were combined into one measure for dyadic problem solving and one for dyadic forcing.

The substantive and relational outcomes of the total conflict interaction were independently rated by the same observers with the help of the effectiveness items from Study 1.

Results

Table 3.1 provides the descriptive statistics. As in Study 1, problem solving and forcing are negatively interrelated, and have opposite relations with effectiveness.

Problem solving and forcing together account for 72% of the variance in dyadic effectiveness ($p < 0.001$). Again, in agreement with our hypothesis, the interaction effect is also significant ($p < 0.01$). Effectiveness is a positive function of problem solving in combination with forcing. Not surprisingly, little problem solving is especially ineffective if combined with much forcing (see Figure 3.2). Additional analyses with A's or B's individual use of problem solving and forcing as predictors of dyadic effectiveness yielded the same pattern of results.

Discussion

Compared to the senior nurses from Study 1, policemen, having a less caring and more confrontative people-processing profession, show a similar pattern of behavioural effectiveness. As in the hospital, in the police organization the mixture of little problem solving and much forcing produced the least substantive and relational outcomes. Interestingly, this time, problem solving does not influence effectiveness at low levels of forcing. Again, this does not support the assumption that modes of handling conflict have mutually independent effects, as the one-best-way, contingency and time perspectives would have it. Again, the assumptions underlying the complexity perspective fare better instead; mixtures of problem solving and forcing do have joint effects. The police managers appear to handle their conflict with a colleague most effectively if they either refrain from forceful behaviour or mix it with problem solving.

This field experiment, using police dyads, obviated some drawbacks with regard to the earlier use of confederates in the hospital context. However, Studies 1 and 2 still do not answer several other questions. Are the findings about dyads working in hospital and police organizations generalizable to dyads in free enterprises? Also, is it problematic that both studies employed a

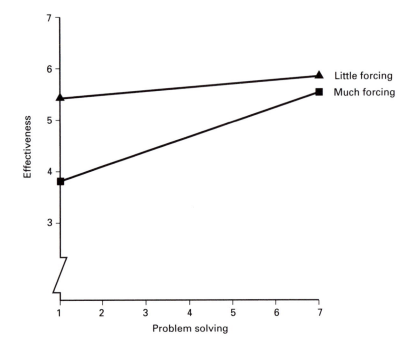

Figure 3.2   *Joint effectiveness of problem solving and forcing: Study 2*

single group of observers for the assessment of the conglomerated conflict behaviour and its effectiveness? Though it is hard to imagine that the observers have artificially caused the consistent pattern of effects of problem solving and forcing, a common source bias cannot be excluded with conviction. With a view to the complexity perspective, the most serious queries concern the distinction between simultaneous and sequential conglomerations of problem solving and forcing. Is the observed interactive effect primarily caused by the juxtaposition or the alternation of the components of problem solving and forcing? And if alternation makes conglomerated conflict behaviour more effective, is this because problem solving precedes or follows forcing? A data set from a concurrent research project enabled us to answer these questions, and also to overcome the sample and measurement restrictions hinted at above.

Study 3

Overview

The last investigation concerned work dyads from a wide variety of industries, consultancy firms and governmental institutions. We designed a general and comprehensible conflict issue to be acted out by the dyads as part of a workshop on conflict management that we organized for them. Each simulation was videotaped and later rated by two independent groups of observers. The first group assessed the occurrence of problem solving and forcing, while the second group assessed the effectiveness of the conglomerated conflict behaviour.

Method

Twenty-four Dutch dyads participated, including eleven male–male, nine male–female and four female–female dyads. All subjects had either a superior–subordinate or a lateral co-working relationship in daily life.

Conflict simulation. Pilot studies resulted in the following role script: 'In the space of two months, two persons A and B form a selection committee to hire a capable candidate for a new job. Because of illness during a vacation in a foreign country, A has been absent for three weeks. When A returns, it appears that B has continued the procedure and that there are only two candidates left. Both A and B feel frustrated because things have not proceeded satisfactorily. B believes that A let B do all the work alone. A feels bypassed by B because the two remaining candidates do not meet the requirements that A finds most important. They have made an appointment to talk things over.'

A one-day workshop on conflict management for co-working dyads was advertised and organized. In separate rooms, experimenters instructed one dyad member to prepare for role A, while the other dyad member was told to prepare for role B. Subjects had eight minutes to read the role script and to have ambiguities clarified, followed by twelve minutes to handle the conflict.

Measurements. Each conflict interaction was videotaped and later transcribed. A transcript contained fifty-five speaking turns on average, whereby a speaking turn is defined as everything a person says between other's last utterance and other's next utterance.

A group of four observers who were unaware of the goals of the study, was trained to assess the occurrence of the behavioural components of problem solving and forcing. Problem solving was operationalized through six prototypical examples of diagnostic explorations, integrative intentions, creative suggestions and breaking out of impasses. Similarly, forcing was operationalized through six prototypical examples of blaming, claiming, threatening and imposing one's will on the opponent. The behavioural rating scales were independently completed for each of A's and B's speaking turns separately (1 = occurred not at all; 3 = occurred to a great extent).

A completely independent group of four observers who were also unaware of the goals of the study, watched the videotapes to assess the substantive and relational outcomes with the help of the items from Study 1 (1 = very ineffective; 7 = very effective). This produced a reliable overall criterion of dyadic effectiveness.

Predictors. Through median splits each speaking turn was categorized as reflecting little or much problem solving as well as little or much forcing. This produced four types of speaking turns. First, *dominant problem solving*: much problem solving and little forcing. Second, *dominant forcing*: little problem solving and much forcing. Third, *concurrence*: much problem solving and much forcing. Fourth, *non-confrontation*: little problem solving and little forcing. Three predictors were then constructed that dealt with the *simultaneous conglomeration* of problem solving and forcing within speaking turns: each dyad's percentages of speaking turns coded as dominant problem solving, dominant forcing and concurrence, respectively. Two additional predictors dealt with the *sequential conglomeration* of problem solving and forcing in one dyad member's speaking turn at time t, and problem solving and forcing in the same dyad member's next speaking turn at time t+2 (after the other dyad member's speaking turn at t+1). The fourth predictor was each dyad's percentage of two subsequent own speaking turns coded as dominant problem solving at time t and dominant forcing at time t+2. Conversely, the fifth and final predictor was each dyad's percentage of two subsequent own speaking turns coded as dominant forcing at time t and dominant problem solving at time t+2.

Table 3.2   *Means, standard deviations and intercorrelations of problem solving, forcing and effectiveness for Study 3*

	M	SD	Y	Z	X/Y	Y/X	E
Simultaneity							
X. Dominant problem solving	11.63	8.72	−0.76**	−0.04	0.19	0.26	0.73**
Y. Dominant forcing	39.86	15.26		−0.22	0.15	0.02	−0.78**
Z. Concurrence	11.64	5.39			0.15	−0.26	−0.01
Sequentiality							
X first, Y next (X/Y)	1.98	1.69				0.46*	0.07
Y first, X next (Y/X)	2.70	2.76					0.35*
Effectiveness (E)	4.81	1.30					

Note: N = 24 dyads; scales indicate percentages of speaking turns (X, Y, Z) or combinations of speaking turns (X/Y, Y/X). The interobserver reliability coefficients are good (problem solving $\alpha = 0.78$; forcing $\alpha = 0.90$; effectiveness $\alpha = 0.96$). The correspondence between the dyad members' average scores across observers and speaking turns (problem solving $r = 0.35$, $p < 0.05$; forcing $r = 0.71$, $p < 0.001$) allow the use of combined measures.
* $p \leq 0.05$.
** $p \leq 0.01$.

Results

Table 3.2 contains the descriptive statistics. Similar to Studies 1 and 2, dominant problem solving and dominant forcing are negatively interrelated and have opposite relations with effectiveness.

Regression analysis showed that dominant forcing ($p < 0.001$) and dominant forcing followed by dominant problem solving ($p < 0.01$) account for 74% of the variance in effectiveness. Dominant forcing appears to undermine effectiveness unless it is followed by dominant problem solving. Or in words that underscore the confirmation of our hypothesis: the dyadic effectiveness of conglomerated conflict behaviour is a negative function of forcing, but a positive function of problem solving preceded by forcing. Due to the extremely high negative correlation between dominant problem solving and dominant forcing, dominant problem solving in and of itself does not contribute to effectiveness over and above the two successful predictors. Also, no unique contribution to effectiveness could be established for concurrent problem solving and forcing, nor for dominant problem solving followed by dominant forcing. Additional analyses with A's or B's individual use of problem solving and forcing as predictors of dyadic effectiveness yielded the same pattern of results.

Discussion

Like the foregoing studies, Study 3 does not support the commonly held assumptions that mutually independent conflict behaviours exist, and that they have mutually independent effects. Instead, once again, it supports the complexity assumption that conglomerated components of conflict behaviour have interdependent effects. More importantly, however, this last study solidifies, generalizes and enriches our understanding of dyadic effectiveness by employing different groups of observers for behavioural components and behavioural effectiveness, by moving beyond the boundaries of hospital and police organizations, and by crossing the boundary between simultaneity and sequentiality. In particular, it introduces the time dimension by examining distinct sequences of behavioural components. This enables us to conclude that problem solving preceded by forcing produces better substantive and relational outcomes for organizational dyads than any other simultaneous or sequential conglomeration of dyadic conflict behaviour.

It is important to note that our successful predictor of forcing followed by problem solving rests on the observation of repeated behavioural patterns rather than once-only behavioural shifts. For that reason, the above conclusion leads to more than the recommendation that one should start competitive and end cooperative. The additional recommendation reads that the sequence of 'first forcing then problem solving' may have to be repeated to enhance effectiveness. That the members of effective dyads do indeed use alternating competition and cooperation is reflected in the positive connection between dominant problem solving followed by dominant forcing, and dominant forcing followed by dominant problem solving (see Table 3.2).

Supplementary analyses of the total 'wave' of forcing–problem solving–forcing–problem solving indicate that effectiveness is especially sensitive to ending with problem solving. Taken together, this represents a crucial specification of the complexity perspective's corollary that employees are more effective to the extent that they use mixtures of dominant problem solving and dominant forcing.

General discussion

This chapter contributes to the literature in several regards. First, at the level of the organizational dyad, the occurrence of problem solving and the occurrence of forcing are studied as twins rather than loners. Breaking away from the prevailing assumption of conflict behaviours as mutually isolated modes of reaction, problem solving and forcing are considered components of complex conflict behaviour (see Falbe & Yukl, 1992; Knapp et al., 1988; Rubin et al., 1994; Van de Vliert et al., 1995; Yukl et al., 1993). Second, the effectiveness of problem solving and the *in*effectiveness of forcing are studied as twins rather than loners. Breaking away from the prevailing assumption of conflict behaviours as mutually isolated determinants of substantive and relational outcomes, it is demonstrated that problem solving and forcing are more effective, or less ineffective, in combination than they are in isolation (see Falbe & Yukl, 1992; Putnam, 1990; Van de Vliert et al., 1995). Third, for the very first time, the simultaneity and the sequentiality of problem solving and forcing are studied as twins rather than loners. Study 3 shows that the simultaneity of much problem solving and little forcing, preceded by the simultaneity of little problem solving and much forcing, is especially effective.

The studies reported here seem to provide additional scientific underpinning of the crude behavioural recommendation that 'constructive controversy' pays (see Johnson et al., 1989; Tjosvold, 1985, 1991). As outlined in our theoretical introduction, problem solving and forcing supplement each other with respect to appropriateness for specific aspects of conflict issues, consistency with the existence of conflict and risks of effectiveness reduction. For those reasons, the mixture of constructive problem solving and controversy in the form of forcing might be very effective. The findings in the last study provide a more refined operationalization of the rule of thumb that integrative and distributive moves should be mixed (see Lax & Sebenius, 1986; Putnam, 1990). In order to be effective, controversy in the form of forcing should precede constructive exploration in the form of problem solving. This resembles the well-documented effectiveness of the 'reformed sinner strategy' (Deutsch, 1973; Harford & Solomon, 1967), and the within-person 'black-hat/white-hat routine' (see Hilty & Carnevale, 1993; Rafaeli & Sutton, 1991). In all such cases, a phase of differentiation precedes a phase of integration (Walton, 1987). On closer consideration, however, the reformed sinner strategy and the strategy of taking off one's black hat and putting on one's white hat address once-only behavioural shifts. In contrast, our findings are based on the alternation of dominant forcing and dominant problem solving. Apparently, the move from forcing to problem solving has a de-escalatory and effective nature, whereas the reverse move from problem solving to forcing is neutral as to joint substantive and relational outcomes.

Future research should tease out why exactly de-escalatory shifts increase effectiveness more than escalatory shifts decrease effectiveness. Considerable progress would be made if the explanation could be fine-tuned to specific operationalizations of problem solving and forcing. A major shortcoming of the present series of studies is the broad domain of coding instructions. Problem solving covers such divergent ways of behaving as exchanging accurate information, working through differences, dealing with each party's concerns, and suggesting creative breakthroughs. Similarly, forcing covers acts of blaming, claiming, using power to win, and imposing one's will. It is unlikely that each alternation of any problem solving element and any forcing element improves the effectiveness in the same way or to the same extent.

An additional weakness of our studies is that they relied on neutral observers exclusively. It is relevant to examine whether the actors themselves experience the apparent effectiveness of dominant forcing followed by dominant problem solving. Similarly, can the results be replicated if the effectiveness is assessed through comparison with one or more objective standards? Finally, efficiency was left out of consideration. What are the costs of dominant forcing followed by dominant problem solving in terms of the time and energy that have to be invested to reach a somewhat higher level of effectiveness?

In spite of these limitations, the systematic pattern of results reported here inspires confidence in the following three main conclusions: First, simultaneous mixtures of problem solving and forcing seem effective if sequentiality is left out of consideration (Studies 1 and 2), but not if sequentiality is also examined (Study 3). Second, simultaneous mixtures of little problem solving and much forcing are *in*effective unless they are followed by simultaneous mixtures of much problem solving and little forcing (Study 3). Third, effective sequential mixtures of dominant forcing preceding dominant problem solving are a cyclical rather than a once-only phenomenon exclusively. This leaves the paradoxical overall impression that the alternation of conflict escalation and de-escalation enhances organizational performance.

References

Axelrod, R. (1984). *The evolution of cooperation*. New York: Basic Books.

Blake, R.R. and Mouton, J.S. (1964). *The managerial grid*. Houston, TX: Gulf.

Blake, R.R. and Mouton, J.S. (1970). The fifth achievement. *Journal of Applied Behavioral Science*, *6*, 413–26.

Borisoff, D. and Victor, D.A. (1989). *Conflict management: a communication skills approach*. Englewood Cliffs, NJ: Prentice-Hall.

Deutsch, M. (1973). *The resolution of conflict: Constructive and destructive processes*. New Haven, CT: Yale University Press.

Falbe, C.M. and Yukl, G. (1992). Consequences for managers of using single influence tactics and combinations of tactics. *Academy of Management Journal*, *35*, 638–52.

Harford, T. and Solomon, L. (1967). 'Reformed sinner' and 'lapsed saint' strategies in the prisoner's dilemma game. *Journal of Conflict Resolution*, *11*, 104–9.

Hilty, J.A. and Carnevale, P.J. (1993). Black-hat/white-hat strategy in bilateral negotiation. *Organizational Behavior and Human Decision Processes*, *55*, 444–69.

Hocker, J.L. and Wilmot, W.W. (1991). *Interpersonal conflict* (3rd edn). Dubuque, IA: William C. Brown.

Janssen, O. and Van de Vliert, E. (1996). Concern for the other's goals: Key to (de) escalation of conflict. *International Journal of Conflict Management*, *7*, 99–120.

Johnson, D.W., Johnson, R.T. and Smith, K. (1989). Controversy within decision making situations, in M.A. Rahim (ed.), *Managing conflict: an interdisciplinary approach*. New York: Praeger, pp. 251–64.

Knapp, M.L., Putnam, L.L. and Davis, L.J. (1988). Measuring interpersonal conflict in organizations: Where do we go from here? *Management Communication Quarterly*, *1*, 414–29.

Lax, D.A. and Sebenius, J.K. (1986). *The manager as negotiator: Bargaining for cooperation and competitive gain*. New York: Free Press.

Pneuman, R.W. and Bruehl, M.E. (1982). *Managing conflict*. Englewood Cliffs, NJ: Prentice-Hall.

Pruitt, D.G. (1981). *Negotiation behavior*. New York: Academic Press.

Putnam, L.L. (1990). Reframing integrative and distributive bargaining: a process perspective, in B.H. Sheppard, M.H. Bazerman and R.J. Lewicki (eds), *Research on negotiation in organizations*. Greenwich, CT: JAI Press, Vol. 2, pp. 3–30.

Rafaeli, A. and Sutton, R.I. (1991). Emotional contrast strategies as means of social influence: Lessons from criminal interrogators and bill collectors. *Academy of Management Journal*, *34*, 749–75.

Rahim, M.A. (1992). *Managing conflict in organizations* (2nd edn). Westport, CT: Praeger.

Rubin, J.Z., Pruitt, D.G. and Kim, S.H. (1994). *Social conflict: Escalation, stalemate, and settlement*. New York: McGraw-Hill.

Thomas, K.W. (1992). Conflict and negotiation processes in organizations, in M.D. Dunnette and L.M. Hough (eds), *Handbook of industrial and organizational psychology* (2nd edn). Palo Alto, CA: Consulting Psychologists Press, pp. 651–717.

Tjosvold, D. (1985). Implications of controversy research for management. *Journal of Management*, *11*, 221–38.

Tjosvold, D. (1991). *The conflict-positive organization: Stimulate diversity and create unity*. Reading, MA: Addison-Wesley.

Van de Vliert, E. (in press). *Theoretical frontiers of complex interpersonal conflict behaviour*. Hove: Erlbaum (UK) Taylor & Francis.

Van de Vliert, E., Euwema, M.C. and Huismans, S.E. (1995). Managing conflict with a subordinate or a superior: Effectiveness of conglomerated behavior. *Journal of Applied Psychology*, *80*, 271–81.

Walton, R.E. (1987). *Managing conflict: Interpersonal dialogue and third-party roles* (2nd edn). Reading, MA: Addison-Wesley.

Walton, R.E., Cutcher-Gershenfeld, J.E. and McKersie, R.B. (1994). *Strategic negotiations: a theory of change in labor-management relations*. Boston, MA: Harvard Business School Press.

Yukl, G., Falbe, C.M. and Young Youn, J. (1993). Patterns of influence behavior for managers. *Group & Organization Management*, *18*, 5–28.

PART II

WITHIN-GROUP CONFLICT AND PERFORMANCE

4

Mitigating Groupthink by Stimulating Constructive Conflict

Marlene E. Turner and Anthony R. Pratkanis

One of the most searing television images of the past decades occurred at 11:38 a.m. on January 8, 1986. Less than a minute after lift-off, the space shuttle *Challenger* exploded, killing all seven people aboard. Although there were ample warning signs that a potential disaster was on the horizon, they were ignored by the elite team at the United States space agency, NASA. Four years later, in a highly publicized event designed to triumphantly proclaim its regained technological pre-eminence, NASA launched the two-billion dollar *Hubble* space telescope. The telescope, however, did not work. As Senator Barbara Mikulski pithily put it, the *Hubble* had a 'cataract' (Chaisson, 1994). Among other problems, its main mirror, critical to approximately 50% of the planned astronomical research to be conducted by the *Hubble*, was flawed, apparently due to a rudimentary failure to implement simple quality assurance tests (see Chaisson, 1994 for a chronicle of the *Hubble* space telescope development).

What do these fiascos have in common? In many respects, they share the characteristics of what Irving Janis called 'groupthink' – the extreme concurrence seeking displayed by decision making groups. When groups are susceptible to groupthink, their goals are transformed from the pursuit of effective problem resolution (i.e. identifying possible problems, evaluating different alternatives) to the suppression of conflict at all costs (i.e. launch despite any concerns or contradictory indications). As the *Challenger* and *Hubble* incidents illustrate, this suppression of conflict and the ensuing curtailment of discussion and evaluation of the decision can be costly, both in terms of loss of financial resources and in terms of loss of human life.

The purpose of this chapter is to explore ways to stimulate discussion and promote constructive conflict in situations where groups might be likely to experience groupthink. To do this, we first briefly evaluate prior research on groupthink and describe our own model of groupthink, the social identity maintenance perspective. Once we understand the social dynamics and forces operating in the groupthink situation, we then offer methods of combating its adverse consequences by effectively stimulating cognitive conflict and reducing pressures towards identity maintenance that impede deliberative discussion.

Groupthink in perspective

Groupthink defined

Janis's classic formulation (Janis, 1972, 1982) as well as his more recent reformulation (see, for example, Janis, 1989) hypothesizes that decision making groups are most likely to experience groupthink when they are highly cohesive, insulated from experts, perform limited search and appraisal of information, operate under directive leadership, and experience conditions of high stress with low self-esteem and little hope of finding a better solution to a pressing problem than that favoured by the leader or influential members.

When present, these antecedent conditions are hypothesized to foster the extreme consensus seeking characteristic of groupthink. This in turn is predicted to lead to two categories of undesirable decision making processes. The first, traditionally labelled symptoms of groupthink, includes illusion of invulnerability, collective rationalization, stereotypes of outgroups, self-censorship, mindguards, and belief in the inherent morality of the group. The second, typically identified as symptoms of defective decision making, involves the incomplete survey of alternatives and objectives, poor information search, failure to appraise the risks of the preferred solution, and selective information processing. Not surprisingly, these combined forces are predicted to result in extremely defective decision making performance by the group.

Examining the evidence for the groupthink phenomenon: a pessimistic appraisal

An analysis of the groupthink literature leads to two paradoxical conclusions. On the one hand, the pervasiveness of the concept is breathtaking. Groupthink is perhaps one of the few social science models that has had a truly interdisciplinary impact. A rudimentary scan of such diverse literatures as political science, management, strategy, marketing, social psychology, organizational theory, health care management, counselling psychology, decision making, communications, information technology, and computer science reveals the striking appeal and conceptual influence of the groupthink theory. On the other hand, however, a meticulous analysis of the empirical research uncovers astonishingly limited support for the model.

Recent reviews of groupthink research draw three major conclusions regarding the state of the groupthink theory. First, case and laboratory research rarely document the full constellation of groupthink effects. For example, although Janis (1972, 1982) provides some support for the full groupthink model, both recent and classic case analyses demonstrate that groupthink can occur in situations where only a limited number of antecedents can be discerned (see, for example, 't Hart, 1990; Longley & Pruitt, 1980; Raven, 1974; for reviews see Aldag & Fuller, 1993; Park, 1990). Other studies suggest that groupthink is not apparent when even most of the antecedents conditions exist (e.g. Neck & Moorhead, 1992). Likewise, laboratory studies, although they have experimentally manipulated only a few groupthink antecedents, rarely provide supporting evidence for the full groupthink model (see, for example, Callaway & Esser, 1984; Callaway, Marriott & Esser, 1985; Flowers, 1977; Leana, 1985). Thus, when laboratory experiments find evidence for groupthink, it tends to be partial – for example, finding that directive leadership does limit discussion but that this does not interact with cohesion and ultimately does not affect other decision processes.

Moreover, both laboratory and case research provide conflicting findings regarding the adequacy of conceptualizations of antecedents. For example, laboratory experiments as well as analyses of both the Nixon White House (Raven, 1974) and the *Challenger* space shuttle decision (Esser & Lindoerfer, 1989) found little evidence for the traditional conception of cohesion as mutual attraction (see Callaway & Esser, 1984; Callaway et al., 1985; Flowers, 1977; Fodor & Smith, 1982; Leana, 1985). Despite its prominence in most groupthink case studies, threat, as operationalized in laboratory experiments, rarely has had any consequences for any group decision making outcomes or processes (see Callaway & Esser, 1984; Callaway et al., 1985; Flowers, 1977; Fodor & Smith, 1982; Leana, 1985).

A second conclusion drawn from groupthink research is that few experimental studies have documented the end result and the hallmark of groupthink: the low quality, defective decisions. For example, studies investigating the effects of cohesion and leadership style show no adverse effects on performance (Flowers, 1977; Fodor & Smith, 1982; Leana, 1985). Studies investigating the effects of social cohesion and discussion procedures (e.g. restricted vs. participatory discussion) similarly provide no evidence of impaired decision performance under groupthink conditions (Callaway & Esser, 1984; Callaway et al., 1985; Courtwright, 1978).

A final conclusion drawn from this literature is that questionable support has been provided for the causal sequences associated with the original model. No research has supported the hypothesized links among the five antecedents, the seven groupthink symptoms, and the eight defective decision making symptoms. Recent theoretical reviews suggest that at least three interpretations of the model can be drawn from groupthink work (see further M.E. Turner, Pratkanis, Probasco and Leve, 1992). A 'strict' interpretation of the groupthink theory holds that groupthink should occur only when all the antecedent conditions are present. An 'additive' interpretation suggests that groupthink should become increasingly more pronounced as the number of antecedent conditions increases. However, no published studies provide evidence for either of these interpretations. A third interpretation of the groupthink theory, the liberal or particularistic model, is more consistent with current evidence. This perspective suggests that groupthink outcomes will depend on the unique situational properties

invoked by the particular set of antecedent conditions found in each groupthink situation.

Taken together, these findings have fostered a variety of evaluations regarding the viability of the groupthink theory. These opinions range from outright
rejection (e.g. Longley & Pruitt, 1980), to reconceptualization of key
antecedents (e.g. McCauley, 1989; Raven, 1974), to improved operationalization of constructs (M.E. Turner et al., 1992), to dropping some antecedents
altogether (Tetlock, Peterson, McGuire, Chang & Feld, 1992), to revising
the concept of groupthink itself ('t Hart, 1990; Whyte, 1989). Other
researchers have extended the groupthink model by incorporating other social
psychological principles such as individual and collective accountability
(Kroon, 't Hart & Van Kreveld, 1991; Kroon, Van Kreveld & Rabbie, 1992).

What, then, are the implications of these conclusions? From a theoretical
standpoint, a pessimistic appraisal would suggest outright rejection of the
groupthink theory. From a practical viewpoint, such an appraisal would suggest that the model is of little consequence for decision making groups.
Indeed, if groupthink has no impact on decision performance, why should its
antecedents, its consequences, and its prevention be of interest?

Examining the groupthink evidence: a more optimistic appraisal

A more optimistic appraisal of the groupthink literature, however, reveals certain critical consistencies in the research evidence. Three consistencies, in
particular, suggest that a refocusing of the groupthink model can illuminate
our understanding of group decision making in significant ways (see M.E.
Turner et al., 1992; M.E. Turner & Pratkanis, 1994b).

First, although research consistently demonstrates that cohesion as con-
ceptualized as mutual attraction (e.g. Lott & Lott, 1965) exerts few if any
influences on groupthink outcomes (e.g. see Esser & Lindoerfer, 1989; Raven,
1974), other formulations of cohesion have been found to be more useful.
Case studies find evidence for a conceptualization of cohesion based on the
self-categorization and social identity literatures. For example, Raven's (1974)
analysis of the Nixon White House handling of the Watergate break-in suggested that cohesion in this instance depended not so much on the presence
of an *esprit de corps* but rather the desire to maintain group membership at all
costs. Others have pointed out that the NASA *Challenger* launch team was a
cohesive group in the sense that they developed a shared identity as members
of an elite NASA core and, like the Nixon White House members, wanted to
remain part of that group (Feynman, 1988; see Moorhead, Ference & Neck,
1991 for another analysis; see Chaisson, 1994 for a similar description of the
NASA *Hubble* group). These analyses suggest a different perspective on
group cohesion – one that defines cohesion in terms of self-categorization or
social identity (Tajfel, 1981; J.C. Turner, Hogg, Oakes, Reicher & Wetherell,
1987). A self-categorization and social identity perspective suggests that the
perception of others as group members rather than as unique individuals
may be a necessary precondition for group cohesion (Tajfel, 1981; J.C. Turner

et al., 1987). Categorization may also operate by reinforcing the similarities between the individual and other group members and making the group identity attractive. The policy making groups originally studied by Janis appear to conform to this precondition. Moreover, many subsequent case studies providing evidence for the predicted effects of cohesion also meet this condition (see especially, for example, Hensley & Griffin, 1986; Neck & Moorhead, 1992).

A second consistency found in groupthink research concerns the importance of threat as an antecedent condition. Although many case analyses document the influence of threat, few laboratory studies find such effects. How can these contradictory findings be reconciled? One possibility lies in the nature of the threats occurring in the various groupthink situations. In each case analysis, the decision making group faced a threatening situation for which effective means of resolution were not immediately apparent (see Janis, 1982 for a discussion of the importance of this antecedent). In contrast, the threats used in many experimental studies, while having both face and ecological validity, actually seemed to involve few personal consequences for the group and frequently were imposed through some internal requirement of the decision making task (e.g. the group had to solve a hypothetical budget crisis in an organizational scenario as opposed to actually facing its own budget cut or other loss with consequences for the group).

A third consistency involves the unique effects associated with specific groupthink antecedents. Procedures designed to limit group discussion (e.g. directive leadership, instructions emphasizing avoiding disagreement) tend to produce fewer solutions, less sharing of information, and fewer statements of disagreement (although they do not adversely affect solution quality measures; e.g. see Flowers, 1977; Leana, 1985). This provides some evidence that particular antecedent conditions may be associated with certain outcomes and that groups may adopt a variety of procedures to resolve groupthink (that is, some support for the liberal or particularistic perspective on groupthink).

These consistencies, we believe, give credence to a more optimistic appraisal of the groupthink literature – one that suggests that the groupthink model is alive and well, albeit a bit reorientated and recast.

Groupthink as social identity maintenance (SIM): towards a reconciliation

Clearly, any attempt to refocus the groupthink model must accomplish several objectives. First, and most critically, it must provide a parsimonious way of accounting for the equivocal results regarding the relationships among the antecedents of groupthink and the predicted effects on decision making performance. Second, it must also provide conceptualizations of those antecedent conditions that are consistent with empirical results and that have predictive utility with respect to various groupthink consequences. Finally, any refocusing should yield insights into intervention strategies that can specify the conditions under which groupthink will not occur – an important requirement for understanding how to mitigate or ameliorate groupthink.

We developed a model of groupthink as social identity maintenance (SIM) to account for the points raised above (see M.E. Turner et al., 1992; M.E. Turner & Pratkanis, 1994b; M.E. Turner & Pratkanis, in press). According to this perspective, groupthink is a process by which members of a cohesive group attempt to maintain a shared positive view of the functioning of the group in the face of a collective threat. In other words, the group attempts to protect its collective identity from the potential failure to adequately handle that threat, often at the expense of effective decision making.

There are at least three critical points about this perspective that differentiate it from other groupthink models. First, it incorporates a self-categorization and social identity approach to cohesion. This entails quite different preconditions than does an interpersonal attraction approach to cohesion. It suggests that members must categorize themselves as a group (rather than simply experiencing mutual attraction). According to social identity theorists, this categorization leads groups to seek positive distinctiveness for the ingroup and to exhibit a motivational bias for positive collective self-esteem (J.C. Turner, 1981). Thus, we see that members tend to develop a positive image of the group and, importantly, are motivated to protect that image (as in, for example, the Nixon White House and the NASA *Challenger* and *Hubble* space telescope decisions).

A second condition highlighted by a SIM perspective is that the group should experience a collective threat that attacks its positive image. This shared threat has critical consequences for intragroup processes. When threatened, individuals and groups tend to narrow their focus of attention to threat-related cues (Kahneman, 1973; M.E. Turner, 1992; M.E. Turner & Horvitz, in press). In this case, the group tends to focus on those cues that can help maintain the shared positive image of the group that is invoked by social categorization. When the task is complex and uncertain (as in most groupthink decisions), this focusing of attention detracts from the decision making process to such an extent that performance is impaired. In a direct test of the SIM perspective, M.E. Turner et al. (1992) found that cohesion (manipulated through the induction of social identity) and threat (manipulation by threatening the group's image) together impaired group decision making effectiveness.

A third factor underscored by an SIM perspective is that members may employ a variety of tactics to protect the group image. For example, Lanzetta (1955) found that groups tend to exhibit more variety in their intragroup processes under threatening than under nonthreatening conditions. Thus, groups can exhibit a variety of groupthink processes and indicators as members attempt to maintain a positive image of the group in the face of a threatening situation that already induces variability into the group process. M.E. Turner et al. (1992) found that cohesion and threat independently (but not interactively) affected self-reports of some groupthink and defective decision making symptoms. Further, these symptoms tended to reflect attempts to put forth the most positive image of the group. Indeed, there are interesting parallels between the symptoms of groupthink and the tactics of social identity maintenance or enhancement. For example, the groupthink symptom of stereotyping of outgroups resembles the outgroup discrimination that can accompany the induction of social identities. Similarly, illusion of invulnerability and rationalization are similar to social identity maintenance strategies involving the selective enhancement of various group characteristics to achieve positive distinctiveness. Finally, pressures toward uniformity and self-censorship induced by groupthink are similar to referent informational influence processes (J.C. Turner, 1982). This partial list illustrates the variety of tactics that are readily available to groups as they attempt to protect their identities. When faced with the complexity of the decision situation and the variability induced by threat, groups have a wide array of options with which to bolster their image. This also lends support to the particularistic or liberal interpretation of groupthink which suggests that unique conceptualizations of antecedents may be associated with specific configurations of outcomes.

Thus, we see that both case and experimental evidence exists for the SIM perspective on groupthink. This perspective accomplishes the first two objectives required of any refocusing of the groupthink model: It has (1) parsimoniously accounted for the relevant empirical research and (2) provided the first experimental evidence for the defective decision performance that heretofore was only hypothetically associated with groupthink. This view of groupthink also accomplishes our third objective: to suggest specific strategies for mitigating groupthink. We discuss these issues in the next section.

Designing interventions

The SIM model is consistent with the view that, as Janis (1982) suggests, one outcome of groupthink seems to be a mutual effort among members of the group to maintain emotional equanimity. In other words, groupthink can be viewed as a SIM strategy: a collective effort designed to protect the positive image of the group. Any interventions designed to mitigate groupthink must be formulated with an understanding of this motivation for identity protection. Let us first examine, from the standpoint of the SIM model, some potential unintended consequences of traditional recommendations for overcoming groupthink.

The inadequacy of some traditional recommendations for mitigating groupthink

The SIM perspective suggests that some traditional recommendations advanced to overcome groupthink may actually exacerbate the groupthink process when SIM pressures exist. Indeed, unless carefully formulated and executed, these procedures may provoke rather than minimize excessive concurrence seeking. A brief examination of the traditional recommendations for mitigating groupthink (see Janis, 1982, 1989) is illustrative. Strategies such as the use of outside experts, second chance meetings, subgroup evaluations of alternatives, devil's advocates and so forth can easily be perceived by the group as remedial procedures designed to assist a group unable to cope with a threatening, challenging situation. This in turn is likely to escalate the group's effort to maintain its positive image. In short, these strategies may have the unintended consequence of aggravating rather than inhibiting group-think processes when SIM pressures exist. Traditional recommendations that involve exposing the group to outsiders (such as outside experts and trusted associates) and to members advocating viewpoints conflicting with the group's preferred solution can result in either the cooptation or marginaliza-tion of these nonconformists. If group members can actively select these outside evaluators (see Janis, 1982), they will be likely to select associates and experts who subscribe to the group's preferred solution and thereby enhance the group's identity. In contrast, when dissenters can not be coopted, they are likely to become objects of outgroup discrimination, be treated as deviants, and be marginalized or even excluded by the group.

In addition, tactics such as assigning the role of critical evaluator to all group members, dividing the original group into subgroups to enhance eval-uation, the use of second chance meetings to re-evaluate the decision, and the construction of alternative scenarios to examine consequences of the pre-ferred decision may have the unintended consequences of structuring the group discussion to support the preferred decision rather than to critically evaluate it. For example, assigning the role of critical evaluator to each member may actually produce superficial conflict around peripheral issues that do not substantially threaten the group's preferred decision or the group's identity. Similar outcomes would be expected with the use of subgroups, second chance meetings, and the construction of alternative scenarios. Some existing case analyses provide evidence for this proposition. For example, in analysing the decision of the Johnson White House to escalate the Vietnam war, Janis (1982) notes that groups can limit objections to issues that do not threaten to shake the confidence of the group members in the rightness of their collective judgments. Interestingly, such a strategy allows the group to report that it actually tolerated dissent and encouraged full evaluation – both positive and negative – of the group decision even though it actually did not. And, this in turn enhances the image of the group as a competent, objective evaluator.

Our analysis of the traditional recommendations further underscores the tightrope one must walk in implementing tactics to mitigate groupthink. On the one hand, the traditional procedures *do* directly stimulate conflict and dis-cussion. On the other hand, they may do so in ways that intensify the negative repercussions of threat and cohesion and further aggravate the group's ten-dency to engage in identity protection. Thus, any attempt to design interventions to mitigate groupthink must be adapted to the unique situa-tional constraints faced by groups experiencing SIM pressures under groupthink conditions.

Situational constraints unique to groups operating under SIM pressures

The social identity maintenance approach underscores three unique constraints that are characteristic of groupthink situations. These constraints set limits on the design and implementation of strategies promoting effective group decision making under groupthink conditions.

First, in most groupthink situations, the group is required to make a common group decision. In short, the group must subscribe to and support a unitary group decision. This requirement makes the use of such strategies as the induction of competitive pressures which foster disunity extremely problematic (unless an authoritarian leader can exert dominance over the group, which in turn likely leads to more groupthink pressures).

Second, a groupthink-type situation involves threat. As we have discussed above, threat has a number of consequences for group decision making. These include the intensified focusing of attention and the self-protective motivation that is enhanced by a social identity. Under groupthink conditions, these consequences have overarching implications for the group's decision process and outcomes. The group's paramount goal becomes the attempt to ward off a negative image implicated by potential failure in responding to a collective threat. For example, the induction of competitive pressures under these conditions is likely to intensify the threat (see Deutsch, 1973 for a discussion of competition effects) which in turn will intensify the focus of attention and aggravate self-protective tendencies.

Finally, the SIM model suggests that a group may adopt a variety of strategies in service of the collective effort to maintain a positive social identity and that these strategies may impair decision processes and outcomes. This in turn highlights the complexity of the groupthink phenomenon and the resulting intricacies of designing and implementing interventions that can adequately handle these myriad self-protective strategies.

Intervention strategies suggested by the SIM perspective

According to the SIM model, the mitigation of groupthink is predicated on two overall goals: the stimulation of constructive, cognitive conflict and the reduction of social identity maintenance pressures (see M.E. Turner & Pratkanis, 1994b). Clearly, the stimulation of constructive conflict is a paramount goal of these interventions. As groupthink arises from the failure to adequately capitalize on controversy, procedures designed to stimulate conflict are unquestionably applicable. However, the SIM perspective highlights the risks of inappropriately implementing interventions. Procedures designed to stimulate cognitive conflict may appear to be effective in warding off groupthink. However, an SIM perspective suggests that they will do so only when they do not intensify the group's tendency to engage in identity protection. In short, these strategies must be designed so that they ideally support or at least do not threaten the group's identity. In the next two sections, we examine two sets of prescriptions for mitigating groupthink. The first provides tactics for reducing pressures toward identity protection; the second concerns procedures for stimulating constructive conflict.

Reducing pressures towards identity protection

The social identity maintenance model of groupthink suggests three interventions that are likely to be capable of diminishing the collective effort directed towards warding off a negative image of the group. These include the provision of an excuse or face-saving mechanism, the risk technique, and multiple role-playing procedures.

Provide an excuse or face-saving mechanism for potential poor performance
One method of reducing the need for groups to engage in identity protection strategies is to provide an excuse for potential poor performance. Research suggests that when faced with a threat to self-esteem, people are likely to self-handicap (actively set up circumstances or claim certain attributes that may be blamed for poor performance; Frankel & M.L. Snyder, 1978; Higgins, 1990; Jones & Berglas, 1978; Miller, 1976; C. R. Snyder, 1990; M. L. Snyder, Smoller, Strenta & Frankel, 1981). Although this often results in poor performance on the task, failure on the task does not reflect poorly on self-esteem because it can be attributed to a volitional self-handicapping.

However, providing threatened individuals with another potential explanation for the expected failure (such as poor lighting) may obviate the need to use self-handicapping strategies for maintaining self esteem and subsequently may ameliorate performance decrements (M.L. Snyder et al., 1981). M.E. Turner et al. (1992) found that groups operating under SIM groupthink conditions (i.e. experiencing a collective threat to a group identity) who were given an excuse for poor performance performed significantly better than groups working under groupthink conditions without such an excuse. Thus, the reduction of identity protection pressures seems to allow groups to mitigate groupthink tendencies and to produce higher quality decisions.

The risk technique   A second effective strategy for reducing pressures towards identity protection is an application of the risk technique (Maier, 1952). The risk technique is a structured discussion situation designed to facilitate the expression and reduction of fear and threat. The discussion is structured so that group members talk about dangers or risks involved in a decision and delay discussion of any potential gains. The process emphasizes a reaction to or reflection of the underlying content of the risks associated with a particular decision or situation. Following this discussion of risks is a discussion of controls or mechanisms for dealing with the risks or dangers. Research with this technique has demonstrated its usefulness in clarifying and reducing fears and threats with a variety of groups including factory workers, students and managers (see Maier, 1952). This technique would seem especially applicable in groupthink situations that produce strong pressures towards identity protection, especially as it encourages objective evaluation and control of these tendencies (see also Tjosvold & Johnson, 1983 for a discussion of managing emotions during controversy).

Multiple role-playing procedures   This process can be accomplished through two procedures. First, group members may assume the perspectives of other constituencies with a stake in the decision. For example, in the *Challenger* and *Hubble* incidents, group members might have been asked to assume the roles of the federal government, local citizens, space crew families, astronomers and so forth. A second approach focuses on the internal workings of the group. Each member can be asked to assume the role or perspective of another group member. This approach facilitates the confrontation of threats and rationales for decisions (see Maier, 1952) and allows the development of multiple perspectives. Fisher, Kopelman & Schneider (1996) recommend that parties adopt perspectives of themselves, of others involved in the situation, and of neutral observers and explore each party's objectives, interests and current positions or favoured recommendations. (See George, 1972 for an application of this technique in governmental settings that uses decision makers with varying initial solution preferences; see also our discussion of dispute resolution below.)

Summary   Face-saving strategies, the risk technique and multiple role-playing procedures can be very beneficial to decision-making groups. Most fundamentally, they can reduce the emotional impact of the group social identity by facilitating the identification and salience of alternative groups. The procedures also serve to legitimate or even institutionalize the expression of threat, emotion and concerns about the group identity. Role playing can provide additional sources of information that can impact the decision itself, provide alternative perspectives on information already at hand, and provide needed perspective on the attack on the group identity. However, alone they are unlikely to be effective in promoting effective decision performance. The following set of recommendations is designed to accomplish that goal.

Procedures for stimulating cognitive conflict under groupthink: a SIM perspective

Both researchers and practitioners have long promulgated the benefits of stimulating cognitive conflict (see, for example, Deutsch, 1973; Fisher, Rayner & Belgard, 1995; Pascale, 1991; Tjosvold, 1991, 1995; Tjosvold & Johnson, 1983; Worchel, Coutant-Sassic & Wong, 1993). Pavitt (1993), for example, suggests that the process of reflective thinking (i.e. problem identification and proposal generation, evaluation of proposals and alternatives, and solution selection), may be characteristic of high quality group decisions (see also Guzzo & Salas, 1995; Moreland & Levine, 1992; see Van de Vliert & De Dreu, 1994, for a discussion of conditions leading to the effective use of conflict stimulation).

   Procedures for stimulating cognitive conflict in groups generally have three objectives: (a) stimulating the generation of objectives and solution alternatives, (b) encouraging the evaluation of alternatives, and (c) influencing optimal solution selection while promoting re-evaluation of decisions. However, these general procedures need to be adapted to groupthink conditions. When implemented in groupthink situations where SIM pressures are operative, these procedures should be designed to facilitate the critical evaluation of ideas, assumptions and plans in ways that are supportive rather than threatening to the group identity. In general, the prescriptions mandated by the SIM model differ in substance (though not necessarily in intent) from the traditional recommendations for overcoming pressures towards uniformity. The SIM model prescriptions for enhancing cognitive conflict tend to be much more detailed so that they serve to structure the decision process to a greater extent than do traditional recommendations. This additional structure may have distinctive advantages for groups operating under groupthink conditions. First, by structuring the decision, they serve to institutionalize the evaluative procedure, thus separating it from the group identity. Indeed, if implemented appropriately, these procedures can enhance the collective pride of the group when linked to the group's identity as a competently functioning team. For example, jury instructions or the scientist's idea of proving oneself wrong rather than right may serve both to bolster the collective self-esteem and to institutionalize sound decision making processes. Second, these procedures provide members with more specific strategies for evaluating alternatives and decisions. This specificity is particularly important when heightened threat serves to narrow the focus of attention (see M.E. Turner, 1992) and when identity protection motivations are exacerbated.

We will now discuss two such techniques for structuring group decisions: structured discussion principles and procedures for protecting minority opinions.

Structured discussion principles   Maier (1952) presents extensive research demonstrating the efficacy of structured discussion in enhancing group effectiveness. Structured discussion techniques provide recommendations for establishing procedures that clarify responsibility, analyse the situation, frame the question or decision, gather information, structure consideration of alternatives, frequently solicit further suggestions, provide evaluation and so forth. The goal of these recommendations is to delay solution selection and to increase the problem solving phase. These interventions attempt to ameliorate premature closure on a solution and to extend problem analysis and evaluation. These recommendations can be given to the group in a variety of ways.

One method is to provide training in discussion principles either for the group leader alone or for all the members. This approach may work well when there is sufficient time, resources and motivation to complete such a programme.

A second method is simply to expose group members to these recommendations. For example, groups may be given guidelines that emphasize (a) the recognition of all suggestions but continued solicitation of solutions, (b) the protection of individuals from criticism, (c) keeping the discussion problem-centred, and (d) listing all solutions before evaluating them. M.E. Turner and Pratkanis (1994a) found that highly cohesive, threatened groups given these types of structured discussion guidelines produced significantly higher quality decisions than did highly cohesive, threatened groups not given these guidelines. Rosenthal & 't Hart (1989) suggest that the management of the decision process was key to the amelioration of groupthink and the overall effectiveness of the resolution of the South Moluccan hostage situation. (See also Maier, 1963 for a discussion and Wheeler & Janis, 1980 for adaptations of these principles.)

A third approach to structured discussion is the constructive controversy approach developed by Tjosvold (see, for example, Tjosvold, 1991, 1995). Under this approach, the superordinate cooperative goal of effective performance is coupled with specific mechanisms ensuring that issues are explored thoroughly, diverse opinions are stimulated, and opposing ideas are sought and integrated into a final solution. Specific tactics include the establishment of norms favouring the expression of opinions, doubts and uncertainty, the consultation of relevant sources (including those who are likely to disagree), the implementation of constructive criticism of ideas rather than people, and the integration of solutions rather than the use of zero-sum choice procedures (see Tjosvold, 1991, 1995 for further details and a persuasive review of the supporting evidence).

A fourth approach useful in orchestrating group discussions can be adapted from the dispute resolution arena. Fisher et al. (1996) provide a particularly detailed list of tactics designed to integratively resolve conflict. Fisher et al. recommend that parties follow certain guidelines that enable the: (a) exploration of partisan perceptions (as in the multiple role-playing procedures outlined above), (b) analysis of perceived choices, (c) generation of fresh ideas, and (d) implementation of a solution. Although initially designed to resolve rather than stimulate conflict, these tactics can be readily adapted to achieve opinion diversity in situations where groups might experience groupthink stemming from SIM pressures. For example, the analysis of perceived choices would entail the systematic appraisal of the consequences (including personal, political, organizational, interpersonal and so forth) of proposed action plans for stakeholders. Particularly useful are the recommendations for generating and considering new alternatives. These tactics include a methodical evaluation of the problem, the causes, general approaches, and specific action plans in the light of precise criteria such as goals, options, legitimacy, commitments and so on that are fully spelled out before the decision process begins. The implementation of a solution likewise involves both a detailed analysis of the preferred recommendation and the solicitation of constructive criticism. We suggest that this general approach might be particularly useful for groups operating under groupthink conditions when it is accompanied by the simultaneous reinforcement of a superordinate goal and the reduction or channelling of emotions stemming from social identity pressures.

A fifth approach used to direct the discussion centres on structuring the decision itself. For example, the developmental discussion technique is a decision aid designed to direct the evaluation into logical steps and into positive action channels. This technique is particularly useful in the development and exploration of ideas, the analyses of barriers and conditions interfering with actions, and for solving problems for which group members have adequate skills but tend to form judgments on an impressionistic basis. The technique involves the solicitation of all opinions and the systematic appraisal of objectives and alternatives (see Maier & Hoffman, 1960a for specific guidelines).

Another strategy for structuring or directing the evaluation process is called the 'two column method'. This technique requires that all aspects of the situation be listed, advantages and disadvantages of each aspect be considered and rated, and finally systematic appraisals of methods for securing the advantages and minimizing the disadvantages take place (see Maier, 1952, 1963).

Finally, one simple technique that may be especially useful when group members operate under time pressure or are resistant to more structured methods is to require groups to identify a second solution or decision recommendation once the first has been submitted. In short, this technique tends to enhance the problem solving and idea generation phases of the discussion and can significantly enhance performance quality (Maier & Hoffman, 1960b).

Establishment of procedures for protecting minority opinions   These procedures are critical because some groupthink research demonstrates that groups can actually generate high quality decision alternatives but frequently fail to adopt them as their preferred solution (Janis, 1982; M.E. Turner et al., 1992). The protection of minority opinions may be one method of facilitating the evaluation and subsequent adoption of more effective solutions. Nemeth (1992) presents evidence that simple exposure to minority opinions can enhance performance by increasing the cognitive resources devoted to the task and by increasing search and evaluation of novel solutions (see also Nemeth & Staw, 1989; Peterson & Nemeth, 1996). Maier & Solem (1952) found that groups simply instructed to encourage discussion and participation of all members produced significantly better decisions than did groups without those instructions.

One pitfall of these procedures may be that members are disinclined to provide their true opinions and are fearful of being marginalized or excluded from the group. When that happens, strategies for protecting minority opinions should ideally be combined with identity protection strategies and with some of the structured decision guidelines discussed above.

Summary   Structured discussion principles and procedures for protecting minority opinions have several advantages for groupthink situations involving SIM conditions. First, they acknowledge that groups must make an interdependent decision. Members are likely to be reluctant to engage in tactics designed to ineluctably split the group or make it appear inadequate. These procedures all clearly contravene that fear. Second, these strategies serve to structure the decision making process. This structure benefits the group by harnessing the effects of threat on the focusing of attention. Thus, rather than focusing solely on the presentation of a positive image induced by identity cohesion, the group concentrates on effectively solving the problem at hand.

When cognitive conflict is threatening: stimulating cognitive conflict and reducing SIM pressures

These approaches do not guarantee success. Much prior research shows that people evaluate conflict extremely negatively (see, for example, O'Connor, Gruenfeld & McGrath, 1993) and are motivated to avoid it. We can predict that groups operating under groupthink conditions would be especially susceptible to these pressures and might interpret conflict as threatening the group identity. And, as we have seen earlier, groups are extremely flexible in the ways in which they can attempt to protect their identity. In order to project an image of an effectively functioning team, a group might superficially adopt these procedures and, for example, structure the discussion around issues that are peripheral to critical evaluation but give the appearance of constructive conflict. In this way, the group maintains unity, supports its image, appears to fully discuss and evaluate the decision, and yet continues to advocate an ineffective solution. In such cases, we offer three pieces of advice: (a) make the intervention early in the groupthink-type situation before collective rationalization becomes the norm, (b) link the intervention strategy to the social identity in a supportive rather than threatening way, and (c) also introduce strategies that can reduce, obviate or redirect identity protection motivations (as discussed above). In this way, the strategies can be introduced as a way of handling the threatening situation. Moreover, they can be implemented in a manner which supports and enhances the group's identity rather than threatening it.

Conclusion

The social identity maintenance model views groupthink as a collective effort to maintain a shared positive view of the functioning of the group in the face of a collective threat. Group members are truly engaged in a struggle to protect their collective identity from the potential failure to adequately handle that threat. This collective identity protection may have disastrous consequences for both the group and for outsiders who experience the consequences of the group's decision. Yet, this perspective also provides some unique insights into overcoming the adverse consequences of groupthink when social identity maintenance pressures exist.

Effective intervention strategies must accomplish two objectives: First, these intervention strategies must promote cognitive conflict. Ideally, they should provide decision making strategies that ensure that critical evaluations of ideas, assumptions and plans are conducted. Second, they must reduce or remove pressures stimulating identity protection. In other words, they must provide groups with mechanisms that either obviate the need for identity protection or provide coping strategies for dealing with the emotional consequences of identity threat. In short, these two objectives entail enhancing the constructive, beneficial aspects of 'cognitive' conflict and diminishing the destructive, adverse aspects of 'affective' conflict (Deutsch, 1973; Jehn, 1994; Walton, 1987). Empirical research on groupthink has just begun to address these strategies (M.E. Turner et al., 1992; M.E. Turner & Pratkanis, 1994a).

The events of recent days argue for the urgency of this research. After the *Challenger* shuttle disaster, volumes of books, magazine and newspaper articles, and Congressional reports were published on the incident. The portrait that emerged revealed a NASA under pressure to launch successful, breathtaking and spectacular mission after mission in order to stay in the public's eye and to secure the needed funding from Congress. The scientists, engineers, astronauts and mission specialists of NASA perceived themselves to be honoured to serve on an elite force that beat the Russians and landed the first person on the moon. With such a team, what could go wrong? Given NASA's past track record, it was a safe bet that any new proposal would take the agency to new heights; there was little doubt otherwise and little need to engage in critical analysis and evaluation of decisions and alternatives.

As Richard Feynman (1988) dramatically pointed out, the technological solution to the *Challenger* disaster was so simple that all one needed to do was dunk an O-ring in a glass of ice water for a few minutes and observe that it easily cracked at low temperatures similar to those at the launch of the *Challenger*. The behavioural solution is not so simple. It involves (a) an understanding of how groups under threat supplant their goals of making high quality decisions with a desire to protect their shared identity and (b) a knowledge of how best to reduce these processes and replace them with constructive, cognitive conflict.

What did NASA learn from the *Challenger* disaster? New O-rings and new launch procedures are now in place to prevent a similar disaster from occurring. However, four years after the *Challenger* launch, NASA placed into orbit the great cataract in the sky, the *Hubble* space telescope. This time the technological solution was a little more difficult to execute, requiring a costly shuttle mission to fix the telescope. And once again, volumes of reports are beginning to appear on why the *Hubble* fiasco occurred. The portrait that emerges, once again, is of a NASA that failed to do the critical evaluations and analyses so necessary for successful decision making. In this case they failed to implement quality assurance tests that would have identified the problem and saved a costly launch. And once again, NASA was under pressure to produce incredible results to secure its funding – this time to see back to the beginning of time and the Big Bang, as the press reports mistakenly proclaimed. And once again, NASA proclaimed its identity as the elite organization that could do no wrong. At the Senate hearings investigating the

Hubble fiasco, one NASA official eloquently expressed the identity protection at the core of groupthink as social identity maintenance: 'We know what we're doing. We're clever' (Chaisson, 1994, p. 191). Clearly, they did not and they were not. Perhaps, with a greater understanding of the social dynamics and forces that can operate when an 'elite' group is threatened, the next time they will.

Note

Financial support for Marlene E. Turner was partially provided by the College of Business Summer Research Grant Program, San José State University. We are grateful to Lisa Iha for research assistance.

References

Aldag, R. and Fuller, S. R. (1993). Beyond fiasco: a reappraisal of the groupthink phenomenon and a new model of group decision processes. *Psychological Bulletin, 113*, 535–52.

Callaway, M.R. and Esser, J.K. (1984). Groupthink: Effects of cohesiveness and problem-solving procedures on group decision making. *Social behavior and personality, 12*, 157–64.

Callaway, M.R., Marriott, R.G. and Esser, J.K. (1985). Effects of dominance on group decision making: Toward a stress-reduction explanation of groupthink. *Journal of Personality and Social Psychology, 4*, 949–52.

Chaisson, E.J. (1994). *The Hubble wars*. New York: HarperPerennial.

Courtwright, J.A. (1978). A laboratory investigation of groupthink. *Communication Monographs, 45*, 229–46.

Deutsch, M. (1973). *The resolution of conflict: Constructive and destructive processes*. New Haven: Yale University Press.

Esser, J.K. and Lindoerfer, J.S. (1989). Groupthink and the space shuttle Challenger accident: Toward a quantitative case analysis. *Journal of Behavioral Decision Making, 2*, 167–77.

Feynman, R.P. (1988). *What do you care what other people think?* New York: W.W. Norton & Co.

Fisher, F., Kopelman, E. and Schneider, A. K. (1996). *Beyond Machiavelli: Tools for coping with conflict*. New York: Penguin.

Fisher, K., Rayner, S. and Belgard, W. (1995). *Tips for teams: a ready reference for solving common team problems*. New York: McGraw-Hill.

Flowers, M.L. (1977). A laboratory test of some implications of Janis's groupthink hypothesis. *Journal of Personality and Social Psychology, 35*, 888–96.

Fodor, E.M. and Smith, T. (1982). The power motive as an influence on group decision making. *Journal of Personality and Social Psychology, 42*, 178–85.

Frankel, A. and Snyder, M.L. (1978). Poor performance following unsolvable problems: Learned helplessness or egotism? *Journal of Personality and Social Psychology, 36*, 1415–23.

George, A.L. (1972). The case for multiple advocacy in making foreign policy. *American Political Science Review, 60*, 761–85.

Guzzo, R.A. and Salas, E. (eds) (1995). *Team effectiveness and decision making in organizations*. San Francisco: Jossey-Bass.

Hensley, T.R. and Griffin, G.W. (1986). Victims of groupthink: the Kent State University board of trustees and the 1977 gymnasium controversy. *Journal of Conflict Resolution, 30*, 497–531.

Higgins, R.L. (1990). Self-handicapping: Historical roots and contemporary approaches, in R.L. Higgins, C.R. Snyder and S. Berglas (eds), *Self-handicapping: the paradox that isn't*. New York: Plenum.

Janis, I.L. (1972). *Victims of groupthink*. Boston: Houghton Mifflin.

Janis, I.L. (1982). *Groupthink: Psychological studies of policy decisions and fiascoes* (2nd edn). Boston: Houghton Mifflin.

Janis, I.L. (1989). *Crucial decisions: Leadership in policymaking and crisis management*. New York: Free Press.

Jehn, K. (1994). Enhancing effectiveness: an investigation of advantages and disadvantages of value-based intragroup conflict. *International Journal of Conflict Management, 5*, 223–38.

Jones, E. E. and Berglas, S. (1978). Control of attributions about the self through self-handicapping strategies. *Personality and Social Psychology Bulletin, 4*, 200–6.

Kahneman, D. (1973). *Attention and effort*. Englewood Cliffs, NJ: Prentice-Hall.

Kroon, M.B.R., 't Hart, P. and van Kreveld, D. (1991). Managing group decision making processes: Individual versus collective accountability and groupthink. *International Journal of Conflict Management, 2*, 91–116.

Kroon, M.B.R., van Kreveld, D. and Rabbie, J.M. (1992). Group versus individual decision making: Effects of accountability and gender on groupthink. *Small Group Research, 23*, 427–58.

Lanzetta, J. (1955). Group behavior under stress. *Human Relations, 8*, 29–52.

Leana, C.R. (1985). A partial test of Janis' groupthink model: Effects of group cohesiveness and leader behavior on defective decision making. *Journal of Management, 11*, 5–17.

Longley, J. and Pruitt, D. G. (1980). Groupthink: a critique of Janis's theory, in L. Wheeler (ed.), *Review of personality and social psychology* (Vol. 1). Beverly Hills: Sage.

Lott, A.J. and Lott, B.E. (1965). Group cohesiveness as interpersonal attraction: a review of relationships with antecedent and consequent variables. *Psychological Bulletin, 64*, 259–309.

Maier, N.R.F. (1952). *Principles of human relations*. New York: John Wiley & Sons.

Maier, N.R.F. (1963). *Problem-solving discussions and conferences*. New York: McGraw-Hill.

Maier, N. R. F. and Hoffman, L. R. (1960a). Using trained 'developmental' discussion leaders to improve further the quality of group decisions. *Journal of Applied Psychology, 44*, 247–51.

Maier, N.R.F. and Hoffman, L.R. (1960b). Quality of first and second solution in group problem solving. *Journal of Applied Psychology, 44*, 278–83.

Maier, N.R.F. and Solem, A.R. (1952). The contribution of a discussion leader to the quality of group thinking: the effective use of minority opinions. *Human Relations, 5*, 277–88.

McCauley, C. (1989). The nature of social influence in groupthink: Compliance and internalization. *Journal of Personality and Social Psychology, 57*, 250–60.

Miller, R.T. (1976). Ego involvement and attribution for success and failure. *Journal of Personality and Social Psychology, 34*, 901–6.

Moorhead, G., Ference, R. and Neck, C.P. (1991). Group decision fiascoes continue: Space shuttle Challenger and a revised groupthink framework. *Human Relations, 44*, 539–50.

Moreland, R. and Levine, J. (1992). Problem identification in groups, in S. Worchel, W. Wood and J.A. Simpson (eds), *Group process and productivity*. Newbury Park, CA: Sage.

Neck, C.P. and Moorhead, G. (1992). Jury deliberations in the trial of US v. John DeLorean: a case analysis of groupthink avoidance and an enhanced framework. *Human Relations, 45*, 1077–91.

Nemeth, C.J. (1992). Minority dissent as a stimulant to group performance, in S. Worchel, W. Wood and J.A. Simpson (eds), *Group process and productivity*, Newbury Park, CA: Sage.

Nemeth, C.J. and Staw, B.M. (1989). The tradeoffs of social control and innovation in groups and organizations, in L. Berkowitz (ed.), *Advances in experimental social psychology*. New York: Academic Press, Vol. 22, pp. 175–210.

O'Connor, K.M., Gruenfeld, D.H. and McGrath, J.E. (1993). The experience and effects of conflict in continuing work groups. *Small Group Research, 24*, 362–82.

Park, W. (1990). A review of research on groupthink. *Journal of Behavioral Decision Making, 3*, 229–45.

Pascale, R.T. (1991). *Managing on the edge: How the smartest companies use conflict to stay ahead*. New York: Simon & Schuster.

Pavitt, C. (1993). What (little) we know about formal group discussion procedures: a review of relevant research. *Small Group Research, 24*, 217–35.

Peterson, R.S. and Nemeth, C.J. (1996). Focus versus flexibility: Majority and minority influence can both improve performance. *Personality and Social Psychology Bulletin, 22*, 14–23.

Raven, B.H. (1974). The Nixon group. *Journal of Social Issues, 30*, 297–320.

Rosenthal, U. and 't Hart, P. (1989). Managing terrorism: the South Moluccan hostage taking, in U. Rosenthal, M.T. Charles and P. 't Hart (eds), *Coping with crises: the management of disasters, riots, and terrorism*. Springfield, IL: Charles C. Thomas Publisher.

Snyder, C.R. (1990). Self-handicapping processes and sequelae, in R.L. Higgins, C.R. Snyder and S. Berglas (eds), *Self-handicapping: the paradox that isn't*. New York: Plenum.

Snyder, M.L., Smoller, B., Strenta, A. and Frankel, A. (1981). A comparison of egotism, negativity, and learned helplessness as explanations for poor performance after unsolvable problems. *Journal of Personality and Social Psychology, 40*, 24–30.

Tajfel, H. (1981). *Human groups and social categories*. Cambridge: Cambridge University Press.

't Hart, P. (1990). *Groupthink in government*. Amsterdam: Swets & Zeitlinger.

Tetlock, P.E., Peterson, R.S., McGuire, C., Chang, S. and Feld, P. (1992). Assessing political group dynamics: a test of the groupthink model. *Journal of Personality and Social Psychology, 63*, 403–25.

Tjosvold, D. (1991). *Team organization: an enduring competitive advantage*. Chichester: John Wiley & Sons.

Tjosvold, D. (1995). Cooperation theory, constructive controversy, and effectiveness: Learning from crisis, in R.A. Guzzo and E. Salas (eds), *Team effectiveness and decision making in organizations*. San Francisco: Jossey-Bass.

Tjosvold, D. and Johnson, D.W. (eds) (1983). *Productive conflict management: Perspectives for organizations*. New York: Irvington Publishers.

Turner, J.C. (1981). The experimental social psychology of intergroup behavior, in J.C. Turner and H. Giles (eds), *Intergroup behavior*. Chicago: University of Chicago Press, pp. 66–101.

Turner, J.C. (1982). Towards a cognitive redefinition of the social group, in H. Tajfel (ed.), *Social identity and intergroup relations*. Cambridge: Cambridge University Press, pp. 15–40.

Turner, J.C., Hogg, M.A., Oakes, P.J., Reicher, S.D. and Wetherell, M.S. (1987). *Rediscovering the human group: a self-categorization theory*. New York: Basil Blackwell.

Turner, M.E. (1992). Group effectiveness under threat: the impact of structural centrality and performance set. *Journal of Social Behavior and Personality, 7*, 511–28.

Turner, M.E. and Horvitz, T. (in press). The dilemma of threat: Group effectiveness and ineffectiveness under crisis, in M. E. Turner (ed.), *Groups at work: Advances in theory and research*. Mahwah, NJ: Lawrence Erlbaum & Associates.

Turner, M.E. and Pratkanis, A.R. (1994a). Effects of structured decision aids on decision effectiveness under groupthink (unpublished raw data). San José State University.

Turner, M.E. and Pratkanis, A.R. (1994b). Social identity maintenance prescriptions for preventing groupthink: Reducing identity protection and enhancing intellectual conflict. *International Journal of Conflict Management, 5*, 254–70.

Turner, M. E. and Pratkanis, M.E. (in press). A social identity maintenance model of groupthink. *Organizational Behavior and Human Decision Processes*.

Turner, M.E., Pratkanis, A.R., Probasco, P. and Leve, C. (1992). Threat, cohesion, and group effectiveness: Testing a social identity maintenance perspective on groupthink. *Journal of Personality and Social Psychology, 63*, 781–96.

Van de Vliert, E. and De Dreu, C.K.W. (1994). Optimizing performance by conflict stimulation. *International Journal of Conflict Management, 5*, 211–22.

Walton, R.E. (1987). *Managing conflict*. Reading, MA: Addison-Wesley.

Wheeler, D. and Janis, I.L. (1980). *A practical guide for making decisions*. New York: Free Press.

Whyte, G. (1989). Groupthink reconsidered. *Academy of Management Journal, 14*, 40–56.

Worchel, S., Coutant-Sassic, D., and Wong, F. (1993). Toward a more balanced view of conflict: There is a positive side, in S. Worchel and J.A. Simpson (eds), *Conflict between people and groups: Causes, processes, and resolutions*. Chicago: Nelson Hall.

5

Minority Dissent in Organizations

Carsten K. W. De Dreu and Nanne K. De Vries

In his seminal work on the social psychology of organizing, Karl Weick (1979) forwards two definitions of organizations. The first one is from Vickers (1967) and reads that organizations are structures of mutual expectation, attached to roles which define what each of its members shall expect from others and from himself. The second is from Hunt (1972) and states that an organization is an identifiable social entity pursuing multiple objectives through the coordinated activities and relations among members and objects. Thus, 'organizing is first of all grounded in agreements concerning what is real and illusory, a grounding that is called consensual validation' (Weick, 1979, p. 3). The fundamental assumption underlying this chapter is that this consensual validation is an ongoing and dynamic activity and that the process of gaining consensus constitutes a very basic source of disagreement and social conflict in groups and organizations (see Taylor, 1992).

Consensus is disrupted by minority factions consisting of one single individual, a temporary coalition of several individuals or subgroups. Minority dissent may be broadly defined as publicly advocating and pursuing beliefs, attitudes, ideas, procedures and policies that go against the 'spirit of the times', that challenge the status quo – the position or perspective assumed by the majority of the group or organization's members. Mundane examples are the decision maker who challenges commonly shared assumptions, the colleague who insists on dropping affirmative action policies, the newly hired medical assistant who consistently advocates implementation of a novel treatment h/she was taught about at school. Other instances, to which we return in the next section, are devil's advocates in decision making groups, whistle blowers, and fact checkers in the publishing industry. Each of these instances of dissent implies nonconformity, disagreement with, resistance and opposition to the majority point of view. Minority dissent is related to 'voice' (Hirschman, 1970), and to initiative at work (Borman & Motowidlo, 1993). But it is not identical to voice since the latter is rooted in dissatisfaction and may have large numerical support whereas minority dissent does not by definition. Minority dissent differs from initiative for the same reasons, and in addition because initiative does not necessarily challenge the status quo. And contrary to voice and initiative, minority dissent implies a perspective on the situation that differs from the common, leading and accepted beliefs, judgments, attitudes or mode of conduct. Minority dissent thus deserves its own place within a theory of organizational behaviour.

Dissent is often costly, time-consuming and sometimes detrimental to interpersonal relations (Schweiger, Sandberg & Ragan, 1986). Being the opposite of compliance, dissent is sometimes explicitly denoted as detrimental to organizational functioning and prototypical of bad organizational citizenship behaviour (Organ, 1988). In other writings, however, it is argued that any organizational culture which values the process of continuous learning fosters dissent as a necessary and desirable part of organizational life (Argyris, 1982; Schilit & Locke, 1982). Indeed, dissent lies at the basis of new ideas, products and procedures. This chapter explores the ambiguous relationship between minority dissent and performance in groups and organizations. Drawing from various literatures in social psychology, organizational behaviour and management sciences, we address three questions: (1) What is the impact of minority dissent on performance? (2) Where does minority dissent come from? and (3) What makes minority dissent effective in influencing majority members' attitudes, judgments and behaviours?

What are the contributions of minority dissent to performance?

The literature identified several instances of organizational dissent which we review below to see whether and how minority dissent may contribute to performance. Performance is a combination of efficiency and effectiveness (Ostroff & Schmitt, 1993) and because minority dissent consumes time and disrupts stability (Schweiger et al., 1986), it is likely to reduce efficiency, especially in the short run. Although the review is not intended to be exhaustive and the various instances of minority dissent are not mutually exclusive, we will show that such reduced short-term efficiency may be compensated by improved long-term effectiveness, resulting in an overall increase in functioning and performance at the organizational, the group and the individual level.

Minority dissent and organizational performance

At the level of organizational functioning and performance, two examples are prominent in the literature. The first one is whistle blowing and impacts organizational functioning. The second one is fact checking, which impacts organizational effective performance. *Whistle blowing* is a form of dissent which may be defined as the disclosure by former or current members of an organization of illegal, immoral or illegitimate practices under the control of their employers, to persons or organizations that may be able to undertake action (Near & Micelli, 1995). Sometimes whistle blowers have the silent approval of the majority of the organization's employees, but sometimes they do not. In any event, whistle blowing is directed at halting a particular wrong-doing, be it an omission such as constant failure to provide safe working conditions, or a commission such as violating particular rules or moral standards. As such, whistle blowing may contribute to organizational functioning in that it may reduce deviation from an ideal state, and deviation from desirable organizational characteristics.

Graham (1986) discusses a specific instance of whistle blowing, namely principled dissent – the effort by individuals in the workplace to protest and/or change the organizational status quo because of their conscientious objection to current policy or practice. Principled dissent deals with violation of a standard of justice, honesty or economy. Graham provides several examples, such as that of the physician member of a drug research team who was concerned about doing human testing of a drug containing high levels of a possible carcinogen. The contribution of principled dissent is in terms of reduced deviation from desirable states as well as in terms of good citizenship behaviour – the tendency to align oneself with the organizational goals and to assist others in reaching these goals.

Fact checkers in the publishing industry are discussed by Cohen and Staw (1995). Fact checkers are tenured, or sometimes freelance employees whose job is to verify the correctness of a writer's story. Fact checkers are supposed to check every single 'fact' presented in an article before it goes to print. They resist the publisher's tendency to write nice, smooth tales that sell, and instead attempt to force the journalist to write accurate articles. The goal of fact checkers is to prevent error and their contribution is reflected in the amount of libel suits filed against journalists. In addition, fact checkers may contribute to a positive public image, which may be a desirable organizational characteristic.

Minority dissent and group performance

To understand the relation between minority dissent and group performance, we may consider procedures that are designed to constrain free communication within groups, and to prevent premature conformity pressures from occurring. Examples are the nominal group technique (Van de Ven, 1974), dialectical inquiry (Mason, 1969), and the procedure of devil's advocacy (Cosier, 1978). For instance, the procedure of *devil's advocacy* refers to the decision aid strategy in which an individual or group formulates a plan, which is subsequently criticized by someone who attempts to find all that is wrong with the plan and to expound the reasons why the plan should not be adopted (e.g. Schwenk, 1990). Devil's advocacy is often encouraged, and sometimes explicitly induced by organizational leaders, and therefore devil's advocates may have some legitimacy and social status. As we will see below this is key to their effectiveness.

Devil's advocacy may be employed in a variety of situations, including production teams and decision making groups. It serves as an alternative to expert-based approaches in which one or several experts make the decision, or to agreement-based approaches in which team members seek agreement upon method and objectives. Compared to expert-based approaches, the procedure of devil's advocacy prevents pressure to conformity and groupthink (Janis, 1972; Turner & Pratkanis, 1994). Compared to agreement-based approaches, devil's advocacy increases the critical evaluation in decision making, and tends to promote commitment to the decision made (Schweiger et al., 1986). Thus, devil's advocates promote decision quality in teams.

Minority dissent and individual performance

Research by Nemeth (1986) suggests that being confronted with minority dissent elicits 'divergent' thinking. When recipients focus on the dissenter's message they attempt to understand why the minority thinks this way and attempt to falsify and counter argue its position. As a result, recipients of dissent take into account multiple perspectives and consider various aspects of the issue under debate (De Dreu & De Vries, 1993; Gordijn, De Vries & De Dreu, 1996; Nemeth, 1995; Nemeth & Kwan, 1985, 1987; Nemeth, Mayseless, Sherman & Brown, 1990; Van Dyne & Saaverda, 1996). In contrast, being confronted with a majority elicits 'convergent' processing of information – recipients focus on verifying the majority position and attempt to justify its viewpoint.

The notion of divergent thinking has interesting consequences for decision making in teams, where minority influence may facilitate the discovery of alternative, sometimes better solutions (Nemeth & Kwan, 1987). But the fundamental implication is at the individual level, in that minority influence and concomitant divergent thinking seems to induce more elaborate clustering strategies in memory and enhanced recall of previously learned information (Nemeth et al., 1990), greater creativity in individual thinking, more novel associations (De Dreu & De Vries, 1993; Nemeth & Kwan, 1985), and more original proposals (Volpato, Maass, Mucchi-Faina & Vitti, 1990).

Related to divergent thinking is that exposure to minority dissent increases individual courage to resist pressures to conformity and the tendency to polarize attitudes towards extreme viewpoints that are undesirable in their consequences (Nemeth & Chiles, 1988). For example, Smith, Scott Tindale and Dugoni (1996) found that in decision making groups in which a minority advocated a deviating position, less extreme and less polarized strategy decisions were made than in groups in which such a resisting minority was absent. In fact, the appointment of devil's advocates to prevent groups from entering a groupthink process (see Janis, 1972) may be thought of as a procedural tool to accomplish exactly this.

Nemeth and Staw (1989) conclude that an important consequence of minority dissent is better scanning of the environment, greater flexibility and higher responsiveness to external change. As summarized in Table 5.1, minority dissent in the form of whistle blowing contributes to organizational functioning, fact checkers enhance organizational effectiveness, devil's advocates promote high quality decisions, and more mundane forms of minority dissent such as the colleague who advocates a novel procedure elicit divergent thinking and provide a model of dissenting behaviour which bolsters the courage of other group members to speak up. In short, minority dissent disrupts stability and consumes time, but may also have significant positive effects on performance.

Table 5.1   *Contributions of minority dissent to organizational, group and individual performance*

Level of analysis	Example	Effect
Organizational	Whistle blowing Fact checkers in publishing industry	Reduced deviation from ideal Reduction in libel suits
Group	Procedure of devil's advocacy	Enhanced decision quality
Individual	Colleague arguing for novel procedure	Divergent thinking, Enhanced individuality Greater creativity

Where does minority dissent come from?

To benefit optimally from the potential contributions of dissent, two conditions are needed: There should be initiatives to dissent, and these initiatives should be noticed and given serious consideration. Only then can a balanced judgment be made and it can be decided whether to pursue dissenting ideas and positions or not. This section deals with group and person factors that are likely to influence the occurrence of minority dissent in groups and organizations. Since there has been little systematic research on antecedents of minority dissent, the following section presents examples of plausible determinants rather than an exhaustive list of everything that may lead to, or promote the likelihood of, minority dissent.

Group factors promoting initiative to dissent

Much managerial effort is focused on preventing and suppressing minority dissent. Cohen and Staw (1995) note that historically, managers have sought a cohesive and homogeneous workforce. This argument parallels the more general proposition made by Schneider (1983) that people tend to be attracted to similar others, tend to select similar others, and that there is much higher turnover among those who deviate rather than among those who are prototypical within a group or organization. This so-called attraction–selection–attrition model points to a tendency in human nature that reduces the likelihood of dissent occurring.

The attraction–selection–attrition argument should apply especially to groups of some duration. However, how long a group has been together is but one of the many group variables that may influence initiative to dissent. Graham (1986) discusses three broad classes of context variables that further inhibit initiative, namely cultural factors, reward systems and organizational prosperity. First, an organizational culture which disrespects individual conscience and which fails to foster interpersonal trust may reduce the occurrence of dissent. Occurrence of dissent may be a function of organizational history regarding treatment of dissent. Whether dissent has been suppressed or rewarded in the past influences the extent to which people press their dissenting point of view (see also Olson-Buchanan, 1996a). Second, reward systems that provide employees with relatively little freedom and with tight daily supervision and/or surveillance tend to reduce occurrence of dissent (Perrucci, Anderson, Schendel & Trachtman, 1980; Zald & Berger, 1978). Third, in situations of trouble and scarcity, authority tends to be more hostile towards dissent, making minority dissent less likely to come out. Graham (1986, p. 34) points out that: 'A benefit of environmental munificence is the organizational slack which is allowed. Slack translated into time can set the stage for reflective activity. Reconsideration of questions long forgotten, recognition of issues which had gone unnoticed, identification of opportunities on the horizon, [and] the generation of genuinely new ideas.'

Person factors promoting initiative to dissent

Initiative to dissent may also be a function of personal motivation, which is partly rooted in the group variables discussed above. Recall that dissent was defined as actively advocating a deviating idea, opinion or course of action. Research identified a variety of factors that may stimulate or inhibit such personal initiative. Personal initiative is defined as a behaviour syndrome resulting in an active and self-starting approach to work and going beyond what is formally required in a given job. It is a function of job control. Higher levels of control contribute to feelings of 'empowerment' which increases feelings of responsibility for one's job (Frese, Kring, Soose & Zempel, 1996; Hackman & Oldham, 1975). The notion of job control is related to Graham's (1986) idea that tight supervision reduces occurrence of dissent. We may expect less initiative to dissent under low levels of job control.

In addition, personal initiative may differ as a function of individual differences in commitment to the organization, perceived importance of one's job, and job satisfaction. For example, high commitment to the organization and low levels of job satisfaction have been shown to contribute to constructive behaviours such as 'voice' (e.g. Rusbult, Farrell, Rogers & Mainous III, 1988). In addition, research on grievance systems in organizations shows that employees who file a grievance after being treated unfairly generally are more satisfied with their performance than those deciding not to file a grievance (Olson-Buchanan, 1996a).

Finally, Santee and Maslach (1982) argued that stable individual differences may be related to initiatives to dissent. In their study, subjects read a series of scenarios presenting a particular problem for which they had to write down solutions. Before doing so, they overheard the solution given by the other three group members. The extent to which subjects gave alternative solutions was positively related to their self-esteem and their private self-consciousness, and negatively related to shyness, social anxiety and public self-consciousness.

What makes minority dissent effective?

Even when minority dissent occurs, its message needs to be attended to and recipients need to think about the minority proposal. This section shows that attending to, and thinking about, a minority proposal is not as evident or as straightforward as we may think. Even when recipients process a minority message and the minority message contains strong, compelling and convincing arguments (e.g. the dissenter shows that her invention actually generates profits), there is no guarantee that recipients will adopt the minority point of view.

In general, whether people engage in thorough and systematic processing of a persuasive message depends on the degree to which they experience a discrepancy between their desired degree of confidence in judgment as exemplified in a 'sufficiency threshold', and their actual degree of confidence (De Vries, De Dreu, Gordijn & Schuurman, 1996; Eagly & Chaiken, 1993). Confidence refers to the belief in the goodness of one's judgment or opinion, as it can be expressed in subjective probabilities about the likelihood of its correctness. Desired confidence refers to the level of confidence the recipient aspires to, incorporating limited capacity and environmental constraints (see Simon's satisficing principle). Such aspirations derive from individual differences such as involvement and uncertainty avoidance, as well as from environmental demands such as high vs. low pressure to reach a decision. When the actual degree of confidence meets or exceeds the sufficiency threshold, recipients will neglect the dissenter's message or process it in a superficial manner. But when the actual degree of confidence falls short of the sufficiency threshold, recipients become motivated to regain certainty. This motivation results in thorough, systematic processing of the message, in which all relevant information is carefully scrutinized (Eagly & Chaiken, 1993).

In the light of the above, a problem with minority dissent is that it is unlikely to induce out of itself a discrepancy between a recipient's desired and actual level of confidence. People tend to operate on the basis of a 'consensus-implies-correctness heuristic' which informs them that minority-based points of view are less likely to be correct and valid than the position endorsed by the majority of one's group or organization (Axsom, Yates & Chaiken, 1987). On the basis of this consensus-implies-correctness heuristic, people reject the dissenting message even without considering it seriously (De Dreu & De Vries, 1993). Thus, additional motivation is needed for individual group members to engage in thorough, systematic processing of a minority point of view. This extra motivation may be rooted in the dissenter, in the framing of the message, in characteristics of the recipient, and in the situation. Each of these variables, which we review below in more detail, is assumed either to lower the actual level of confidence, or to increase the desired level of confidence. The net result is a greater discrepancy between the two and thus a greater probability that the dissenting message will be attended to.

Factors promoting systematic processing

Features of the dissenter, as well as its strategy, may lower the recipient's actual level of confidence. For example, when the dissenter has high status, he/she is more likely to draw attention to his/her position and to influence actual level of confidence (see Eagly & Chaiken, 1993). Or when the dissenter is categorized as belonging to one's ingroup instead of to a (less competent and less prestigious) outgroup, he/she is more likely to cause uncertainty and thus to induce thorough processing of his/her message (David & Turner, 1996). A minority dissenter who advances a surprising and unexpected position is more likely to gain attention and to have impact (Baker & Petty, 1994). And consistent with the finding that negotiators are most effective when they are flexible about means but rigid about their goals (Lax & Sebenius, 1986), research demonstrated that minority dissent elicits more systematic processing when flexibility on means is combined with rigidity on position (e.g. Mugny, 1982). Finally, and perhaps most important is that dissent should be consistent over time (Moscovici, Lage & Naffrechoux, 1969). In organizations where a minority fights pay discrimination, such dissent will be most influential when arguments are repeated consistently on every relevant occasion.

Characteristics of the recipients as well as situational demands are expected to moderate the influence of minority dissent because they augment recipients' desired level of confidence. For instance, research shows that as the recipient's personal involvement with a specific topic or theme increases, dissent gains more attention and elicits more systematic processing of its message (De Dreu & De Vries, 1996). When someone blows the whistle on employers' unwillingness to contribute to health insurance and there is a recent history of accidents in the workplace, the whistle blower is likely to gain more attention than when the topic of health insurance and safe work conditions is less salient and involving. In addition, minority dissent may be more influential when recipients assume the existence of one and only one correct solution (unitary perspective) rather than that multiple judgments, attitudes and opinions may co-exist (pluralistic perspective) (Butera & Mugny, 1995; De Dreu & De Vries, 1993, Exp. 2; Sanchez-Mazas, 1996; see also Laughlin & Ellis, 1986). In the case of a unitary perspective, recipients may have a higher desired level of confidence than in the case of a pluralistic perspective, and thus dissent is more likely to induce a discrepancy between actual and desired level.

Pressures to resist minority influence and attitude change

Attention to the minority, and strong and compelling arguments provided by the minority are both necessary but not sufficient conditions for minority influence to occur. The problem with dissent is that it colours, or biases the processing of information. As discussed before, research by Nemeth (1986) demonstrated that people process minority messages in a divergent manner, in which they focus on falsification rather than on confirmation of content and in which they attempt to identify other solutions than the one forwarded by the dissenter him or herself. Although this may lead to the discovery of better strategies (Nemeth & Kwan, 1987) and improved performance (Van Dyne & Saaverda, 1996), it also diverts from the dissenting message itself so that its intended impact is reduced. In addition, there seems to be a general tendency to avoid identification with the minority (Mugny, Kaiser, Papastamou & Perez, 1984), and this also biases the processing of information.

Minority dissent often implies a change in relative status and power, and is therefore likely to be met with considerable resistance among the more influential and powerful players within the organization (Pfeffer, 1981). Frost and Egri (1991) discuss cases in which organizations cover up evidence given in support of the dissenter, sabotage the minority's functioning, or manage external committees in ways that automatically silence the dissenter. Other research indicates that group members direct a substantial amount of their communication towards the dissenting party, put pressures on the dissenter to change his or her point of view, or expel the minority from further participation (e.g. Levine, 1980). To prevent themselves from being exposed to these normative pressures, people generally avoid endorsing the dissenting point of view in public, and even in private they resist its deviating judgment (Deutsch & Gerard, 1955; Moscovici, 1980; Wood, Lundgren, Quellette, Busceme & Blackstone, 1994). In fact, early research by Festinger, Gerard, Hymovitch, Kelley and Raven (1952) already showed that people in minority positions are quite reluctant themselves to communicate with majority members.

Although fear for these (normative) pressures certainly inhibits the transition from processing a message to actually adopting the minority point of view, it does not mean that dissent has no influence. Minority influence research distinguishes between three types of response: Public agreement with the minority message, private agreement with the minority message (focal change), and private change on topics related to the focal issue by associative content (De Vries et al., 1996; Moscovici, 1980; Wood et al., 1994). When a co-worker blows the whistle on hazardous work conditions, colleagues and supervisors may both in public and in private resist such changes, but at the same time change their opinions regarding the amount of health insurance covered by the organization. Thus, dissent may influence attitudes at each of these levels independently, or even provoke much resistance at for instance the public level while simultaneously inducing considerable private acceptance on related matters (De Vries et al., 1996; Wood et al., 1994).

Research repeatedly demonstrated that the influence of dissent is present at related issues where identification with the minority source seems less obvious (De Dreu & De Vries, 1993, 1996; De Vries et al., 1996; Moscovici, 1980; Mugny, 1982; Wood et al., 1994). Such change on related issues may well precede more overt change on the focal issue, for two reasons. First, as time goes by people may dissociate the source of influence from the position advocated: Avoiding identification with the minority now is less of a barrier in thinking about, and approaching, the dissenting point of view. Thus, we

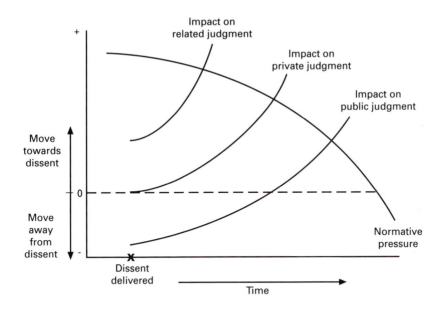

Figure 5.1 *Impact of minority dissent on opinions and judgments on related and focal issues as a function of time passed*

propose a so-called 'sleeper effect' (Pratkanis, Greenwald, Leippe & Baumgardner, 1988), in that minority influence on focal issues becomes apparent only after some time (see Figure 5.1). In addition, it seems reasonable to assume that people desire an internally consistent and coherent system of beliefs, attitudes and judgments (Eagly & Chaiken, 1993). Changing one's attitude on one topic augments internal inconsistency and thus promotes change on related topics as well. Thus, the fact that minority influence enhances divergent thinking and change on related topics after some time 'spreads out' towards the focal issues.

The relation between resistance and influence is depicted in Figure 5.1, which shows that over time, when the minority source and its message become dissociated and changes in attitudes at one level spread out to affect related attitudes, the likelihood of the minority position being accepted in public increases. In a sense, this brings us back by the starting point of this chapter, that minority dissent disrupts consensus, but if effective installs a new consensus as well.

Conclusions

Although dissent disrupts stability and smooth social interaction, some instances of minority dissent such as devil's advocates, whistle blowers and fact checkers may contribute positively to group performance and organizational productivity. In addition, we invoked research by Nemeth (1986) to demonstrate that minority dissent in groups and organizations may make a general contribution to performance at the individual level: It is likely to induce divergent thinking which increases creativity and enhances the courage to resist pressure to conformity. Thus, a first general conclusion that follows from our discussion is that dissent in groups and organizations tends to reduce efficiency especially in the short run, but may improve long-term effectiveness at the individual, group or organizational level.

The second part of this chapter dealt with the issue of effective dissent – what makes a dissenter effective in getting its message along? We identified two main barriers to dissenter effectiveness, the first being the fact that majority members usually reject minority viewpoints on a heuristic basis, and the second being that if minority viewpoints are processed, it happens in a biased manner orientated towards disconfirmation. To overcome the first barrier, the dissenter needs to take care of its strategy (e.g. being consistent over time), employ whatever high status cues it possesses, ensure that it is categorized as a member of the recipient's ingroup, and so on. Then, the dissenting minority message may be picked up, and processed in a thorough, systematic way. To overcome the second barrier (i.e. bias towards disconfirmation), the dissenter should be even more careful to deliver high quality arguments than regular persuasive sources should be.

Two questions received little and only indirect attention. First, what happens to the minority dissenters after they voice their discrepant point of view? We speculate that the outcome of the debate between dissenter and majority members is crucial: When the dissenter proves right and influences majority members, consequences for the dissenter may be much more positive than when the debate is decided in favour of the status quo. Van Dyne and Saaverda (1996) offer interesting qualitative material that supports the idea that consequences of dissent to the minority may be either bad – increased stress, conflict, exclusion from the group – or good – admiration from fellow group members, increased self-confidence. Research on filing grievance suggests that managers tend to give lower performance ratings to subordinates who file a grievance, which in part may be attributed to actual decrease in performance following the filing of a grievance (Olson-Buchanan, 1996b). This literature underlines that those in organizations who deviate have a hard time, and suggests the intriguing possibility that minority dissenters attract so much critique partly because they are (temporarily) performing suboptimally.

A second question awaiting further research is the role of minority dissent in group functioning at various stages of group life. Worchel, Coutant-Sassic and Wong (1993) distinguish between a development phase, in which groups form their identity, a production phase, in which groups focus on productivity issues and performance, and a desegregation phase, in which group boundaries are weakened, subgroups are formed and the group falls apart. Minority dissent seems most naturally occurring in the desegregation phase, and its impact will be small. It seems unlikely in the development phase.

Minority dissent may be most likely, and most beneficial, in the productivity phase. However, research is needed to test these speculations.

Summary

Minority dissent often leads to disagreement and irritation. Although detrimental consequences of such conflict to short-term productivity are readily acknowledged, we tried to demonstrate that conflict due to minority dissent may contribute to long-term organizational performance. Dissent should be given room to come out, and should be given attention and careful consideration. It was argued that careful consideration follows from an (induced) discrepancy between the recipient's actual and his/her desired level of confidence in judgment. Source-related, strategy and recipient-related variables that increase such discrepancy were discussed. Some of these factors, such as the categorization of the dissenter as belonging to the organization's ingroup, the recipient's personal involvement, and lack of tight supervision are more or less under the control of management. Thus, we argued that dissent should be fostered as a necessary and desirable part of organizational life, we indicated where managers may intervene to increase attendance to dissent and we also suggested ways in which management may work to decrease normative pressures that prevent the influence of minority dissent to come out in public.

Note

Parts of this chapter were written while Carsten K.W. De Dreu was at the Yale School of Management. Our work is financially supported by a Royal Netherlands Academy of Sciences fellowship awarded to Carsten De Dreu, and a Dutch National Science Foundation Grant (NWO #575-75-085) awarded to Nanne De Vries. This chapter benefited from discussions with, comments by and help from Michael Frese, Ernestine Gordijn, Bert Klandermans and Steve Motowidlow.

References

Argyris, C. (1982). *Reasoning, learning, and action: Individual and organizational.* San Francisco: Jossey-Bass.

Axsom, D., Yates, S. and Chaiken, S. (1987). Audience response as a heuristic cue in persuasion. *Journal of Personality and Social Psychology, 53,* 30–40.

Baker, S.M. and Petty, R.E. (1994). Majority and minority influence: Source-position imbalance as a determinant of message scrutiny. *Journal of Personality and Social Psychology, 67,* 5–19.

Borman, W.C. and Motowidlo, S.J. (1993). Expanding the criterion domain to include elements of contextual performance, in N. Schmitt and W.C. Borman (eds), *Personnel selection.* San Francisco: Jossey-Bass, pp. 71–98.

Butera, F. and Mugny, G. (1995). Conflict between incompetencies and influence of a low-expertise source in hypothesis testing. *European Journal of Social Psychology, 25,* 457–62.

Cohen, L. and Staw, B.M. (1995). *'Fun's over, fact-finders are here'. A case study of institutionalized dissent.* Paper presented at the Academy of Management meetings, Vancouver, BC, August 11–14.

Cosier, R.A. (1978). The effects of three potential aids for strategic decision making on prediction accuracy. *Organizational Behavior and Human Performance, 22,* 295–306.

David, B. and Turner, J.C. (1996). Studies in self-categorization and minority conversion: Is being a member of an out-group an advantage? *British Journal of Social Psychology, 35*, 179–200.

De Dreu, C.K.W. and De Vries, N.K. (1993). Numerical support, information processing and attitude change. *European Journal of Social Psychology, 23*, 647–62.

De Dreu, C.K.W. and De Vries, N.K. (1996). Differential processing and attitude change following majority and minority arguments. *British Journal of Social Psychology, 35*, 77–90.

De Vries, N.K., De Dreu, C.K.W., Gordijn, E. and Schuurman, M. (1996). Majority vs. minority influence: a dual-role interpretation, in W. Stroebe and M. Hewstone (eds), *European Review of Social Psychology* (Vol. 7). Chichester: John Wiley & Sons.

Deutsch, M. and Gerard, H.B. (1955). A study of normative and informational social influences upon individual judgment. *Journal of Abnormal and Social Psychology, 51*, 629–36.

Eagly, A. and Chaiken, S. (1993). *The psychology of attitudes.* New York: Harcourt Brace Jovanovich.

Festinger, L., Gerard, H.B., Hymovitch, B., Kelley, H.H. and Raven, B.H. (1952). The influence process in the presence of extreme deviates. *Human Relations, 5*, 327–46.

Frese, M., Kring, W., Soose, A. and Zempel, J. (1996). Personal initiative at work: Differences between east and west. *Academy of Management Journal, 39*, 154–69.

Frost, P.J. and Egri, C.P. (1991). The political process of innovation, in B.M. Staw and L.L. Cummings (eds), *Research on organizational behavior.* Greenwich, CT: JAI Press, Vol. 13, pp. 229–95.

Gordijn, E.H., De Vries, N.K. and De Dreu, C.K.W. (1996). Minority influence: the impact of expanding and shrinking minorities and argument quality on attitudes and information processing. Unpublished manuscript, University of Amsterdam.

Graham, J.W. (1986). Principled organizational dissent, in B.M. Staw and L.L. Cummings (eds), *Research on organizational behavior.* Greenwich, CT: JAI Press, Vol. 8, pp. 1–52.

Hackman, J.R. and Oldham, G.R. (1975). Development of a job diagnostic survey. *Journal of Applied Psychology, 60*, 159–70.

Hirschman, A.O. (1970). *Exit, voice, and loyalty: Responses to decline in firms, organizations, and states.* Cambridge, MA: Harvard University Press.

Hunt, J.W. (1972). *The restless organization.* Sydney: John Wiley & Sons.

Janis, I.L. (1972). *Victims of groupthink: a psychological study of foreign-policy decisions and fiascos.* Boston: Houghton Mifflin.

Laughlin, P.R. and Ellis, A.L. (1986). Demonstrability and social combination processes on mathematical intellective tasks. *Journal of Personality and Social Psychology, 22*, 177–89.

Lax, D. and Sebenius, J. (1986). *The manager as negotiator: Bargaining for cooperation and competitive gain.* New York: Free Press.

Levine, J.M. (1980). Reaction to opinion deviance in small groups, in P. Paulus (ed.), *Psychology of group influence.* Hillsdale, NJ: Lawrence Erlbaum, pp. 375–430.

Mason, R.O. (1969). A dialectical approach to strategic planning. *Management Science, 15*, 403–14.

Moscovici, S. (1980). Toward a theory of conversion behaviour, in L. Berkowitz (ed.), *Advances in experimental social psychology.* New York: Academic Press, Vol. 13, pp. 209–39.

Moscovici, S., Lage, E. and Naffrechoux, M. (1969). Influence of a consistent minority on the responses of a majority in a color perception task. *Sociometry, 32*, 365–80.

Mugny, G. (1982). *The power of minorities.* London: Academic Press.

Mugny, G., Kaiser, C., Papastamou, S. and Perez, J.A. (1984). Intergroup relations, identification and social influence. *British Journal of Social Psychology, 23*, 317–22.

Near, J.P. and Micelli, M.P. (1995). Effective whistle-blowing. *Academy of Management Review, 20*, 679–708.

Nemeth, C. (1986). Differential contributions of majority and minority influence processes. *Psychological Review, 93*, 10–20.

Nemeth, C. (1995). Dissent as driving cognition, attitudes, and judgments. *Social Cognition, 13*, 273–91.

Nemeth, C. and Chiles, C. (1988). Modelling courage: the role of dissent in fostering independence. *European Journal of Social Psychology, 18*, 275–80.

Nemeth, C. and Kwan, J. (1985). Originality of word associations as a function of majority versus minority influence. *Social Psychology Quarterly, 48*, 277–82.

Nemeth, C. and Kwan, J. (1987). Minority influence, divergent thinking and detection of correct solutions. *Journal of Applied Social Psychology, 17*, 786–97.

Nemeth, C., Mayseless, O., Sherman, J. and Brown, Y. (1990). Exposure to dissent and recall information. *Journal of Personality and Social Psychology, 58*, 429–37.

Nemeth, C. and Staw, B.M. (1989). The tradeoffs of control and innovation in groups and organizations, in L. Berkowitz (ed.), *Advances in experimental social psychology*. New York: Academic Press, Vol. 22, pp. 175–210.

Olson-Buchanan, J.B. (1996a). *To grieve or not to grieve: Factors related to voicing discontent in an organizational simulation*. Paper presented at the ninth annual meeting of the International Association for Conflict Management, Ithaca (NY), June 2–5.

Olson-Buchanan, J.B. (1996b). Voicing discontent: What happens to the grievance filer after the grievance? *Journal of Applied Psychology, 81*, 52–63.

Organ, D.W. (1988). *Organizational citizenship behavior*. Lexington, MA: Lexington Books.

Ostroff, C. and Schmitt, N. (1993). Configurations of organizational effectiveness and efficiency. *Academy of Management Journal, 36*, 1345–61

Perrucci, R., Anderson, R.M., Schendel, D.E. and Trachtman, L.E. (1980). Whistle-blowing: Professionals' resistance to organizational authority. *Social Problems, 28*, 149–64.

Pfeffer, J. (1981). *Power in organizations*. Marshfield, MA: Pitman.

Pratkanis, A.R., Greenwald, A.G., Leippe, M.R. and Baumgardner, M.H. (1988). In search of reliable persuasion effects: III. The sleeper effect is dead. Long live the sleeper effect. *Journal of Personality and Social Psychology, 54*, 203–18.

Rusbult, C.E., Farrell, D., Rogers, G. and Mainous III, A.G. (1988). Impact of exchange variables on exit, voice, loyalty, and neglect: an integrative model of responses to declining job satisfaction. *Academy of Management Journal, 31*, 599–627.

Sanchez-Mazas, M. (1996). Minority influence under value conflict: the case of human rights and xenophobia. *British Journal of Social Psychology*, 169–78.

Santee, R. and Maslach, C. (1982). To agree or not to agree: Personal dissent amid social pressure to conform. *Journal of Personality and Social Psychology, 42*, 690–700.

Schilit, W.K. and Locke, E.A. (1982). A study of upward influence in organizations. *Administrative Science Quarterly, 27*, 304–16.

Schneider, B. (1983). An interactionist perspective on organizational effectiveness, in L.L. Cummings and B. Staw (eds), *Research in Organizational Behavior*. Greenwich, CT: JAI Press, pp. 1–31.

Schweiger, D.M., Sandberg, W.R. and Ragan, J.W. (1986). Group approaches for improving strategic decision making: a comparative analysis of dialectical inquiry, devil's advocacy, and consensus. *Academy of Management Journal, 29*, 51–71.

Schwenk, C.R. (1990). Conflict in organizational decision making: an exploratory study of its effects in for-profit and not-for-profit organizations. *Management Science, 36*, 436–48.

Smith, C.M., Scott Tindale, R. and Dugoni, B.L. (1996). Minority and majority influence in freely interacting groups: Qualitative versus quantitative differences. *British Journal of Social Psychology, 35*, 137–50.

Taylor, R.N. (1992). Strategic decision making, in M.D. Dunnette and L.M. Hough (eds), *Handbook of industrial and organizational psychology* (2nd edn). Palo Alto, CA: Consulting Psychologists Press, pp. 651–717.

Turner, M.E. and Pratkanis, A.R. (1994). Social identity maintenance prescriptions for preventing groupthink: Reducing identity protection and enhancing intellectual conflict. *International Journal of Conflict Management, 5*, 254–70.

Van de Ven, A.H. (1974). *Group decision making effectiveness*. Ken, OH: Center for Business and Economic Research Press.

Van Dyne, L. and Saaverda, R. (1996). A naturalistic minority influence experiment: Effects on divergent thinking, conflict, and originality in work-groups. *British Journal of Social Psychology, 35*, 151–68.

Vickers, G. (1967). *Towards a sociology of management*. New York: Basic Books.

Volpato, C., Maass, A., Mucchi-Faina, A. and Vitti, E. (1990). Minority influence and social categorization. *European Journal of Social Psychology*, *20*, 119–32.

Weick, K.E. (1979). *The social psychology of organizing*. New York: Random House.

Wood, W., Lundgren, S., Quellette, J.A., Busceme, S. and Blackstone, T. (1994). Minority influence: a meta-analytical review of social influence processes. *Psychological Bulletin*, *115*, 323–45.

Worchel, S., Coutant-Sassic, D. and Wong, F. (1993). Toward a more balanced view of conflict: There is a positive side, in S. Worchel and J.A. Simpson (eds), *Conflict between people and groups: Causes, processes, and resolutions*. Chigaco: Nelson Hall, pp. 76–89.

Zald, M.N. and Berger, M.A. (1978). Social movements in organizations: Coup d'état, insurgency, and mass movements. *American Journal of Sociology*, *83*, 823–61.

6

Affective and Cognitive Conflict in Work Groups: Increasing Performance Through Value-Based Intragroup Conflict

Karen A. Jehn

Conflict can be detrimental and beneficial in organizational task groups. Much has been written about the negative effects of conflict and how to resolve differences between the parties involved (Brett, 1984; Brown, 1983; Pondy, 1967; Schmidt & Kochan, 1972). In contrast to this approach, I focus on the advantages of conflict and how to promote productive conflict in organizational groups. For instance, two members of a marketing department may similarly conflict over issues related to cooperation, task allocation, and also activities external to work. Whether the conflict turns out to benefit or to harm the relationship or productivity of the parties involved depends on the type of conflict, the situation surrounding the conflict and the outcomes desired.

While many things can cause conflict (i.e. incompatible goals, limited resources, irreconcilable personalities), the basis of many organizational conflicts can be described by the underlying values regarding work such as being rule-orientated, being innovative, and being attentive to details (Bar-Tal, 1989; Eisenhardt & Schoonhoven, 1990; Watson, Kumar & Michaelsen, 1993). In this chapter, a model is presented which focuses on the different types of work group conflicts that help and hinder individual and group productivity. The different types of conflict are described (affective conflict, cognitive conflict). The underlying value compatibility among group members and between group members and interested superiors is discussed in relation to the type of conflict it influences. The links between conflict and performance are described and the different contextual factors that influence whether or not the different types of conflict will be beneficial in the group setting are identified. Some recent studies are then discussed to substantiate the various links in the model and to identify the gaps in the research and need for future study.

Intragroup conflict

It is essential to examine conflict within groups since individuals generally interact and perform in groups daily (i.e. management teams, organizational departments, the family, social clubs, sports teams). The group is the most immediate social environment and therefore has a large impact on individual perceptions and behaviour. Conflict can be broadly defined as an awareness by the parties involved that there are discrepancies, or incompatible wishes or desires present (Boulding, 1963). Behaviours that occur are the consequences of perceived discrepancies between parties, yet conflict can be present without any outward display (Pondy, 1967).

Based on past research and typologies of conflict (Cosier & Rose, 1977; Guetzkow & Gyr, 1954; Haiman, 1951; Jehn, 1991; Kabanoff, 1991), I focus on affective and cognitive conflict. Interpersonal relationships have been postulated to have various dimensions, such as relationship, or emotional aspects and task-orientated aspects (Deutsch, 1973; Pinkley, 1990; Thomas, 1979). Functions in groups have also been divided into two components: the functions that contribute to group relationship maintenance and those regarding task accomplishment (Ancona & Caldwell, 1988; Bales, 1958; McGrath, 1984).[1]

Cognitive conflict pertains to conflict of ideas in the group and disagreement about the content and issues of the task. One member of a task group provided me with the following example of cognitive conflict: 'The discussion was about how to correctly calculate relative capacity utilization. We could not agree. Everyone had their own viewpoint and argued for it.' The disagreement is about a work-related topic – calculating relative capacity utilization. The situation has also reached a certain intensity – it is not just a 'disagreement' of viewpoints, but is worthy of 'argument'. Another example was provided by a second employee: 'Some people were sure that the future strategy should be to focus on the super premium market, while others felt the focus should be the minority market. There were different interpretations of the key issues. We debated a long time.' This work-related conflict is about the differing interpretations of the future strategy and was described by the group member as one of the major conflicts the group had experienced internally.

Affective conflict exists when personal and relationship components within the group are characterized by friction, frustration and personality clashes within the group. For example, one group member states: 'There was confrontation about things not related to work at all, silly things like clothes. The people in the team just didn't get along. The group felt a lack of trust, frustration, and insecurity. There was anger and even tears' (Jehn, 1994). The level of intensity of this nonwork conflict is demonstrated by the emotional displays that the employee describes. Another employee states: 'Some group members were so inconsiderate. They played the radio too loud. There were different personalities too – shy and dominant people. This created an imbalance and people became annoyed with each other.'

Group culture

Groups, as well as organizations, have specific, identifiable cultures (McFeat, 1974; Sackman, 1992). One defining aspect of group culture that guides actions is the sharing of knowledge and values among group members (Enz, 1988; Levine & Moreland, 1991; Sathe, 1983; Schein, 1985). In this study, two dimensions of group culture are addressed, group value consensus (GVC) and group value fit (GVF). GVC is the extent to which group members have similar work-related values. GVF is the degree to which the values of group members match the ideal group values envisioned by external parties with control over the group. Values are the beliefs held by an individual regarding choices involving one mode of behaviour over another, as in choosing business actions and objectives (Enz, 1988; Rokeach, 1973). Specific examples of group values include: being innovative, being careful, showing autonomy, adaptability and informality (O'Reilly, Chatman & Caldwell, 1991).

The research examined here addresses the question of how the similarity or diversity of group members and their similarity with external forces stimulate conflict, and in turn, influence group effectiveness. Research on group diversity (e.g. regarding demographics, values, work experience) and productivity has provided contradictory results. Some evidence has indicated that groups with low levels of diversity have higher levels of satisfaction (Lott & Lott, 1965), lower turnover rates (Jackson, Brett, Sessa, Cooper, Julin & Peyronnin, 1991; Wiersema & Bird, 1993), increased performance (Clement & Schiereck, 1973; Watson et al., 1993) and creativity (Kent & McGrath, 1969). In contrast, other research has demonstrated that diversity is sometimes positive (Bantel & Jackson, 1989). More specifically, value consensus and value fit have been associated with both positive outcomes such as high productivity (Weiss, 1978; Wilkins & Ouchi, 1983) and negative outcomes such as groupthink (Liedtka, 1989; Nemeth & Staw, 1989). Strong cultures and intensely held norms have been associated with increased performance (Deal & Kennedy, 1982; Denison, 1984), original products (Van Dyne & Jehn, 1993), and increased satisfaction (Kemelgor, 1982; O'Reilly & Caldwell, 1985). Alternatively, value consensus decreased satisfaction and quality care in a study of nurses (Kramer & Hafner, 1989) and may inhibit necessary change (Wilkins & Dyer, 1988; Zammuto & O'Connor, 1992).

In addition, it is not only the level of diversity within the group but also diversity across levels or with external elements such as supervisors and managers that may impact conflict and performance (Ancona & Caldwell, 1988; Enz, 1988). The value fit between individuals and superiors has also provided inconsistent results predicting both positive (Weiss, 1978) and negative effects (Liedtka, 1989; Nemeth & Staw, 1989). Examining conflict as a mediator between value consensus and value fit on the one hand and outcomes on the other may reconcile these controversial findings, and explain the inconsistent findings regarding conflict and group effectiveness.

A model of intragroup conflict

A recent study (Jehn, 1994) examined the mediating effect of intragroup conflict on the relationship between two of the above dimensions of group culture

(GVC and GVF) and individual and group productivity. The field study utilized functioning strategy consulting groups performing comparable tasks to examine the relations among group values, conflict, individual satisfaction and group performance. The team members spent their time together performing organizational activities such as task distribution, analysis of company reports and financial data, problem identification, discussion of strategic alternatives and report preparation. They met with the organization's employees and executives, took part in organizational meetings and made formal presentations. Their final product was a report identifying a problem area in strategy formulation within the firm, analysing the problem, and making specific recommendations to the executives.

This study examined two of the group culture dimensions as causes of affective and cognitive conflict (see Figure 6.1). Group value consensus (GVC) was defined as the extent to which group members had similar work-related values. Group value fit (GVF) was defined as the match between the values of the group and its immediate superior. This is the degree to which the values of the group members were consistent with the values envisioned by superiors (external parties with control over the group regarding work load and rewards) to be ideal for the group in its operating environment.

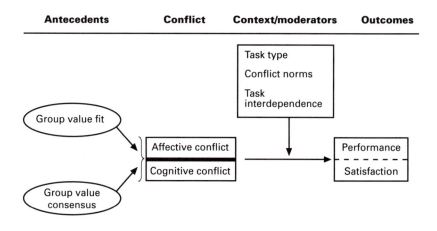

Figure 6.1   *A model of intragroup conflict*

Group value consensus and intragroup conflict

Group value consensus (GVC) or the degree to which group members agreed on the importance of various work values to the group, is negatively related to affective conflict among members. When a group has a high level of GVC, members will agree on norms and values regarding work which will promote goal similarity and harmony (Nemeth & Staw, 1989). If group members agree on the importance of various work values such as being innovative, being careful, showing adaptability and autonomy, just to mention a few, they will be less likely to dislike one another. According to Schneider (1983), the similarity of values among members will influence attraction and therefore decrease interpersonal tension. In a strong culture, defined as the intense sharing of values (O'Reilly, 1989), members develop emotional attachment and understanding which decreases affective conflict. When low GVC exists, members' core values and beliefs about their everyday work are challenged, causing friction and emotional upset (Schein, 1986). The disagreement about values causes animosity among group members (Bar-Tal, 1989).

GVC also influences cognitive conflict. Research has shown that groups with members who have similar values have more effective interaction processes than groups with dissimilar values (Watson et al., 1993). Shared values increase the likelihood that members will have coordinated action plans regarding the task (Denison, 1984), thus decreasing task-related conflict. When work-related values are shared, misunderstandings are decreased. Differing values cause group members to perceive situations differently and therefore members may have different goals regarding the task. Individuals may differ in their beliefs about what is important to the job and what should be done. In addition, value diversity is associated with differing points of view which also encourages cognitive conflict (Eisenhardt & Schoonhoven, 1990).

Group value fit and intragroup conflict

Group value fit (GVF), or the degree to which the content of the group's values and the ideals of the governing superiors are similar, also affects conflict. While members may agree within the group (high GVC), they may, as a whole, disagree with their manager (low GVF), which can cause uneasiness and friction within the group. This is similar to Liedtka's (1989) concept of value congruence which suggests that low levels of fit between an individual and the corporation can have negative results such as turnover and absenteeism. Similarly, research has shown that incompatible values between merging organizations (Cartwright & Cooper, 1993) and between individuals and organizations (Chatman, 1988) can influence negative emotions. More specifically, value contradictions between leaders and their followers can be a continuous source of tension and affective conflict for the group of followers (Gray, Bougon & Donnellon, 1985). Research has indicated that when groups, or departments, possess values that are different from those of upper management, conflict or nonharmonious situations and perceptions are more likely to arise (Gregory, 1983; Kemelgor, 1982). When a group and its manager share values, the group will be more secure in its actions (Enz, 1988), thus decreasing the likelihood of cognitive conflict. If the values of the group do not match the supervisor's vision for the group, there will be discrepancies concerning how the work should be carried out. Members may disagree about whether they should follow the values of the group or the different goals advocated by the manager.

Intragroup conflict and group outcomes

Research on group conflict, similar to the research on values and diversity, has demonstrated that conflict can have both negative and positive consequences on groups and individuals. In the current study, affective and cognitive conflict are examined to determine their varying effects on behaviour and attitudes. Conflict may threaten performance and productivity (Brown, 1983; Pondy, 1967). Research has demonstrated that affective, personal attacks decrease group performance (Evan, 1965). When group members are upset with one another, feel antagonistic towards one another and are experiencing affective conflict, their performance and productivity can suffer (Argyris, 1962). Group members will tend to focus their efforts on resolving or ignoring the interpersonal conflicts, rather than concentrating on task completion (Kelley, 1979).

On the other hand, disagreement of ideas within a group can be beneficial. Evidence has shown that conflict within teams can improve decision quality and strategic planning (Cosier & Rose, 1977; Mitroff, Barabba & Kilmann, 1977; Schweiger, Sandberg & Rechner, 1989). Conflict may also lead to innovation, re-evaluation of the status quo, and thus adaptation to one's situation and increased productivity (Coser, 1970; Nemeth & Staw, 1989; Thomas, 1979; Roloff, 1987). In the view of systems theorizing, specifically the concept of requisite variety, disagreement and variety are necessary for systems to adapt to their environment and perform well (Ashby, 1956). Further, when members agree with other group members about concepts or actions without presenting dissenting viewpoints, superior alternatives may be overlooked and thus performance may be suboptimal (Janis, 1982; Tjosvold, Dann & Wong, 1992; Turner, Pratkanis, Probasco & Leve, 1992).

Conflict typically creates uncomfortable feelings and unhappiness. When people sense personality clashes and friction among group members, they are typically unsatisfied with their group and fellow group members (Baron, 1990; Surra & Longstreth, 1990). Cognitive conflict, while potentially beneficial to performance, can still cause anxiety and uncomfortable feelings among group members. When a group argues about who does what, the actual task will take longer, members will be dissatisfied because of this uncertainty, and they will also feel a greater desire to leave the group (Hoffman, 1978; Roloff, 1987). Disputes regarding resources and responsibilities may also cause members to perceive unfairness which will decrease members' satisfaction with being part of the group (Kabanoff, 1991; Lind & Tyler, 1988). Inconsistent task responsibilities interfere with efficient task completion (Herbert, 1976) and foster feelings of role ambiguity. Such ambiguities may, in turn, cause dissatisfaction and turnover among members (Katz & Kahn, 1966; Schein, 1985). Sometimes changes in job assignment and responsibility allocation are necessary and even beneficial. For example, one member may be better qualified to do a cost/benefit analysis than others. In this instance, disagreement about who should do what may promote the discussion of technical qualifications which raises the likelihood that the most able person is assigned to the appropriate task. It is the additional and chronic conflicts regarding allocation of duties and resources that can be detrimental.

A study of 105 work groups and management teams in the corporate headquarters of a Fortune 500 company provides evidence for the complex relationships between conflict and team outcomes (Jehn, 1991). In this study, 633 employees in seven departments of a freight transportation firm reported on their levels of cognitive and affective conflict. It is not surprising that in this study also, affective conflict was associated with a decrease in individual satisfaction; however, contrary to expectations, cognitive conflict did not have a negative impact on satisfaction. Cognitive conflict may increase members' curiosity and perceptions of 'voice', thus generating positive attitudes (Deutsch, 1969). In addition, if the conflicts are not presented as personal attacks they can actually intensify the relationships (Coser, 1970) and increase satisfaction (Hoffman, 1978). These positive attributes of cognitive conflict may have outweighed the negative impact in this study. The relationship between cognitive conflict and employee attitudes such as satisfaction may be more complex, and thus warrant future investigation.

Another study (Jehn, 1995) also supports these links of the model. In this field study of intragroup conflict, over 600 employees of an international firm were asked about the level of conflict within their work units. Multiple methods were used to examine the impact of conflict on group performance and individual member satisfaction. Interviews, surveys and ethnographic observation provided the basis for triangulating the relationship between conflict and objective performance (i.e. performance appraisals, team productivity reports, error reports, total quality measurements). Affective conflict was negatively related to satisfaction but not to performance. Cognitive conflict was positively related to performance in groups performing nonroutine types of tasks like strategy formation and management teams but negatively related to performance in routine task groups.

Contextual factors that influence the relationship between intragroup conflict and group outcomes

Brehmer (1976) has suggested that the type of task a group performs influences the relationship between conflict and effectiveness. Not surprisingly, whether or not cognitive conflict is beneficial may well depend on the type of task that the group performs. A task is defined as the work-related activities that group members perform (Goodman, 1986). Routine tasks have a low level of task variability, defined as the amount of variety in methods and repetitiveness of task processes (Hall, 1972), are generally familiar, and are done the same way each time with predictable results (Thompson, 1967). In contrast, nonroutine tasks require problem-solving, have few set procedures, and have a high degree of uncertainty (Mason & Mitroff, 1981; Van de Ven, Delbecq & Koenig, 1976). Groups performing nonroutine tasks benefit from diverse ideas of group members. When members agree with other group members about concepts or actions at the expense of presenting dissenting viewpoints, superior alternatives may be overlooked (Janis, 1982). Thoughtful consideration of criticism and alternative solutions enhances decision making and productivity in groups with complex tasks (Allison, 1971; Tjosvold et al., 1992). As such, differing viewpoints should be encouraged and alternative consequences considered in groups performing primarily nonroutine tasks. Cognitive conflict also increases stimulation, curiosity (Tjosvold, 1991) and perceptions of 'voice', which may lead to positive attitudes (Deutsch, 1969). According to Coser (1970), conflict which is not conveyed as a personal attack can contribute to group preservation by intensifying interpersonal relationships. Based on the negative effects that a lack of cognitive conflict has (i.e. conformity and complacency) and on the benefits of cognitive conflict (i.e. the increased number of ideas and opinions), cognitive conflict should be positively related to effectiveness in nonroutine tasks.

In contrast to the effects of conflict on groups performing nonroutine tasks, conflict regarding content issues will hinder groups performing routine tasks by interfering with efficient processing (Barnard, 1938; Guzzo, 1986). When groups consistently perform the same activities in the same manner day after day, conflicts which arise regarding the issues of the task may be counterproductive, time-consuming and frustrating. Some conflict, however, can increase re-evaluation of current ideas and standards (Tjosvold, 1991), thus causing changes that upgrade the quality of the product and enhance group effectiveness. Therefore, it is predicted that an absence of conflict will be detrimental to effectiveness and a small amount of conflict will be beneficial in groups performing routine tasks. A greater degree of conflict, after that point, will be increasingly detrimental.

The relationship between conflict and effectiveness will be influenced by other factors such as the interdependence of members and the specific group norms regarding conflict. There are many different forms of interdependence relevant to groups. Task interdependence as used in this model exists to the extent that group members are reliant upon one another to perform and complete their individual jobs (Thompson, 1967; Van de Ven et al., 1976). Increased interaction and dependence among members causes conflict to have an intensified effect on group outcomes (Brett, 1984; Schmidt & Kochan, 1972). Groups with low levels of task interdependence will be less affected by conflict, while groups with high levels of interdependence will experience a strong relationship between conflict and effectiveness. For example, affective conflict will have a greater negative impact on group outcomes in highly interdependent groups than in other groups. When group members do not depend on one another to complete their work and are not required to work closely with one another, interpersonal problems will not be as detrimental as they are in groups that are highly interdependent. The impact of task interdependence and group conflict norms on the relationship between conflict and effectiveness are quite complex. Interdependence increases the negative impact of affective conflict, as expected, but decreases the negative impact of cognitive conflict (Jehn, 1991). It may be that the group members realize that they must work together and agree on content issues in order to complete the group task, therefore lessening the tendency for them to be negatively influenced by arguments regarding the actual task. The stress and pressure to conform in interdependent groups may then be manifested in affective conflicts. This outcome-interdependence based pressure to agree suggests an intrinsic paradox for groups that require constructive criticism and cognitive conflict to perform well.

Group norms about conflict will also have an impact on the relationship between intragroup conflict and effectiveness. Norms, as defined by Bettenhausen and Murnighan (1985), are standards that regulate behaviour. Tjosvold (1991) discusses 'openness norms' (i.e. open confrontation, open discussion) which encourage people to express their doubts, opinions and uncertainties. Similarly, Brett (1991) addresses effective discussion norms and states that a very important norm for a group to develop is tolerance of differing viewpoints. Therefore, conflict norms can encourage openness and acceptance of disagreement (i.e. communication about conflict is encouraged within this group; disagreements are accepted within this group) and can, therefore, augment the positive effects of conflict or decrease the negative effects. For instance, effectiveness in groups performing tasks requiring problem solving and decision making will be enhanced when there are disagreements of opinions and ideas; these benefits will be increased when norms encourage open communication of ideas because there will be more options discussed. On the other hand, groups may have conflict norms that are not open in that they foster conflict avoidance and the perception that conflict is harmful (i.e. conflict should be avoided at all costs). Such norms will increase the negative influence of conflict and decrease the positive effects. For example, affective conflict will cause decreases in performance and the view that conflict is harmful will intensify this. In this case, even constructive criticism and disagreements may be responded to with defensiveness and animosity, thus interfering with productivity and satisfaction within the group.

Jehn (1995) hypothesized that open conflict norms would increase the beneficial aspects of conflict and that closed norms would increase the detrimental effects. In actuality, open norms did increase the beneficial aspects of cognitive conflict (i.e. individual and group performance). They also increased the negative impact of affective conflict (i.e. groups with closed norms regarding affective conflict were more effective than groups with open norms). The qualitative data revealed that the open norms about affective conflict increased the number and intensity of affective conflicts but the openness regarding conflict did not provide an atmosphere of acceptance and forgiveness among members. In fact, the conflict escalated as the number and intensity of episodes increased. This is consistent with Murnighan and

Conlon's finding (1991) that successful string quartets did not openly discuss heated, interpersonal conflicts, recognizing that these conflicts could be counter-productive.

Implications for managers and team leaders

Past theorizing has suggested that conflict may have beneficial as well as a detrimental function in organizations. This chapter demonstrates the various roles of conflict in different types of organizational groups ranging from production groups to executive decision making teams. A practical contribution of this research is its assistance in helping practitioners determine (1) under which circumstances they should encourage brainstorming and voicing multiple points of view, (2) what types of conflict they need to be concerned with given the group's goal(s), and (3) when they should intervene and diffuse the group's conflict. Managers and group leaders need to first identify the type of task the group is performing, the goal of the group (i.e. group member satisfaction, performance, or long-term functioning), the level of interdependence in the group, and the norms in the group surrounding conflict and conflict management before determining whether or not to resolve or encourage conflict. Managers must also consider the dynamic role of conflict in work groups and take into account the possibility that one type of conflict may change into another type. For example, cognitive conflict that is not resolved may be transformed into affective conflict. Or an affective conflict may be manifested in a cognitive conflict episode. Also, not only does conflict influence effectiveness, but past effectiveness may influence the level and type of conflict in the group.

Other perceptions and attitudes, while not the focus of this chapter, will affect the nature and level of conflict (e.g. the regard for good group relationships, and the level of respect and trust among members). If group members have a high level of respect for one another, they will be able to endure a high level of cognitive conflict without interpreting the conflict as being a relationship problem. If there is a lot of concern in the group with trust and relationship maintenance, members may disagree in ways that are based in intelligent arguments rather than attacking issues on a personal basis. This concern also includes the degree to which members believe they are competing rather than working together to complete the group project. If members sense intense competition, low levels of trust, and are not concerned with relationship continuation, conflict regarding interpersonal relationships will increase. In addition, past research suggests that group size, tenure with the firm, group composition, group goals, and degree of conflict resolution influence performance and individual reactions (Nieva, Fleishman and Rieck, 1978). Future research should more closely examine the role of conflict types as a mediator between these influences and group outcomes.

Summary

Group value consensus, or the extent to which group members share values, and group value fit, or the degree to which the culture of the group matches the ideal culture envisioned by external parties with control over the group, decreased conflict. In examining work groups, it was found that groups with low levels of value similarity among members and between the group and governing superiors had higher levels of conflict than groups with high levels of value similarity.

While managers typically cannot alter the fundamental values of employees, they often have control over who will work with whom. To produce a high level of performance, a group should consist of members with varying values, but the process by which these differences are manifested will need to be carefully managed since value differences can also increase affective conflict. If the diverse values of members provoke discussions of various options and constructive criticism, increased effectiveness is likely in nonroutine task groups; however, if the differing values cause interpersonal tensions, interference with task completion and effectiveness may occur. In addition, when the values of group members and those of their superiors are too similar, a groupthink situation may occur which can decrease the effectiveness of the group (Allison, 1971; Janis, 1982). The critical evaluation that occurs when groups challenge their manager or leader can enhance task performance. According to the results of this study, in order to reduce detrimental conflict (i.e. affective conflict) and to increase productive, cognitive conflict, group members and their superiors need to recognize and manage not only the type of values the group shares but the discrepancies in norms and values as well.

Note

1. There are many labels of task-related conflict (e.g. task, cognitive, realistic) and relationship conflict (emotional, socio-emotional, personal, interpersonal, people). There have also been many critiques of the various terms. For instance, many task conflicts have an 'emotional', affective aspect to them as well which makes distinguishing between task and emotional conflict confusing. Using the term personal conflict might assume that the conflict resides in stable traits and this is not necessarily so, conflict can be very situational. There is also a problem with the term 'interpersonal conflict' in that both types of conflict occur between people. The various terms have been a continued source of difficulty in this literature. I have chosen affective conflict because it seems to be the term that most closely represents the aspect of conflict that focuses on interpersonal incompatibilities related to the relationships among people (separate from the task).

References

Allison, G. (1971). *Essence of decision: Explaining the Cuban missile crisis*. Boston, MA: Little, Brown.
Ancona, D.G. and Caldwell, D.F. (1988). Beyond task and maintenance: Defining external functions in groups. *Group and Organization Studies, 13*, 468–94.

Argyris, C. (1962). *Interpersonal competence and organizational effectiveness*. Homewood, IL: Dorsey.

Ashby, W.R. (1956). *An introduction to cybernetics*. London: Methuen.

Bales, R.F. (1958). Task roles and social roles in problem solving groups, in E.E. Macoby, T.M. Newcomb and E.C. Hartley (eds), *Social psychology*. New York: Holt, pp. 437–47.

Bantel, K.A. and Jackson, S.E. (1989). Top management and innovations in banking: Does the composition of the top team make a difference? *Strategic Management Journal, 10*, 107–24.

Barnard, C.I. (1938). *The functions of the executive*. Cambridge, MA: Harvard University Press.

Baron, R. (1990). Countering the effects of destructive criticism. The relative efficacy of four interventions. *Journal of Applied Psychology, 75*, 235–45.

Bar-Tal, D. (1989). *Group beliefs: a conception for analyzing group structure, processes, and behavior*. New York: Springer-Verlag.

Bettenhausen, K. and Murnighan, J.K. (1985). The emergence of norms in competitive decision-making groups. *Administrative Science Quarterly, 30*, 350–72.

Boulding, K. (1963). *Conflict and defense*. New York: Harper & Row.

Brehmer, B. (1976). Social judgement theory and the analysis of interpersonal conflict. *Psychological Bulletin, 83*, 985–1003.

Brett, J.M. (1984). Managing organizational conflict. *Research and Practice, 15*, 644–78.

Brett, J.M. (1991). Negotiating group decisions. *Negotiation Journal, 3*, 291–310.

Brown, L.D. (1983). *Managing conflict at organizational interfaces*. Reading, MA: Addison-Wesley.

Cartwright, S. and Cooper, G.L. (1993). The role of culture compatibility in successful organizational marriage. *Academy of Management Executive, 7*, 57–70.

Chatman, J.A. (1988). Matching people and organizations: Selection and socialization in public accounting firms. Unpublished doctoral dissertation. School of Business Administration, University of California Berkeley.

Clement, D.E. and Schiereck, J.J. (1973). Sex composition and group performance in a visual signal detection task. *Memory & Cognition, 1*, 251–5.

Coser, L.A. (1970). *Continuities in the study of social conflict*. New York: Free Press.

Cosier, R. and Rose, G. (1977). Cognitive conflict and goal conflict effects on task performance. *Organizational Behavior and Human Performance, 19*, 378–91.

Deal, T.E. and Kennedy, A.A. (1982). Culture: a new look through old lenses. *Journal of Applied Behavioral Science, 19*, 498–505.

Denison, D.R. (1984). Bringing corporate culture to the bottom line. *Organizational Dynamics, 13*, 5–22.

Deutsch, M. (1969). Conflicts: Productive and destructive. *Journal of Social Issues, 25*, 7–41.

Deutsch, M. (1973). *The resolution of conflict*. New Haven, CT: Yale University Press.

Eisenhardt, K. and Schoonhoven, C. (1990). Organizational growth: Linking founding team, strategy, environment, and growth among US semiconductor ventures, 1978–1988. *Administrative Science Quarterly, 35*, 504–29.

Enz, C. (1988). The role of value congruity in intraorganizational power. *Administrative Science Quarterly, 33*, 284–304.

Evan, W. (1965). Conflict and performance in R&D organizations. *Industrial Management Review, 7*, 37–46.

Goodman, P.S. (1986). *Designing effective work groups*. San Francisco, CA: Jossey-Bass.

Gray, B., Bougon, M.G. and Donnellon, A. (1985). Organizations as constructions and destructions of meaning. *Journal of Management, 11*, 83–98.

Gregory, K. (1983). Native-view paradigms: Multiple cultures and culture conflicts in organizations. *Administrative Science Quarterly, 28*, 331–8.

Guetzkow, H. and Gyr, J. (1954). An analysis of conflict in decision-making groups. *Human Relations, 7*, 367–81.

Guzzo, R.A. (1986). Group decision making and group effectiveness in organizations, in P.S. Goodman (ed.), *Designing effective workgroups*. San Francisco, CA: Jossey-Bass, pp. 34–71.

Haiman, F.S. (1951). *Group leadership and democratic action*. Boston, MA: Houghton Mifflin.

Hall, R.H. (1972). *Organizations, structure, and process*. Englewood Cliffs, NJ: Prentice-Hall.

Herbert, T. (1976). *Dimensions of organizational behavior*. New York: Macmillan.

Hoffman, L.R. (1978). The group problem-solving process, in L. Berkowitz (ed.), *Group Processes*. New York: Academic Press, pp. 101–14.

Jackson, S.E., Brett, J.F., Sessa, V.I., Cooper, D.M., Julin, C. and Peyronnin, S. (1991). Some differences make a difference: Individual dissimilarity and group heterogeneity as correlates of recruitment, promotions, and turnover. *Journal of Applied Psychology, 76*, 675–89.

Janis, I.L. (1982). *Groupthink*. Boston, MA: Houghton Mifflin.

Jehn, K. (1991). *The benefits and detriments of conflict*. Paper presented at the Academy of Management meeting, Miami Beach, FL.

Jehn, K. (1994). Enhancing effectiveness: an investigation of advantages and disadvantages of value-based intragroup conflict. *International Journal of Conflict Management, 5*, 223–38.

Jehn, K. (1995). A multimethod examination of the benefits and detriments of intragroup conflict. *Administrative Science Quarterly, 40*, 256–82.

Kabanoff, B. (1991). Equity, equality, power, and conflict. *Academy of Management Review, 16*, 416–41.

Katz, D. and Kahn, R.L. (1966). *The social psychology of organizations*. New York: John Wiley & Sons.

Kelley, H.H. (1979). *Personal relationships: their structure and prophecies*. Hillsdale, NJ: Erlbaum.

Kemelgor, B.H. (1982). Job satisfaction as mediated by the value congruity of supervisors and their subordinates. *Journal of Occupational Behavior, 3*, 147–60.

Kent, R.N. and McGrath, J.E. (1969). Task and group characteristics as factors influencing group performance. *Journal of Experimental Social Psychology, 5*, 429–40.

Kramer, M. and Hafner, L.P. (1989). Shared values: Impact on staff nurse job satisfaction and perceived productivity. *Nursing Research, 38*, 172–7.

Levine, J.M. and Moreland, R.L. (1991). Progress in small group research. *Annual Review of Psychology, 41*, 585–634.

Liedtka, J. (1989). Managerial values and corporate decision-making: an empirical analysis of value congruence in two organizations. *Research in Corporate Social Performance and Policy, 11*, 55–91.

Lind, A. and Tyler, T. (1988). *Procedural justice*. New York: John Wiley & Sons.

Lott, A.J. and Lott, B.E. (1965). Group cohesiveness as interpersonal attraction. *Psychological Bulletin, 64*, 259–309.

Mason, R.O. and Mitroff, I.I. (1981). *Challenging strategic planning assumptions*. New York: John Wiley & Sons.

McFeat, T. (1974). *Small-group cultures*. New York: Pergamon Press.

McGrath, J.E. (1984). *Groups: Interaction and performance*. Englewood Cliffs, NJ: Prentice-Hall.

Mitroff, J., Barabba, N. and Kilmann, R. (1977). The application of behavior and philosophical technologies to strategic planning: a case study of a large federal agency. *Management Studies, 24*, 44–58.

Murnighan, J. K. and Conlon, D.E. (1991). The dynamics of intense work groups: a study of British string quartets. *Administrative Science Quarterly, 36*, 165–86.

Nemeth, C.J. and Staw, B.M. (1989). The tradeoffs of social control in groups and organizations, in L. Berkowitz (ed.), *Advances in Experimental Social Psychology*, New York: Academic Press, Vol. 22, pp. 175–210.

Nieva, V.F., Fleishman, E.A. and Rieck, A. (1978). *Team dimensions: their identity, their measurement, and their relationships*. Final Technical Report for Contract No. DAHC19-78-C-0001. Washington, DC: Advanced Research Resources Organizations.

O'Reilly, C.A. (1989). Corporations, culture, and commitment: Motivation and social control in organizations. *California Management Review, 31*, 9–25.

O'Reilly, C. A. and Caldwell, D.F. (1985). The commitment and job tenure of new employees: Some evidence of postdecisional justification. *Administrative Science Quarterly, 26*, 597–616.

O'Reilly, C.A., Chatman, J.A. and Caldwell, D.F. (1991). People, jobs, and organizational culture. *Academy of Management Journal, 34*, 487–516.

Pinkley, R.L. (1990). Dimensions of conflict frame: Disputant interpretations of conflict. *Journal of Applied Psychology, 75*, 117–26.

Pondy, L.R. (1967). Organizational conflict: Concepts and models. *Administrative Science Quarterly, 12*, 296–320.

Rokeach, M. (1973). *The nature of human values*. New York: Free Press.

Roloff, M.E. (1987). Communication and conflict, in C.R. Berger and S.H. Chaffee (eds), *Handbook of communication science*. Newbury Park, CA: Sage, pp. 484–534.

Sackman, S.A. (1992). Culture and subcultures: an analysis of organizational knowledge. *Administrative Science Quarterly, 38*, 140–61.

Sathe, V. (1983). *Culture and related corporate realities*. Homewood, IL: Irwin.

Schein, E. H. (1985). *Organizational culture and leadership*. San Francisco, CA: Jossey-Bass.

Schein, E.H. (1986). What you need to know about organizational culture. *Training and Development Journal, 8*, 30–3.

Schmidt, S.M. and Kochan, T.A. (1972). Conflict: Toward conceptual clarity. *Administrative Science Quarterly, 17*, 359–70.

Schneider, B. (1983). An interactionist perspective on organizational effectiveness, in L.L. Cummings and B.M. Staw (eds), *Research in organizational behavior*. Greenwich, CT: JAI Press, pp. 1–31.

Schweiger, D., Sandberg, W. and Rechner, P. (1989). Experimental effects of dialectical inquiry, devil's advocacy, and other consensus approaches to strategic decision making. *Academy of Management Journal, 32*, 745–72.

Surra, C. and Longstreth, M. (1990). Similarity of outcomes, interdependence, and conflict in dating relationships. *Journal of Personality and Social Psychology, 59*, 501–16.

Thomas, K.W. (1979). Organizational conflict, in S. Kerr (ed.), *Organizational behavior*. Columbus, OH: Grid Publishing, pp. 151–84.

Thompson, J. (1967). *Organizations in action*. Chicago, IL: McGraw-Hill.

Tjosvold, D. (1991). Rights and responsibilities of dissent: Cooperative conflict. *Employee Responsibilities and Rights Journal, 4*, 13–23.

Tjosvold, D., Dann, V. and Wong, C. (1992). Managing conflict between departments to serve customers. *Human Relations, 45*, 1035–54.

Turner, M.E., Pratkanis, A.R., Probasco, P. and Leve, C. (1992). Threat, cohesion, and group effectiveness: Testing a social identity maintenance perspective on groupthink. *Journal of Personality and Social Psychology, 63*, 781–96.

Van de Ven, A.H., Delbecq, A. and Koenig, R. (1976). Determinants of coordination modes within organizations. *American Sociological Review, 41*, 322–38.

Van Dyne, L. and Jehn, K. (1993). *Value and demographic diversity in work groups: Effects on group process and group originality*. Paper, annual meeting of the Academy of Management, Atlanta, GA.

Watson, W.E., Kumar, K. and Michaelsen, L. K. (1993). Cultural diversity's impact on interaction process and performance: Comparing homogeneous and diverse task groups. *Academy of Management Journal, 36*, 590–602.

Weiss, H.M. (1978). Social learning of work values in organizations. *Journal of Applied Psychology, 63*, 711–18.

Wiersema, M. and Bird, A. (1993). Organizational demography in Japanese firms: Group heterogeneity, individual dissimilarity, and top management team turnover. *Academy of Management Journal, 36*, 996–1025.

Wilkins, A.L. and Dyer, W.G. (1988). Toward culturally sensitive theories of culture change. *Academy of Management Review, 13*, 522–33.

Wilkins, A.L. and Ouchi, W.G. (1983). Efficient cultures: Exploring the relationship between culture and organizational performance. *Administrative Science Quarterly, 28*, 468–81.

Zammuto, R.F. and O' Connor, E.J. (1992). Gaining advanced manufacturing technologies benefits: the roles of organization design and culture. *Academy of Management Review, 17*, 701–28.

7

The Effects of Conflict on Strategic Decision Making Effectiveness and Organizational Performance

Allen C. Amason and David M. Schweiger

Most scholars and practitioners agree that the complexities and pressures of strategic decision making can often produce conflict (Carter, 1971; Hickson, Butler, Cray, Mallory & Wilson, 1986; Mintzberg, Raisinghani & Theoret, 1976). The effect this conflict has on the decision making process, however, is unclear (Eisenhardt & Zbaracki, 1992). Traditional wisdom holds that conflict hinders decision making. Conflict can disrupt the exchange of information among the team of decision makers, reducing decision quality. Conflict can undermine the commitment that is needed to get the decision properly implemented. Finally, conflict can reduce satisfaction and affective acceptance among the team members, threatening cohesion and the prospects for future decisions (Schweiger, Sandberg & Ragan, 1986; Schweiger & Sandberg, 1991). However, there is also reason to believe that conflict improves decision making. Conflict can enhance decision quality by encouraging thorough evaluation of more and different alternatives. Conflict can also improve understanding among the members of the decision making team, thereby improving the chances that decisions will be implemented as intended (Cosier & Schwenk, 1990; Schweiger, Sandberg & Rechner, 1989; Schwenk, 1990).

These inconsistencies have arisen from an inadequate understanding of the role conflict plays in strategic decision making. In this chapter, we will discuss the differing effects of conflict on decision making. Specifically, we will examine two types of conflict, cognitive and affective, and review recent research suggesting that, while they often occur together, these different types of conflict have very different effects on decision quality, team consensus and team member affective acceptance.

Decision making and performance

Strategic decisions address important issues and involve significant sums of resources. As a consequence, the quality of each decision is important. Similarly, because it can facilitate the implementation of a decision, consensus among the members of the decision making team is also important.

Finally, to be effective decision makers over the course of time, teams must develop and sustain positive affective relationships among their members. These by-products of the decision making process are all necessary for enhanced organizational performance. As such, they have all been the subject of considerable research.

Perhaps most prominent among this research is the work that has been done on decision quality. This research has consistently shown that high quality decisions have two principal antecedents, the cognitive resources of the decision making team and the interaction processes that the team uses to produce its decisions.

Cognitive resources are the various skills, abilities, knowledge and perspectives held by a team's members. In general, more resources are thought to provide more potential for high quality decisions. Thus, diverse teams are thought to have more potential to produce high quality decisions than less diverse teams. Bantel and Jackson (1989) and Murray (1989), for instance, both found that diverse teams make more innovative and higher quality decisions than do less diverse teams. Indeed, Bantel and Jackson state that 'when solving complex, non-routine problems, groups are more effective when composed of individuals having a variety of skills, knowledges, abilities and perspectives' (1989, p. 109).

Cognitive diversity, however, represents little more than the potential for high quality strategic decisions. To realize that potential, a team's diverse skills, abilities and perspectives must be identified, evaluated and combined into a decision. Research has shown that dialectically styled interaction techniques can produce high quality decisions by synthesizing a team's many different and sometimes conflicting viewpoints. The underlying principle of dialectical interaction is that rigorous debate of opposing positions produces a synthesis that is qualitatively superior to the initial positions themselves (Churchman, 1971). A great deal of research has accumulated on techniques which encourage this sort of critical interaction process (Cosier, 1978; Schweiger et al., 1986; Schwenk & Cosier, 1980; Schwenk, 1990). This research indicates that teams that utilize some type of structured debate process, like dialectical inquiry (DI) (Mason, 1969) or devil's advocacy (DA) (Cosier, 1978), produce higher quality decisions than teams that do not (Schweiger et al., 1989; Schwenk, 1989).

Of course, high quality decisions are of little value without effective implementation and Child states that implementation 'depends on securing the cooperation of other parties to the decision . . .' (1972, p. 10). So some have argued that, in addition to high quality decisions, the decision making process must also produce consensus among a team's members (Bourgeois, 1980; Dess, 1987; Guth & MacMillan, 1986; Wooldridge & Floyd, 1989).

Consensus, however, is more than simple agreement. As Child (1972) suggests, effective implementation is likely to require active cooperation among the members of the decision making team. This is important because strategic decisions are so complex and ambiguous that they are difficult to articulate in complete detail (Mason & Mitroff, 1981; Mintzberg et al., 1976).

Numerous complications can arise as the implementation process unfolds and the details of the decision are ironed out. To usher a decision through this complex web of details, team members must do more than simply agree to or comply with the decision. Team members must both understand and commit to the decision if it is to be implemented effectively (Wooldridge & Floyd, 1989, 1990).

Understanding is particularly important during this process because it provides common direction for the team members. Common understanding of a decision gives the team members the ability to act independently but in a way that is consistent with the actions of others and with the spirit of the decision itself. Commitment is also important because implementing a strategic decision takes time and may involve overcoming some resistance or opposition (Allison, 1971; Mason & Mitroff, 1981; Mintzberg et al., 1976). Commitment among the team members reduces the likelihood that a decision will become the target of cynicism or counter-effort (Guth & MacMillan, 1986). Each decision process must build consensus among the team members because without understanding and commitment, successful implementation of the decision is unlikely.

Finally, it is important to remember that, over time, teams will make many decisions. As Hurst, Rush and White state 'the long term maintenance/existence of the business requires the ongoing (re)creation of the business and the logic by which it is managed' (1989, p. 88). To be truly effective, teams must consistently produce high quality decisions while also consistently reaching consensus on those decisions. Thus, it is important that team members maintain affective relationships that allow them to continue working together. Team members with strong negative sentiments towards one another or towards the team in general are less likely to participate fully and sincerely in the decision making process. Researchers have suggested that the effects of such negativity can linger and threaten future team interactions (Amason, Thompson, Hochwarter & Harrison, 1995). Thus, forces that undermine affective acceptance among team members will, in the long run, hinder strategic decision making effectiveness.

Conflict and decision making

Although decision quality, consensus and affective acceptance are all necessary for enhanced organizational performance, they are not completely complementary. For instance, the antecedents of high quality decisions, cognitive diversity and structured debate, appear to make the realization of consensus and the maintenance of team member affective acceptance more difficult. Likewise, the pursuit of consensus or affective acceptance appears to reduce decision quality. A paradox results whereby decision quality, consensus and affective acceptance are, together, necessary for enhanced organizational performance. Yet, individually, decision quality, consensus and affective acceptance appear to be incompatible.

For example, consider a cognitively diverse team whose interaction processes are designed to elicit confrontation and debate. Bringing the differences of this group into contradistinction over an issue of great importance will be likely to produce acrimony. Acrimony, however, may attenuate consensus (Guth & MacMillan, 1986; Priem, 1990). Indeed, researchers have found that techniques which can improve a decision's quality can also reduce team member commitment to that decision (Schweiger et al., 1986; Schwenk, 1990). As a consequence, while the team may produce a high quality decision, that decision will be difficult to implement because the team lacks consensus.

However, eliminating the acrimony by eliminating its antecedents may reduce decision quality. For instance, reducing diversity may reduce the potential for acrimony. Research has shown that teams that lack diversity experience less contentiousness than do more diverse teams. However, the absence of diversity means fewer capabilities and thus less potential for high quality decisions (Bantel & Jackson, 1989; Priem, 1990). Similarly, interaction processes designed to minimize confrontation may increase consensus and affective acceptance. However, such techniques may lower decision quality by encouraging teams to pursue only those alternatives that can be readily agreed upon (Janis, 1982; Tjosvold & Field, 1983). For example, the nominal group technique produces high levels of team member satisfaction by restricting direct criticism. However, those restrictions seem to reduce decision quality. As Frankel states, the nominal group technique does 'not provide a mechanism for developing synergistic solutions' (1987, p. 547). Similarly, Hegedus and Rasmussen conclude that the technique produces a 'tendency to resolve differences by averaging rankings without logically resolving the divergent rationales . . .' (1986, p. 547).

Clearly, combining diversity with rigorous examination can produce conflict. The evidence, however, indicates that such conflict can increase the quality of a team's decisions (Cosier & Schwenk, 1990). However, by also undermining consensus and affective acceptance, that conflict may negate the effects of those high quality decisions. Thus, conflict can enhance decision quality and, at the same time, threaten consensus and affective acceptance. However, pursuing consensus and affective acceptance by restraining conflict can threaten decision quality. Thus, the dilemma, posed by Schweiger and colleagues, 'on the one hand, conflict improves decision quality; on the other, it may weaken the ability of the group to work together . . .' (1986, p. 67).

Understanding conflict: the crux of the conundrum

This conundrum arises from an incomplete understanding of conflict. Often, when conflict appears in strategic decision making research, it is portrayed as a monolithic construct that varies only in degree (Eisenhardt & Zbaracki, 1992). Thus, much of the research has focused on questions related to 'how much' conflict a team has or should have and what effect that conflict has when present. However, the evidence suggests that conflict is multi-dimensional

(Amason, 1996; Jehn, 1995; Rahim, 1983). That being the case, it is possible that conflict may produce obstacles to consensus on some occasions but produce no such obstacles on other occasions. Conflict may improve decision quality in some instances, yet fail to do so in others. Indeed, without first knowing how different types of conflict influence strategic decision making, it is impossible to know when conflict will be functional and when it will be dysfunctional.

Applying a multi-dimensional conceptualization of conflict, recent research has begun to address this issue of functionality (Amason, 1996; Jehn, 1994, 1995). The findings of this research support the idea that the effect conflict has on decision making depends largely upon the type of conflict that is experienced. In other words, conflict can be both functional and dysfunctional depending upon its form. One form, cognitive conflict, is functional and in many cases enhances decision quality, consensus and affective acceptance. The other form, affective conflict, is dysfunctional and, in many cases, reduces decision quality, consensus and affective acceptance. Thus, questions about how much conflict teams should create are less important than questions about what types of conflict teams should create. Before continuing, however, we will clearly define and more thoroughly discuss these two forms of conflict.

Cognitive conflict

Cognitive conflict is task orientated and arises from differences in judgment (Amason & Schweiger, 1994; Brehmer, 1976; Jehn, 1994). Cognitive disagreements are inevitable during strategic decision making because, as Mitroff (1982) states, 'different positions see different environments' (p. 375). As such, team members will often disagree over how to best accomplish their common objectives (Astley, Axelsson, Butler, Hickson & Wilson, 1982). As discussed earlier, however, these diverse perspectives are needed to produce higher quality decisions (Bantel & Jackson, 1989; Hoffman & Maier, 1961; Murray, 1989). Cognitive conflict, then, is an important part of the process through which managers identify, extract and combine their diverse skills, abilities and perspectives to produce high quality decisions (Schweiger & Sandberg, 1989; Turner & Pratkanis, 1994).

The evidence supports this contention. Amason (1996) studied the effects of conflict on the decision making processes of fifty-three teams. In each team, Amason (1996) measured the quality of a recent strategic decision and the cognitive conflict that the team experienced while making that decision. As expected, there was a strong relationship between the cognitive conflict a team experienced and the subsequent quality of the team's decision. Jehn (1995) also found evidence of this relationship. Jehn (1995) examined 105 work groups and management teams in a large organization and found that cognitive (task) conflict contributed to group productivity in instances where the groups were performing complex, nonroutine tasks. Thus, both researchers concluded that cognitive conflict can improve the quality of complex and ambiguous decisions.

There is also evidence that cognitive conflict can enhance consensus by contributing to team member understanding. By engaging in cognitive debate, managers gain a more thorough understanding of the rationale underlying their decisions (Cosier, 1978). In a laboratory study of the effects of different decision making techniques, Schweiger and colleagues (1986) found that conflict encouraged a more exhaustive evaluation of the assumptions underlying different decision alternatives. As such, team members had a better overall understanding of the rationale for their final decision. Amason (1996) extended this finding. Using a distance measure developed by Dess (1987) and Wooldridge and Floyd (1990), Amason found that cognitive conflict contributed to the similarity with which team members understood the basic rationale of their decision. Again, these findings support the idea that cognitive conflict improves understanding by exposing decision makers to a range of diverse and potentially conflicting alternatives and assumptions.

There is also reason to expect that cognitive conflict will enhance satisfaction and affective acceptance. The presence of open expression and the tolerance of diverse viewpoints may have symbolic significance for team members, suggesting to them that the decision making process is fair and accommodating. By entering into the debate, individual managers gain an opportunity to shape the final decision in a way that is accommodating to their own interests. As the individual managers exercise greater personal 'voice' in the decision making process, they may become more accepting of the process and of the team in general (Folger, 1977; Greenberg & Folger, 1983; Korsgaard, Schweiger & Sapienza, 1995). Indeed, Korsgaard et al. (1995) found that such perceptions contribute to individual feelings of satisfaction with and attachment to the team. Again, consistent with and supporting this finding, Amason (1996) found that high levels of cognitive conflict contributed to the affective acceptance team members felt for their teams and for the decision making process itself.

Taken together these findings suggest that cognitive conflict can be and, in fact, often is functional. Cognitive conflict can improve decision quality, the understanding team members have of their decisions, and the affective acceptance team members feel for the team and for the decision making process in general.

Affective conflict

Unlike cognitive conflict, affective conflict involves personalized disagreement or individual disaffection (Amason & Schweiger, 1994; Brehmer, 1976; Jehn, 1994). As mentioned earlier, differing perspectives among the members of a decision making team make cognitive disagreements almost inevitable. Affective conflict emerges when this cognitive disagreement is misinterpreted as personal criticism. Brehmer (1976) explained that cognitive disagreements can often arouse affective conflict because decision makers can never fully justify their preferences. As a consequence, distrust and suspicion may develop between decision makers who hold different opinions. As distrust and

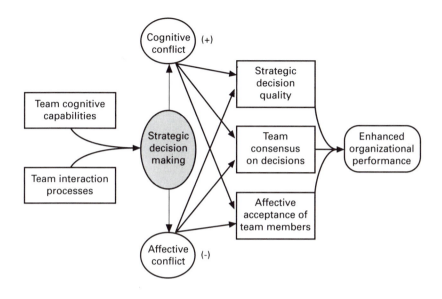

Figure 7.1   *The effects of cognitive and affective conflict on strategic decision making and organizational performance*

suspicion creep into the process, cognitive differences can produce 'full-scale emotional conflict' (1976, p. 986). This explanation is consistent with the findings of Baron, who reports that, 'often, what starts as a rational exchange of opposing views deteriorates into an emotion-laden interchange . . . in which strong negative feelings are aroused' (1984, p. 272).

The propensity to mistake cognitive disagreement for personal animosity is especially high in instances where the issues are serious and there is the potential for great personal gain or loss. Often, rather than being seen as a cognitive exercise, disagreement or criticism will be interpreted as a sinisterly motivated effort to expand the influence of some at the expense of others. Such (mis)interpretation can trigger affective conflict. The offended team members respond to what they perceive to be personally motivated criticism with personal attacks of their own and, by so doing, trigger more affective conflict. This downward spiral produces animosity and an unwillingness to tolerate opposition or to continue working together.

Support for this was found by both Jehn (1995) and Amason (1996). Jehn (1995), for instance, found a strong relationship between the levels of relationship (affective) conflict and members' satisfaction with and intent to remain with their groups. Jehn explained that 'the negative reactions associated with relationship (affective) conflict arouse uncomfortable feelings and dejection among members, which inhibits their ability to enjoy each other and their work in the group' (1995, p. 258). Amason (1996) also found strong negative relationships between the affective conflict a team experiences and the quality of the team's decisions and the affective acceptance among the team's members.

So, the evidence suggests that, while cognitive conflict is functional with respect to strategic decision making, affective conflict is dysfunctional. As Figure 7.1 illustrates, cognitive conflict improves decision quality, consensus and team member affective acceptance. Affective conflict, on the other hand, reduces decision quality and undermines the affective relationships among team members.

Managing cognitive and affective conflict

While the consistent, yet contradictory, effects of cognitive and affective conflict are easily explained, advice on how to manage those effects is easier to give than to take. Indeed, both Jehn (1994) and Amason (1996) found cognitive and affective conflict to be positively correlated, suggesting that as teams experience increased levels of one they also tend to experience increased levels of the other. This seems to support Tjosvold's (1985) admonition that the conditions which produce cognitive conflict may also produce affective conflict. Of course, the danger of this is that encouraging disagreement may yield results that are no better and may well be worse than avoiding conflict altogether. To produce superior results, teams must work diligently to encourage cognitive conflict. At the same time, however, teams must work just as diligently to avoid affective conflict.

The problem is that our ability to stimulate conflict outstrips our knowledge of how to manage its effects. For instance, much of the literature on conflict inducing interaction techniques, such as DI (Mason, 1969) and DA (Cosier, 1978), suggests that, while the techniques do produce conflict, some of that conflict is affective. Note, for example, the reduced affective acceptance and satisfaction among team members observed by Cosier and Rose (1977), Schweiger and colleagues (1986, 1989), and Schwenk (1990). Likewise, researchers have noted that heterogeneity among team members often produces double-edged effects (Cho, Hambrick & Chen, 1994; Nemeth & Staw, 1989). The contrasting ideas and perspectives that accompany heterogeneity can produce conflict (Wagner, Pfeffer & O'Reilly, 1984). While that conflict may allow heterogeneous teams to make better decisions (Bantel & Jackson, 1989), those teams also experience cohesional and communicational difficulties because of their diverse attitudes and understanding (Cho et al., 1994; Smith, Smith, Olian, Sims, O'Bannon & Scully, 1994).

Indeed, many researchers and conflict theorists have concluded that cognitive and affective conflict often occur together because decision makers are unable to distinguish one from the other (Brehmer, 1976; Faulk, 1982; Torrance, 1957). Thus, by establishing the conditions for cognitive conflict, teams may unwittingly trigger affective conflict. This raises two interesting and important questions. Can cognitive conflict flourish in the absence of affective conflict? And, if so, how can teams learn to disagree and disagree strongly on matters of substance without allowing that disagreement to provoke affective conflict?

In answer to the first question, certainly there is evidence that some teams manage conflict better than others. Eisenhardt (1989), for example, describes how the most successful teams in her sample were able to engage in a vigorous 'aeration' of diverse ideas and opinions without allowing those differences to arouse personal animosity or political gamesmanship. These teams were able to use disagreement to produce quick, yet well thought-out, decisions. However, their disagreements stopped short of producing affective conflict. Tjosvold, Dann and Wong (1992) found that effective teams were those that could discuss their different and conflicting views in an open and frank manner without losing their collective orientation or cooperative focus. Additionally, Amason et al. (1995) reported that successful and creative strategic decisions resulted when the teams in their sample openly discussed different and conflicting ideas but kept those discussions task focused and did not allow them to become personal and affective in nature.

If teams can engage in cognitive conflict without also arousing affective conflict, the question for theorists and practitioners alike becomes, how can teams encourage the one while avoiding the other (Eisenhardt & Zbaracki, 1992)? This question is just beginning to receive the sort of research attention needed to provide a clear answer. However, existing research has provided some interesting and potentially valuable insights.

For instance, Tjosvold and colleagues (Tjosvold & Deemer, 1980; Tjosvold & Field, 1983), and Deutsch (1949, 1968, 1969), studied the effects of the reward context on conflict. Their findings suggest that a cooperative reward context can reduce conflict and that a competitive reward context can arouse conflict. A competitive reward context increases the likelihood that dissention and criticism will be seen as self-serving and distrustful. This increases the likelihood that team members will respond to any and all disagreement with affective conflict. A cooperative context, on the other hand, provides assurance that the interests of a team's members are mutually linked. This increases the likelihood that team members will view criticism or dissent as a cognitive exercise that serves the collective purposes of the entire group.

Likewise, the procedural justice literature (Folger, 1977; Greenberg & Folger, 1983) may have implications for the selective management of cognitive and affective conflict. In addition to providing protection against premature closure and groupthink (Janis, 1982), the willingness to tolerate and even encourage frank and open discussion may provide symbolic reassurance that the decision making process is forthright and fair (Korsgaard et al., 1995). Thus, over time, openness may desensitize team members to the discomfort of disagreement, diminishing the chances for negative reactions. Team members may come to see criticism and dissent as natural parts of the decision making process and not as individual attacks that threaten them personally. Indeed, earlier research has shown an experiential effect whereby teams that are experienced with conflict are less likely to have negative responses to it (Cosier & Rose, 1977; Schweiger et al., 1989).

In a recent study, Amason and Sapienza (in press) found evidence of an interaction effect between the degree to which team members are mutually accountable and responsible for their decisions and the openness of team interactions. More specifically, while openness has been shown to be an effective means of stimulating cognitive conflict, by itself it does little to restrain affective conflict (Jehn, 1995). On the other hand, while mutuality appears to repress affective conflict, by itself it does little to encourage and may actually repress cognitive conflict (Janis, 1982). Amason and Sapienza (in press) found that, when combined, mutuality and openness can interact and produce an atmosphere where cognitive conflict can flourish while affective conflict remains relatively inert. In their sample, those teams with high levels of both openness and mutuality showed the largest gap between the levels of cognitive and affective conflict experienced during the consideration of a recent decision.

This is a potentially significant finding that may shed new light on the difficulties of managing conflict. A great deal of attention has been given to structural issues such as team heterogeneity, team size and team tenure and their effects on decision making effectiveness. One observation that has been consistently drawn from this body of research is that these structural characteristics often produce double-edged effects. For instance, larger teams tend to experience both more cognitive and more affective conflict (Amason & Sapienza, in press). Thus, it is questionable just how efficacious coarse-grained changes in a team's structural context can be to the effective management of cognitive and affective conflict. As Amason and Sapienza's (in press) findings suggest, effectively managing conflict may also require the active cultivation of a social context to govern the team's interactions. This social context could establish and reinforce a set of norms that would encourage cognitive conflict but discourage affective conflict. So, as Figure 7.2 illustrates, the combination of structural and social forces, together, determine both the amount and the type of conflict a team experiences. Focusing on one but ignoring the other may limit understanding; acting on one but ignoring the other may invite trouble.

In essence, what we are suggesting by this is that it is probably unrealistic to expect managers to recognize and distinguish cognitive from affective conflict while they are embroiled in the details of a decision. Thus, the management of conflict during decision making must be exercised before decision making actually begins, through the establishment of a context that encourages open, frank and even critical disagreement but that holds in check the natural tendency for that disagreement to arouse personal animosity. As Tjosvold states, to be effective, teams must 'argue, debate, and disagree, but must also create facilitative interpersonal conditions: namely, cooperative goal interdependence . . .' (1985, p. 32). The critical responsibility for creating such conditions must fall disproportionately on the formal leader of the team (e.g. the CEO). Simply put, it is the leader who will explicitly or implicitly set the tone as to what types of behaviour (e.g. conflict) will and will not be tolerated.

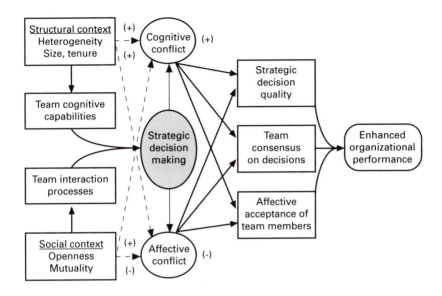

Figure 7.2   *The antecedents of conflict in strategic decision making*

Conclusion

Our own research, along with that of others, has provided considerable evidence that two types of conflict, cognitive and affective, influence the outcomes of strategic decision making. This emerging body of research explains that, while these two types of conflict often occur together, they have dramatically different effects on decision quality, team consensus and team member affective acceptance. From this review, we concluded that the effective management of conflict is not so much an issue of magnitude as it is an issue of variety. In other words, how much conflict a team experiences is of secondary importance to the type of conflict it experiences. Given a choice between cognitive conflict and no conflict at all, teams should choose the former. Given a choice between affective conflict and no conflict at all, teams should choose the latter. Unfortunately, the value of these simple instructions is diminished by the relationship that seems to exist between the antecedents of cognitive conflict and the antecedents of affective conflict. While teams may know that they should encourage some conflict and that they should discourage other conflict, they often have trouble acting on that knowledge.

As a consequence, some theorists have suggested and indeed some practitioners may well have concluded that decision quality, consensus and affective acceptance will never peacefully coexist. The argument that then follows from this conclusion is that, since the benefits of conflict will not be gained without costs, those benefits should be pursued only in limited situations. In other situations, where the benefits of conflict are not needed, it is not necessary to arouse conflict and risk bearing its costs. Thus, in some instances teams should limit the antecedents of conflict in the hope of gaining greater consensus and satisfaction. In other instances, teams will need the antecedents of conflict to produce high quality decisions and thus must be willing to suffer the consequences of the conflict that will arise.

Our contention is that teams need not trade away the benefits of conflict only to avoid its potential costs. Indeed, the benefits of conflict are important for all strategic decisions. What team would not benefit from increasing its cognitive potential? Likewise, what team would not benefit from rigorous debate of the competing alternatives and hidden assumptions of its decisions? Not only is it unnecessary to trade away the antecedents of conflict, it is also unproductive. A considerable amount of anecdotal testimony and a growing body of empirical evidence suggests that teams can manage their differences so as to simultaneously encourage cognitive conflict and discourage affective conflict. Thus, we believe that teams can gain the benefits of conflict without also incurring its costs.

Accomplishing this, it seems, involves cultivating a team environment that is open to and tolerant of diverse and dissenting viewpoints, whereby the natural differences among team members can be expressed and examined without reservation. This may be done through the adoption of any number of conflict inducing interaction techniques or simply through the active encouragement of the team's leader. In addition to openness, however, a cooperative norm must be established and reinforced to prevent those disagreements that will occur only too naturally during open and frank discussion from being misinterpreted as personal attacks or political manoeuvring. Developing this sort of mutuality will also likely necessitate active participation on the part of the team's leader and may well require changes in the team's reward system.

Our reading of the literature along with the findings of our own research leads us to suspect that, in an atmosphere of openness and mutuality, the various antecedents of conflict such as team heterogeneity and dialectical interaction will cease to cut both ways. However, this relationship bears direct testing. There is little doubt that cognitive conflict can be very beneficial to strategic decision making. Likewise, there is little doubt that affective conflict can be just as detrimental to decision making. This is good news indeed because there are strong indications that teams can in fact embrace cognitive conflict while also holding affective conflict in abeyance. The question currently left unanswered is how this can be done. It is that question that future research should concentrate on answering.

References

Allison, G.T. (1971). *The essence of decision: Explaining the Cuban missile crisis.* Boston, MA: Little, Brown.

Amason, A.C. (1996). Distinguishing the effects of functional and dysfunctional conflict on strategic decision making: Resolving a paradox for top management teams. *Academy of Management Journal, 39*, 1.

Amason, A.C. and Sapienza, H.J. (in press). The effects of top management team size and inter-action norms on cognitive and affective conflict. *Journal of Management.*

Amason, A.C. and Schweiger, D.M. (1994). Resolving the paradox of conflict, strategic decision making and organizational performance. *International Journal of Conflict Management, 5*, 239–53.

Amason, A.C., Thompson, K.R., Hochwarter, W.A. and Harrison, A.W. (1995). Conflict: an important dimension in successful management teams. *Organizational Dynamics, 23*, 20–35.

Astley, G.W., Axelsson, R., Butler, J., Hickson, D.J. and Wilson, D.C. (1982). Complexity and cleavage: Dual explanations of strategic decision making. *Journal of Management Studies, 19*, 357–75.

Bantel, K.A. and Jackson, S.E. (1989). Top management and innovations in banking: Does the composition of the top team make a difference? *Strategic Management Journal, 10*, 107–12.

Baron, R.A. (1984). Reducing organizational conflict: an incompatible response approach. *Journal of Applied Psychology, 69*, 272–9.

Bourgeois, L.J. (1980). Performance and consensus. *Strategic Management Journal, 1*, 227–48.

Brehmer, B. (1976). Social judgement theory and the analysis of interpersonal conflict. *Psychological Bulletin, 83*, 985–1003.

Carter, E. (1971). The behavioral theory of the firm and top-level corporate decisions. *Administrative Science Quarterly, 16*, 413–28.

Child, J. (1972). Organizational structure, environment, and performance: the role of strategic choice. *Sociology, 6*, 1–22.

Cho, T.S., Hambrick, D.C. and Chen, M. (1994). *Effects of top management team characteristics on competitive behaviors of firms.* Best Paper Proceedings of the Academy of Management.

Churchman, C.W. (1971). *The design of inquiring systems: Basic concepts of systems and organizations.* New York: Basic Books.

Cosier, R.A. (1978). The effects of three potential aids for making strategic decisions on prediction accuracy. *Organizational Behavior and Human Performance, 22*, 295–306.

Cosier, R.A. and Rose, R.L. (1977). Cognitive conflict and goal conflict effects on task performance. *Organizational Behavior and Human Performance, 19*, 378–91.

Cosier, R.A. and Schwenk, C.R. (1990). Agreement and thinking alike: Ingredients for poor decisions. *The Academy of Management Executive, 4*, 69–74.

Dess, G.G. (1987). Consensus on strategy formulation and organizational performance: Competitors in a fragmented industry. *Strategic Management Journal, 8*, 259–77.

Deutsch, M. (1949). An experimental study of the effects of cooperation and competition upon group process. *Human Relations, 2*, 199–232.

Deutsch, M. (1968). The effects of cooperation and competition upon group processes, in D. Cartwright and A. Zander (eds), *Group dynamics*. New York: Harper & Row, pp. 461–82.

Deutsch, M. (1969). Conflicts: Productive and destructive. *Journal of Social Issues, 25*, 7–41.

Eisenhardt, K.M. (1989). Making fast strategic decisions in high-velocity environments. *Academy of Management Journal, 32*, 543–76.

Eisenhardt, K.M. and Zbaracki, M.J. (1992). Strategic decision making. *Strategic Management Journal, 13*, 17–37.

Faulk, G. (1982). An empirical study measuring conflict in problem solving groups which are assigned different decision rules. *Human Relations, 35*, 1123–38.

Folger, R. (1977). Distributive and procedural justice: Combined impact of 'voice' and improvement of experienced inequity. *Journal of Personality and Social Psychology, 35*, 108–19.

Frankel, S. (1987). Methodological observations on applied behavioral science. *Journal of Applied Behavioral Science, 23*, 543–51.

Greenberg, J. and Folger, R. (1983). Procedural justice, participation, and the fair process effect in groups and organizations, in P.B. Paulus (ed.), *Basic group processes*. New York: Springer-Verlag, pp. 235–56.

Guth, W.D. and MacMillan, I.C. (1986). Strategy implementation versus middle management self-interest. *Strategic Management Journal, 7*, 313–27.

Hegedus, D.M. and Rasmussen, R.V. (1986). Task effectiveness and interaction process of a modified nominal group technique in solving an evaluation problem. *Journal of Management, 12*, 545–60.

Hickson, D.J., Butler, R.J., Cray, D., Mallory, G.R. and Wilson, D.C. (1986). *Top decisions: Strategic decision-making in organizations.* San Francisco, CA: Jossey-Bass.

Hoffman, L.R. and Maier, N.R.F. (1961). Quality and acceptance of problem solutions by members of homogeneous and heterogeneous groups. *Journal of Abnormal and Social Psychology, 62*, 401–7.

Hurst, D.K., Rush, J.C. and White, R.E. (1989). Top management teams and organizational renewal. *Strategic Management Journal, 10*, 87–105.

Janis, I.L. (1982). *Groupthink: Psychological studies of foreign policy decisions and fiascoes* (2nd edn). Boston, MA: Houghton Mifflin.

Jehn, K. (1994). Enhancing effectiveness: an investigation of advantages and disadvantages of value-based intragroup conflict. *International Journal of Conflict Management, 5*, 223–38.

Jehn, K. (1995). A multimethod examination of the benefits and detriments of intragroup conflict. *Administrative Science Quarterly, 40*, 256–82.

Korsgaard, M.A., Schweiger, D.M. and Sapienza, H.J. (1995). Building commitment, attachment, and trust in top management teams: The role of procedural justice. *Academy of Management Journal, 38*, 60–84.

Mason, R.O. (1969). A dialectical approach to strategic planning. *Management Science, 15*, 403–14.

Mason, R.O. and Mitroff, I.I. (1981). *Challenging strategic planning assumptions.* New York: John Wiley & Sons.

Mintzberg, H., Raisinghani, D. and Theoret, A. (1976). The structure of unstructured decision processes. *Administrative Science Quarterly, 21*, 246–75.

Mitroff, I.I. (1982). Talking past one's colleagues in matters of policy. *Strategic Management Journal, 3*, 374–5.

Murray, A.I. (1989). Top management group heterogeneity and firm performance. *Strategic Management Journal, 10*, 125–41.

Nemeth, C.J. and Staw, B.M. (1989). The tradeoffs of social control in groups and organizations. *Advances in Experimental Social Psychology, 22*, 175–210.

Priem, R.L. (1990). Top management team group factors, consensus, and firm performance. *Strategic Management Journal, 11*, 469–78.

Rahim, M.A. (1983). Measurement of organizational conflict. *Journal of General Psychology, 109*, 189–99.

Schweiger, D.M. and Sandberg, W.R. (1989). The utilization of individual capabilities in group approaches to strategic decision-making. *Strategic Management Journal, 10*, 31–43.

Schweiger, D.M. and Sandberg, W.R. (1991). A team approach to top management's strategic decisions, in H.E. Glass (ed.), *Handbook of business strategy.* New York: Warren, Gorham, & Lamont, pp. 6-1–6-20.

Schweiger, D.M., Sandberg, W.R. and Ragan, J.W. (1986). Group approaches for improving strategic decision making: a comparative analysis of dialectical inquiry, devil's advocacy and consensus. *Academy of Management Journal, 29*, 51–71.

Schweiger, D.M., Sandberg, W.R. and Rechner, P.L. (1989). Experiential effects of dialectical inquiry, devil's advocacy, and consensus approaches to strategic decision making. *Academy of Management Journal, 32*, 745–72.

Schwenk, C.R. (1989). A meta-analysis on the cooperative effectiveness of devil's advocacy and dialectical inquiry. *Strategic Management Journal, 10*, 303–6.

Schwenk, C.R. (1990). Conflict in organizational decision making: an exploratory study of its effects in for-profit and not-for-profit organizations. *Management Science, 36*, 436–48.

Schwenk, C.R. and Cosier, R.A. (1980). Effects of the expert, devil's advocate, and dialectical inquiry methods on prediction performance. *Organizational Behavior and Human Performance, 26*, 409–24.

Smith, K.G., Smith, K.A., Olian, J.D., Sims, H.P., O'Bannon, D.P. and Scully, J.A. (1994). Top management team demography and process: the role of social integration and communication. *Administrative Science Quarterly, 39*, 412–38.

Tjosvold, D. (1985). Implications of controversy research for management. *Journal of Management, 11*, 21–37.

Tjosvold, D., Dann, V. and Wong, C. (1992). Managing conflict between departments to serve customers. *Human Relations, 45*, 1035–54.

Tjosvold, D. and Deemer, D.K. (1980). Effects of controversy within a cooperative or competitive context on organizational decision making. *Journal of Applied Psychology, 65*, 590–5.

Tjosvold, D. and Field, R.H.G. (1983). Effects of social context on consensus and majority vote decision making. *Academy of Management Journal, 26*, 500–6.

Torrance, E.P. (1957). Group decision making and disagreement. *Social Forces, 35*, 314–18.

Turner, M.E. and Pratkanis, A.R. (1994). Social identity maintenance prescriptions for preventing groupthink: Reducing identity protection and enhancing intellectual conflict. *International Journal of Conflict Management, 5*, 254–70.

Wagner, W.G., Pfeffer, J. and O'Reilly, C.A. (1984). Organizational demography and turnover in top management groups. *Administrative Science Quarterly, 29*, 74–92.

Wooldridge, B. and Floyd, S.W. (1989). Strategic process effects on consensus. *Strategic Management Journal, 10*, 295–302.

Wooldridge, B. and Floyd, S.W. (1990). The strategy process, middle management involvement, and organizational performance. *Strategic Management Journal, 11*, 231–41.

PART III

BETWEEN-GROUP CONFLICT AND COMPETITION

8

The Enhancing Effect of Intergroup Competition on Group Performance

Gary Bornstein and Ido Erev

Rewarding all group members equally, regardless of their contributions to the group's effort, eliminates the need to assess individual inputs, which is often quite costly or even impossible. The equal payoff rule may also, under certain conditions, promote group harmony and cohesion (Leventhal, 1976; Yamagishi, 1988). Yet this reward scheme has a serious drawback. When they are rewarded collectively, and their personal contributions are not assessed, individual group members do not work as hard as they could. Instead, they use the opportunity to take a free ride on the contributions of others by reducing their own contributions to the group's effort. As a result, the group typically fails to realize its potential level of performance and the rewards associated with it (Dashiell, 1935; Kerr, 1983, 1986; Kerr & Bruun, 1983; Latane, Williams & Harkins, 1979; Steiner, 1972; Yamagishi, 1988). In formal terms, the equal payoff rule creates a social dilemma (Dawes, 1980) where the dominant individual strategy (to take a free ride) is associated with a suboptimal collective outcome (the group fails).

Much research has been motivated by the desire to find a solution to the free rider problem (Kerr, 1986; Messick & Brewer, 1983). The present chapter examines one such solution, which has received little theoretical and empirical attention. This solution involves competition between groups and is most applicable to organizational settings where small groups of approximately the same size perform comparable tasks. An aircraft carrier, a motor-car factory, an elementary school, or a hi-tech research and development firm are familiar examples of such multi-group work environments.

Intergroup competition in the laboratory

To study the effect of intergroup competition on group cooperation and productivity, Bornstein, Erev & Rosen (1990) conducted a laboratory experiment in which they compared behaviour under two conditions: a single-group condition in which subjects in groups of three participated in a social dilemma game (Bonacich, 1972; Dawes, 1980), and an intergroup competition condition in which two groups, each engaged in a separate social dilemma, competed for an additional reward. The reward was provided to the more cooperative (and, consequently, more productive) of the two groups and was divided equally among all of its members regardless of their contribution to the group's success.

The payoff matrix for the individual player in the two conditions appears in Table 8.1. Each subject had to decide privately between: (NC) taking IS 3 (3 Israeli shekels, approximately \$2 at the time the experiment took place) for himself or herself, and (C) giving IS 3 (of the experimenter's money) to each of the other two members of his or her group. The table shows that player i is always better off taking the money (making the noncooperative choice) regardless of what the other group members do. However, if none of the players cooperates, each ends up with IS 3, whereas if all players cooperate, each receives IS 6. The intragroup game is thus a social dilemma where the choice of a dominant strategy results in a deficient equilibrium (an equilibrium is an outcome that allows none of the players to benefit from a unilateral change of strategy if all the remaining players adhere to the equilibrium strategy).

In the intergroup competition condition there were two three-person groups, each engaged in a separate social dilemma game as described above. In addition, a reward of IS 9 was paid to each member of the group with

Table 8.1 *Individual payoff matrix for the single-group and intergroup conditions*

		Single-group dilemma		
		Number of cooperators not including player i		
		0	1	2
player i's choice	C	0	3	6
	NC	3	6	9

		Intergroup competition		
		$m_{A\backslash i} < m_B - 1$	$m_{A\backslash i} = m_B - 1$	$m_{A\backslash i} = m_B$	$m_{A\backslash i} > m_B$
player i's choice	C	x+0	x+4.5	x+9	x+9
	NC	x+3	x+3	x+7.5	x+12

Note: C denotes contribution, NC denotes no contribution; $m_{A\backslash i}$ denotes the number of cooperators in group A excluding player i; m_B denotes the number of cooperators group B; x denotes the payoff for player i in the intragroup dilemma game ($x = 3m_{A\backslash i}$).

more contributors, regardless of his or her own decision. In case of an equal number of contributors in both groups, the reward was divided among the six players and each received IS 4.5. As opposed to the case of the single-group dilemma, player i has no dominant strategy in the intergroup competition game. Rather, as a rational player, player i should give when this is critical for tying or winning the game (shown in columns 2 and 3 in the matrix, respectively), but not otherwise. Moreover, when the competing groups are of equal size, as in the present case, the unique equilibrium solution of the game is for all players to choose the cooperative option (C). That is, when all the other players cooperate, no individual player can benefit from a unilateral defection.

Thus, by rewarding the better performing group, the intragroup payoff structure is transformed from a social dilemma where defection is the dominant individual strategy into a step-level public-goods problem where contribution is the rational individual choice. Bornstein et al. demonstrated that this structural change had a significant effect on subjects' choice behaviour. Namely, when given the opportunity to win an additional reward for out-performing the rival group, 78.3% of the subjects cooperated, as compared to only 46.7% of the subjects in the single-group dilemma ($Z = 2.84$, $p < 0.01$).

Intergroup competition in the field

Simple experimental games like those employed by Bornstein et al. place subjects in an unfamiliar strategic environment where well-rehearsed habits are not readily available and factors that affect behaviour in more natural settings, such as social norms, attitudes and social motives, have relatively little impact (Hamburger, 1979). To what extent are the results generalizable beyond the artificial laboratory setting?

The problem of external validity is regarded by Pruitt and Kimmel (1977) as 'one of the biggest problems of [the experimental games] tradition'. In their review of the first twenty years of game research, they note that 'most researchers who use games simply report their results with no attempt to speculate about the real-life implications' and argue that, as a result, 'questions have been raised about the relevance [of game research] to real-life settings and to other parts of the field of social psychology' (p. 367).

To examine the effects of intergroup competition in a realistic work environment, Erev, Bornstein and Galili (1993) conducted an experiment in an orange grove. The experiment employed a within-subject design in which groups of four subjects participated in an orange-picking task. Each group worked under three payoff conditions (the order of which was balanced across groups). In the *personal* condition, the container was divided into four personal sections and each subject was paid according to the quantity of oranges he himself picked. In the *team* condition, the container was not divided and each worker received an equal share of the group's payoff based on overall group production. Finally, in the *competition* condition, the container was divided into two equal parts, the group was randomly divided into two dyads, and each dyad was assigned one section of the container. At the end of the competition, each member of the more productive dyad earned a bonus. Members of the less productive dyad received no bonus. In the case of equally productive dyads, the bonus was divided equally between the two groups.[1]

Each experimental condition lasted forty minutes. The dependent variable was the quantity of oranges picked. This quantity was measured twice during each condition. The first measurement was taken after twenty minutes of work and the second after forty minutes. The quantity was measured by volume (proportion of container filled), which was later converted into weight in kilograms (kg). The average net weight of a full container is about 400 kg.

Based on a structural analysis of the three experimental conditions described above, Erev et al. predicted that: (1) rewarding group members on a collective basis would lead to a production loss as compared to the individually-based payoff scheme; (2) dividing the group into two teams and creating a competition between the teams by paying a bonus to the more productive team would eliminate free riding and restore production levels; and (3) the intergroup competition would be more effective the more similar the competing teams were as regards the overall ability of their respective members.

The results strongly support all three predictions. Figure 8.1 presents the average performance in each payoff condition as measured after twenty and forty minutes of work. It shows that subjects were more productive in the personal condition than in the team condition; the average group picked a total of 376 kg in the personal condition as compared to an average of 280 kg in the team condition [$F(1,11) = 46.2, p < 0.0001$]. A closer look at Figure 8.1 reveals that in the first twenty minutes the difference in productivity between the two conditions was relatively small. The average group picked 190 kg in the personal condition as compared to 160 kg in the team condition [$F(1,11) = 6.84, p < 0.015$]. The difference in productivity increased greatly in the last twenty minutes. During this period, the average group picked 186 kg in the personal condition as compared to only 120 kg in the team condition [$F(1,11) = 30.8, p < 0.0002$]. The payoff scheme by time interaction is highly significant [$F(2,10) = 30.4, p < 0.0001$], using the group as the unit of analysis.

As predicted, subjects were more productive in the competition condition than in the team condition. The average group picked a total of 380 kg in the competition condition as compared to a total of 280 kg in the team condition [$F(1,11) = 39.7, p < 0.0001$]. The difference between the competition and team conditions is especially apparent in the second twenty-minute period. During that period, the average group picked 208 kg in the competition condition, almost twice as much as the 120 kg picked in the team condition [$F(1,11) = 69.3, p < 0.0001$]. The reason for this, as can be seen in Figure 8.1, is that production increased over time in the competition condition, while decreasing over time in the team condition. These data support

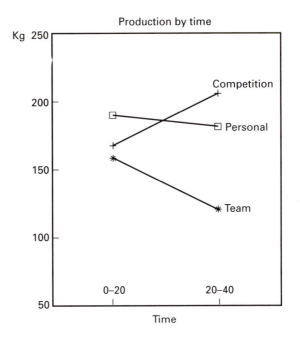

Figure 8.1   *The average performance in the three conditions as measured after twenty and forty minutes of work*

the hypothesis that, as they gained more experience with the task, subjects learned the payoff structure of the situation and their behaviour converged on the equilibria of the respective games.

What learning rule might account for these results? Consider a simple learning rule which states the following: At each decision point a player modifies his behaviour to maximize earnings while assuming that the behaviour of all the other players remains constant. This fictitious play rule hypothesizes that individuals modify their behaviour in an adaptive fashion until they reach an equilibrium point (where a unilateral change of behaviour is no longer adaptive), without relying on the game-theoretic assumption of common rationality.

Assume that player i chooses an initial working speed and, at a certain point (perhaps when he/she empties their basket), re-evaluates his/her strategy. In the team condition, he/she notices that there are already quite a few oranges in the container and realizes that if everyone else keeps up the good work he/she can slow down without suffering a big loss in payoff. If everyone follows this learning rule, the model predicts that work speed will decrease with time. The exact 'learning curve' depends on the frequency and magnitude of the adaptive adjustments.

The same learning rule has different implications in the competition condition. Suppose that when player i empties his basket he/she notices that the amount of oranges the two teams have already picked is approximately the same. If player i assumes that the other players will maintain the same work speed, he/she may decide to work a little faster in order to win the competition and acquire the reward. If the competition is still tied the next time around, he/she may try to increase his/her work speed a little more. If all players use this decision rule, the game will remain tied while the work speed will gradually increase.[2]

To examine the effect of differential abilities on productivity we calculated two difference scores for each group. One score involved the absolute difference in ability between the two dyads as reflected by the respective performance of their members in the personal condition. The other score involved the effectiveness of the intergroup competition and was calculated by subtracting the group's productivity (the number of kg picked) in the team condition from that in the competition condition. As predicted, there was a strong negative correlation between the two difference scores ($r = -0.74$, $p <$ 0.006), indicating that the intergroup competition was less effective in reducing free riding when the two dyads were more different in their abilities.[3]

The Erev et al. experiment demonstrates that the effect of intergroup competition on group performance is not restricted to simple experimental games and can be generalized to a typical work environment. In our orange-picking task, as in most real-life settings, contribution was continuous rather than binary. That is, rather than choosing between contributing and not contributing, each player could choose any level of contribution. Like most situations outside the laboratory, the orange-picking task involved long-term interaction in which the decision of whether (or how much) to contribute towards the group's effort was a recurring one. The fact that the interaction was repeated, rather than one-shot, created an opportunity for subjects to learn the structure of the game and adapt their behaviour accordingly. Finally, whereas in our laboratory experiment the players were symmetrical in the sense that all had the same ability to contribute, our field experiment created a more realistic situation where the players differed with respect to this ability.

Some practical considerations

We attributed the effect of intergroup competition on group productivity to changes in the intragroup payoff structure. Specifically, we argued that the competition between the groups changed the situation within each group from a social dilemma, where defection is the individually rational choice, into a problem of step-level public-goods provision, where self-interested individuals ought to cooperate. It could be argued that intergroup competition is not necessary for creating this structural change. Instead, the intragroup dilemma can be eliminated by simply providing an extra bonus to a (single) group if the overall production of its members exceeds a certain level. While this is indeed true, the single-group solution creates a major difficulty which the intergroup solution circumvents. The difficulty arises from the fact that the provision level in the single-group case must be determined exogenously (the group itself cannot be trusted to make this decision, since group members have an obvious interest in setting the level as low as possible) and, to effectively reduce free riding, it must be carefully calibrated, taking into account the difficulty of the task and the capability of the group. Setting the provision point too high or too low could result in loss of productivity (since in both cases the criticality of individual group members is diminished).

In contrast, the provision level in intergroup competition is determined endogenously. Being of relative (rather than absolute) nature, it adapts itself automatically to the characteristics of the task and the ability of the groups as well as to changing circumstances (such as experience and fatigue). Rather than setting and updating work quotas, intergroup competition requires only that the competing teams be compatible in terms of their members' overall abilities (Rapoport, Bornstein & Erev, 1989). This can be often achieved by randomly assigning individuals to groups.

Another important issue is the cost factor. Intergroup competition constitutes a practical solution to social dilemmas only to the extent that it is cost-effective. However, in order for the competition to eliminate free riding, the rewards associated with winning must be sufficiently high so that free riding is no longer the dominant individual choice. In our experiments we paid our subjects a bonus to ensure that their private benefits from contribution exceeded its cost. Paying such a bonus, it can be argued, renders intergroup competition too costly to be a practical solution to social dilemmas outside the laboratory. This, however, is not necessarily the case. The present study, like other game experiments, operationalized the rewards for winning the intergroup competition in monetary terms. Intergroup competitions may, however, involve other types of material (Olympic gold medals, merit badges, T-shirts) and social (group pride, positive social identity) rewards. Such rewards, while being powerful incentives for the participants, often involve little or no cost for the individual or institution organizing the competition.

A structural vs. a motivational explanation

For the sake of parsimony, we chose to concentrate on the structural effect of intergroup competition and ignore its other potential effects on individual choice behaviour. However, since both of our experiments confounded changes in the intragroup payoff structure with the presence of intergroup competition, we cannot rule out the possibility that, in addition to changing in the actual incentives, or 'given matrix', the intergroup competition transformed our subjects' motivation, or the 'effective matrix' (Kelley & Thibaut,

1978). Specifically, the competition between the groups could have enhanced intragroup cooperation by increasing group-based altruism (or 'patriotism') among our subjects (Campbell, 1965; Coser, 1956; Kramer & Brewer, 1986; Rabbie, 1982).

To distinguish between group altruism, on the one hand, and narrow self-interest, on the other, as reasons for contribution, the intragroup payoff structure must be kept constant. The only way to establish that cooperation increases due to a motivational rather than a structural effect of the inter-group conflict is to compare subjects' behaviour in the same social dilemma, with and without intergroup conflict. A recent experiment by Bornstein and Ben-Yossef (1994) implemented such a contrast. This study employed the Intergroup Prisoner's Dilemma (IPD) game (Bornstein, 1992) to simulate intergroup conflict and compared it with a single-group Prisoner's Dilemma (PD) game. The IPD game is structured in such a way that the intragroup payoff structure is a Prisoner's dilemma, regardless of what the outgroup does, and thus it can be directly compared with a single-group dilemma.

The IPD game, as operationalized in this study, involved six subjects randomly divided into two equal-sized teams. Each player received an endowment of 5 Israeli shekels and had to decide whether to keep the money or contribute it for his or her team's benefit. A bonus was paid to each member of a team depending on the difference between the number of ingroup and outgroup contributors. The payoff to player i (i being a member of group A) in the IPD game, as a function of player i's decision to contribute (C) or not contribute (NC) and the number of ingroup contributors (m_A) and outgroup contributors (m_B), is shown in Figure 8.2.

As can be seen in the figure, the defecting or noncontributing (NC) payoff function is above the contributing (C) function for every contingency in the IPD game, meaning that the dominating individual strategy in this game is to withhold contribution. However, the right-hand extreme of the contributing (C) function is above the left-hand extreme of the noncontributing (NC) function for any number of outgroup contributors, meaning that the optimal group strategy is for all group members to contribute. These two properties define the intragroup payoff structure in the IPD game (for any number of outgroup contributors) as an n-person Prisoner's Dilemma (PD) game or a social dilemma (Dawes, 1980).

Figure 8.2 shows that the four intragroup PD games (corresponding to 0, 1, 2 and 3 outgroup contributors in the IPD game) are structurally identical. Therefore, any one of these games could have been chosen to serve as a con-trol condition. Nevertheless, to prevent possible effects of the absolute level of rewards, we included two such control conditions: a high payoff condition corresponding to the PD game played by group A when there are no con-tributors in group B, and a low payoff condition corresponding to the game played by group A when all members of group B contribute (see Figure 8.2).

The IPD manipulation necessarily involves the co-presence of two distinct groups. Therefore, to exclude the possibility that the categorization of subjects into groups rather than the real conflict of interests between the groups is

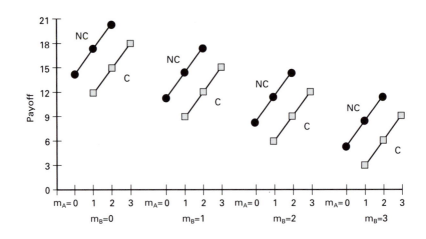

Figure 8.2 *Payoff for a member of group A in the IPD game as a function of his/her decision to contribute (C) or not to contribute (NC) and the number of ingroup contributors (m$_A$) and outgroup contributors (m$_B$)*

responsible for any potential effects, we included two groups in the PD control conditions as well. However, rather than competing against each other, each group in the control conditions was engaged in a separate (independent) PD game.

Subjects in each condition made ten consecutive decisions between contributing and not contributing. Subjects had no opportunity to communicate, and no feedback was provided between one decision and the next. Each decision was recorded on a separate page in a decision booklet and at the end of the experiment one page was chosen randomly and the payoffs were determined by the decisions made by the six members of the set (in the IPD condition) or the three members of the team (in the PD conditions) on that particular page.

The average number of investments out of the ten decisions was 5.47 in the IPD experimental condition, and 2.37 and 3.07 in the high and the low PD control conditions, respectively. The number of contributions in the IPD game was significantly higher than in the PD games [$F(1,87) = 12.95$, $p <$ 0.0005]. The difference between the two PD control conditions was not significant.

The experiment design used by Bornstein and Ben-Yossef kept constant the utilitarian value of cooperation to the acting individual as well as the external payoffs to the ingroup resulting from his/her choice. Therefore, the increase in cooperation observed in the IPD condition cannot be dismissed in terms of either individual or group rationality. In other words, the increase in cooperation cannot be attributed to structural effects of the intergroup competition. Moreover, since we included two groups in the control as well as the experimental condition, the observed increase in cooperation must be due to the real conflict of interests that exists in the IPD game rather the mere categorization of the subjects into groups.

Having established that real intergroup conflict increases intragroup cooperation, and having ruled out all plausible structural explanations for this effect, we have to provide a motivational explanation for our results. We assume that real intergroup conflict serves as a unit-forming factor that enhances group identification beyond categorization and labelling alone (Campbell, 1965; Rabbie, Schot & Visser, 1989). Enhancing group identification, in turn, increases cooperation by blurring the distinction between self-interest and group interest (Brewer & Kramer, 1986; Kramer & Brewer, 1984). This interpretation is supported by the findings that (a) subjects in the IPD condition viewed themselves as less motivated by self-interest than those in the PD control conditions (5.77 and 6.47, respectively, on a seven-point scale; $F(1,84) = 7.07$, $p < 0.001$) and more motivated by the collective group interest than those in the PD conditions (4.55 and 2.59, respectively; $F(1,84) = 19.00$; $p < 0.0001$), and (b) subjects' contribution behaviour was negatively correlated with the motivation to maximize their own payoffs [$r(90) = -0.35$, $p < 0.001$] and positively correlated with the motivation to maximize the collective payoffs of their group [$r(89) = 0.43$, $p < 0.001$].

Enhanced group identification may also increase subjects' motivation to differentiate themselves in a positive way from the outgroup (Tajfel, 1982). This somewhat different interpretation of positive group identity also receives support from the data, which indicate that (a) subjects in the IPD condition were more motivated to maximize the difference between the two groups than those in the PD conditions (3.47 and 1.48, respectively; $F(1,84) = 37.36$, $p < 0.0001$), and (b) the decision to cooperate was positively correlated with this competitive intergroup orientation [$r(90) = 0.34$, $p < 0.001$]. Thus, whereas this study enables us to conclude that intergroup conflict *changes* the individual's motivation, we do not know whether this change involves an increase in the weight assigned to the ingroup's outcome, a decrease in the weight assigned to the outgroup's outcome, or both.

Constructive competition vs. distractive conflict

The Bornstein and Ben-Yossef study directs our attention to another important point. In single-group dilemmas, contribution is consistent with the collective welfare (contribution and cooperation are synonymous in this context). Indeed, much of the research on social dilemmas, having been stimulated by intragroup problems such as resource depletion, pollution and overpopulation, has been concerned with how to get people to cooperate (consume less energy, buy recyclable products, have fewer children). In intergroup conflicts, on the other hand, contribution is good for the group, but is not necessarily good for the larger collective (the one including all members of both groups). The intergroup competition in the experiments of Bornstein et al. and Erev et al. was designed so that contribution was optimal at both the group and the collective level. However, in other types of intergroup conflicts (such as those modelled by the IPD game), contribution, although optimal from the group's perspective, results in an outcome that is collectively deficient. War is the most common example of this destructive class of intergroup conflicts. Each side has an interest in investing maximum effort in order to secure for itself a larger share of the resources at stake. However, the effort invested in fighting a war (in terms of human lives, lost property and other sacrifices) is eventually wasted, and both sides would be better off if they resolved the conflict and divided the resources peacefully. Free commercial competition between firms or nations, on the other hand, is an example of constructive competition between groups. By increasing productivity within each group, such competition often contributes to the collective welfare of all those involved.

Summary

This chapter examines the effect of intergroup competition on intragroup cooperation. Three experiments are reviewed. The first experiment (Bornstein et al., 1990) establishes that intergroup competition can effectively increase intragroup cooperation in a laboratory setting where symmetric players make binary decisions in one-shot dilemma games. The second experiment (Erev et al., 1993) shows that this constructive effect of intergroup competition is generalizable to a real-life setting in which asymmetric players make continuous decisions in an ongoing interaction. The third experiment (Bornstein & Ben-Yossef, 1994) demonstrates that the increase in intragroup cooperation can be accounted for at least in part by motivational, rather than structural, effects of the intergroup competition. Theoretical and practical issues concerning the applications of these findings are discussed.

Notes

The research reported in this chapter was supported by grants from the Israel Foundations Trustees (92–94, 94–96) to Gary Bornstein and by a grant from the British Technion Society to Ido Erev. This text was previously published in the *International Journal of Conflict Management, 5*, 271–84.

1. The group's total payoff in each condition was based on a fixed sum, plus a piece-work fee per container. Thus, for each condition the four group members were paid a total of IS 8 + 24P, where P is the portion of the container filled by the group. In the *personal* condition the individual payoff consisted of (a) a flat payment of IS 2, and (b) a fee of 6P, where P is the portion of the personal section filled by the subject. For example, if a subject filled three-quarters of his section of the container (three-sixteenths of the whole container) he received a total payment of IS 2 + IS 24($\frac{3}{16}$) = IS 6.5. In the *team* condition, each worker received a payment of IS 2 bonus plus one-quarter of the group's piece-work fee. That is, if the group filled three-quarters of the container each worker received IS 2 + IS 4.5 = IS 6.5. In the *competition* condition, after the outcome of the competition was determined, the divider was removed and subjects received a piece-work fee identical to that in the team condition (that is, 24P/4). For example, if the two

members in Dyad A filled up their section of the container, whereas the members of Dyad B filled only half of their section, each member in A received IS 4 + IS 24($\frac{3}{4}$)/4 = IS 8.5, whereas each member in B received only IS 24($\frac{3}{4}$)/4 = IS 4.5.

2. Although the fictitious play rule does well in explaining the present results, it is by no means the only conceivable explanation. There exist other learning rules that predict convergence on the equilibrium point. Although our data support the notion that subjects learned the situation's payoff structure and adapted their behaviour to approximate the game's equilibrium solution, they do not enable us to spell out the exact learning rule that is responsible for this process.

3. For instance, if the members of dyad A picked 96 kg and 104 kg, respectively, whereas the members of dyad B picked 100 kg and 110 kg, the ability difference score is $|(110 + 100) - (96 + 104)| = 10$. And if a group picked 304 kg in the team condition and 396 kg in the competition condition, the effectiveness-of-competition score is 396 − 304 = 92.

References

Bornstein, G. (1992). The free rider problem in intergroup conflicts over step-level and continuous public goods. *Journal of Personality and Social Psychology*, *62*, 597–606.

Bornstein, G. and Ben-Yossef, M. (1994). Cooperation in intergroup and single-group social dilemmas. *Journal of Experimental Social Psychology*, *30*, 52–67.

Bornstein, G., Erev, I. and Rosen, O. (1990). Intergroup competition as a structural solution for social dilemmas. *Social Behavior*, *5*, 247–60.

Bonacich, P. (1972). Norms and cohesion as adaptive responses to potential conflict: an experimental study. *Sociometry*, *35*, 357–75.

Brewer, M.B. and Kramer, R.M. (1986). Choice behavior in social dilemmas: Effects of social identity, group size, and decision framing. *Journal of Personality and Social Psychology*, *50*, 543–9.

Campbell, D.T. (1965). Ethnocentric and other altruistic motives, in D. Levine (ed.), *Nebraska symposium of motivation*. Lincoln: University of Nebraska Press, pp. 289–311.

Coser, L. (1956). *The functions of social conflict*. New York: Free Press.

Dashiell, J.F. (1935). Experimental studies of the influence of social situations on the behavior of individual human adults, in C. Murchison (ed.), *A handbook of social psychology*. Dorchester, MA: Clark University Press, pp. 1097–1158.

Dawes, R.M. (1980). Social dilemmas. *Annual Review of Psychology*, *31*, 169–93.

Erev, I., Bornstein, G. and Galili, R. (1993). Constructive intergroup competition as a solution to the free rider problem: a field experiment. *Journal of Experimental Social Psychology*, *29*, 463–78.

Hamburger, H. (1979). *Games as models of social phenomena*. San Francisco: Freeman.

Kelley, H.H. and Thibaut, J.W. (1978). *Interpersonal relations: a theory of interdependence*. New York: John Wiley & Sons.

Kerr, N.L. (1983). Motivational losses in groups: a social dilemma analysis. *Journal of Personality and Social Psychology*, *45*, 819–28.

Kerr, N.L. (1986). Motivational choices in task groups: a paradigm for social dilemma research, in H. Wilke, D.M. Messick and C. Rutte (eds), *Experimental social dilemmas*. Frankfurt-on-Main: Lang, pp. 1–22.

Kerr, N.L. and Bruun, S. (1983). The dispensability of member effort and group motivation losses: Free rider effects. *Journal of Personality and Social Psychology*, *44*, 78–94.

Kramer, R.M. and Brewer, M.B. (1984). Effects of group identity on resource use in simulated social dilemma. *Journal of Personality and Social Psychology*, *46*, 1044–57.

Kramer, R.M. and Brewer, M.B. (1986). Social group identity and the emergence of cooperation in resource dilemmas, in H. Wilke, D.M. Messick and C. Rutte (eds), *Experimental social dilemmas*. Frankfurt-on-Main, Germany: Lang, pp. 206–31.

Latane, B., Williams, K. and Harkins, S. (1979). Many hands make light the work: the causes and consequences of social loafing. *Journal of Personality and Social Psychology*, *37*, 823–32.

Leventhal, G.S. (1976). The distribution of rewards and resources in groups and organizations, in L. Berkowitz and E. Walster (eds), *Advances in experimental social psychology*. New York: Academic Press, pp. 92–129.

Messick, D.M. and Brewer, M.B. (1983). Solving social dilemmas: a review, in L. Wheeler and P. Shaver (eds), *Review of personality and social psychology*. Beverly Hills, CA: Sage, Vol. 4, pp. 11–44.

Pruitt, D.G. and Kimmel, M.J. (1977). Twenty years of experimental gaming: Critique, synthesis, and suggestions for the future. *Annual Review of Psychology, 28*, 363–92.

Rabbie, J.M. (1982). The effects of intergroup competition and cooperation on intragroup and intergroup relationship, in V.J. Derlega and J. Grzelak (eds), *Cooperation and helping behavior: Theories and research*. New York: Academic Press, pp. 123–49.

Rabbie, J.M., Schot, J.C. and Visser, L. (1989). Social identity theory: a conceptual and empirical critique from the perspective of behavioral interaction model. *European Journal of Social Psychology, 19*, 171–202.

Rapoport, A., Bornstein, G. and Erev, I. (1989). Intergroup competition for public goods: Effects of unequal resources and relative group size. *Journal of Personality and Social Psychology, 56*, 748–56.

Stein, A.A. (1976). Conflict and cohesion. *Journal of Conflict Resolution, 20*, 143–72.

Steiner, I.D. (1972). *Group processes and productivity*. New York: Academic Press.

Tajfel, H. (1982). Social psychology of intergroup relations. *Annual Review of Psychology, 33*, 1–39.

Yamagishi, T. (1988). Exit from the group as an individualistic solution to the free rider problem in the United States and Japan. *Journal of Personality and Social Psychology, 35*, 1–11.

9

Good News About Competitive People

Peter J. Carnevale and Tahira M. Probst

Whether it is because of their behaviour, or their beliefs and perceptions, or even their facial expressions, competitive people, compared to cooperative people, get a lot of bad press. The bad news includes:

1   Competitive people are less in tune with social reality, and more likely to misattribute the causes of another's behaviour (Kelley & Stahelski, 1970a, 1970b).
2   Competitive people are likely to act in a self-interested manner and project their competitive motivations onto others (Kuhlman & Marshello, 1975; Kuhlman & Wimberly, 1976; Messick & McClintock, 1968).
3   Competitive people are likely to adopt social strategies characterized by mistrust (McClintock & Liebrand, 1988).
4   Competitive people are likely to take a greater share of a common resource (Kramer, McClintock & Messick, 1986; Liebrand & Van Run, 1985).
5   Competitive people are less likely to make concessions in negotiation, and are less likely to see others as fair and considerate (De Dreu & Van Lange, 1995; Olekalns, Smith & Kibby, 1996).
6   Competitive people define interdependence in terms of power, and see cooperation as weak and unintelligent and noncooperation as strong and intelligent (Liebrand, Jansen, Rijken & Suhre, 1986; McClintock & Liebrand, 1988).
7   Competitive people have angry facial expressions even when they talk about positive life events (Kuhlman & Carnevale, 1984).
8   Competitive people are less likely to volunteer for psychological experiments than cooperative people (McClintock & Allison, 1989).

Indeed, the line on competitive people is not a happy one. But, as will be seen in this chapter, the news is not all bad. This chapter presents a theoretical analysis, and the results of several recent studies, that suggest that competitive people, in some contexts, may be especially flexible, creative and cooperative. The data to be presented are consistent with the general proposition that competitive people can enhance the likelihood of group goal-attainment and group survival. In a sense, the present analysis is an extension of the framework developed by Bornstein and Erev (1994; see also their chapter in this book).

Cooperative people and competitive people

Most of the work on cooperative people and competitive people stems from studies of social value orientation (MacCrimmon & Messick, 1976; Messick & McClintock, 1968; McClintock, Messick, Kuhlman & Campos, 1973). Social value orientation refers to stable preferences for certain patterns of outcome distributions to oneself and others in situations of mixed-motive interdependence. Although many social value orientations can be identified, three have received the greatest attention from researchers: individualism, cooperation and competition. Individualists are concerned with maximizing their own gain without regard to the gains or losses of the other party; cooperators aim to maximize the joint gain of both parties, where joint gain is defined as the sum of the two individual gains; competitors prefer a pattern of outcomes in which relative gain, the difference between own outcomes and the other's outcomes, is maximized (Knight & Dubro, 1984; Messick & McClintock, 1968). Data presented later in this chapter will show how this individual differences variable can interact with situational characteristics of cooperation and competition.

Another perspective on individual differences in cooperativeness stems from work on the psychological correlates of culture. Kelley, Sure, Deutsch, Faucheux, Lanzetta, Moscovici, Nuttin and Rabbie (1970) found that various cultural regions of the world differ in terms of the salience of cooperative and competitive perceptions. Recent theoretical developments in the study of culture also focus on issues of cooperation and competition, with the bulk of the work related to collectivism and individualism (e.g. Fiske, 1990, 1992; Hofstede, 1980; Kagitcibasi & Berry, 1989; Markus & Kitayama, 1991; Schwartz, 1990; Triandis, 1989, 1994, 1995).

Recent research has shown that people identified as 'vertical individualists' are singularly competitive (Singelis, Triandis, Bhawuk & Gelfand, 1995). Data to be presented later in this chapter will show the relationship between collectivism and individualism, and their vertical and horizontal elements, and the social value orientations detailed by Messick and McClintock (1968), as well as how the culture concepts relate to cooperative behaviour.

Cooperative and competitive situations

It is well known that competitive and cooperative situations can affect attitudes and behaviour (Deutsch, 1969, 1994). The term 'competitive situation' is used here to denote hostile, aversive social interaction, as may occur in contrient (negative) interdependence or escalating conflict (Pruitt, 1981). It has been shown that competition can produce an aversive drive-like arousal state (Steigleder, Weiss, Balling, Wenninger & Lombardo, 1980). Moreover, Lanzetta and Englis (1989) have shown that competitive situations elicit a 'counter-empathy response', where a smile on an opponent's face elicits a grimace, and vice versa.

In addition, there is evidence that the experience of conflict can produce 'rigid' or 'black and white thinking', which entails restricted judgment and an inability to consider alternative perspectives (Deutsch, 1969; Jervis, 1976; Judd, 1978; White, 1984). Social conflict has been shown to decrease the complexity of thought of national leaders (Suedfeld & Tetlock, 1977). Consistent with this, many laboratory studies of bilateral negotiation have shown that negotiators placed in conflict contexts, compared to cooperative contexts, are less likely to see relationships among the issues, and less likely to understand that these relationships can form the basis of trade-offs and mutually beneficial, integrative agreements (Carnevale & Pruitt, 1992).

Conflict situations and cognitive organization

In a series of experiments on conflict and cognition, we (Carnevale & Probst, 1997) found that cooperation and conflict situations can influence fundamental cognitive operations such as creative ingenuity and categorization. In our first two experiments, we detailed the impact of cooperation and conflict in Duncker's (1945) functional-fixedness task and Rosch's (1975) categorization task. The general hypothesis tested was that social conflict affects how people categorize and process material in memory leading to more rigid thinking.

Conflict cognition Conflict cognition, i.e. 'black and white thinking' or 'rigid' thinking (Judd, 1978; White, 1984), involves a narrower range of attention and fewer, narrower, or less integrated mental categories. There is a reduced tendency to perceive relationships among items and to group things together. Conflict cues negative material in memory. In addition, ideas are less likely to be seen as related or holding implications for one another when there is conflict.

Cooperation cognition involves more or broader mental categories, more integrated categories, and a broader range of attention. There is an increased tendency to see relationships among items and to group things together. Cooperation can cue positive material in memory, and ideas are more likely to be seen as similar or holding implications for one another (see Carnevale & Isen, 1986; cf. Isen & Daubman, 1984).

Conflict and creativity In our first experiment, participants were led to expect either cooperation or conflict in a buyer–seller negotiation, or had no expectations of a negotiation (a control condition). In the conflict expectation condition, the participants were told that they would participate in a negotiation where they were to try to attain a better outcome than their opponent. A prize of twenty dollars was promised to the one person in the study that did the best. In the cooperation expectation condition, the participants were told to make as much combined profit in the negotiation as they could for the two of them, and to work for the good of both negotiators. A prize of twenty dollars was promised to each person of the negotiation team that earned the highest joint profit compared to any other team. This form of cooperation involves the participants working together, cooperatively, to do better than another group. Thus, the incentive is to compete, but as a group rather than as an individual. As an individual, the incentive is to cooperate with the other person. In the no-expectation control condition, there was no mention of a negotiation, and the participants were given only the cognitive task.

Just before the negotiation was to begin, the participants were asked to individually solve Duncker's (1945; Adamson & Taylor, 1954) functional-fixedness task. They each were given a book of matches, a small cardboard box full of tacks, and one small candle. The problem was to attach the candle to the partition in front of them so that the candle could burn properly and not drip wax onto the table. They were asked to write their solution on a piece of paper. One solution, identified by Duncker to be creative, was to remove the tacks from the box, tack the box to the partition, and use it as a platform for the candle. This solution requires that the concept 'box of tacks' be unbundled into 'tacks' and 'box', for the box to be used creatively as a platform.

The data indicated that subjects who expected conflict were less likely to discover the creative solution (25%) than those who were in the control condition (58%). However, the participants in the cooperative condition were equally likely to discover the creative solution (58%) compared to those in the control condition.

In other words, the results were consistent with the proposition that conflict expectations can influence general problem solving abilities, and the idea that conflict expectations are associated with less integrated cognitive structures and the failure to perceive relationships among cognitive material. The solution to Duncker's candle task requires the ability to see new aspects of the objects presented, or to see among them potential relationships other than the existing ones. It necessitates accessing a novel function of the box such as seeing a relationship between the concepts 'box' and 'platform' (Glucksberg & Danks, 1968).

The findings confirm in another manner the suggestion that conflict can inhibit seeing relationships among stimuli. In the candle task, it is seeing the relevant novel function, rather than the separate component, that is crucial in its solution. The results suggest a heightened 'black–white' or rigid style of thinking in conflict contexts, akin to what White (1984) has described. The lack of difference between the cooperation expectation condition and the control condition suggests that cooperative expectations did not enhance, or hinder, general problem solving abilities.

Conflict and categorization   A second study was designed to more directly assess the influence of cooperative and competitive/conflict expectations on negotiator cognition, specifically on the variable of categorization. The task was based on Rosch's (1975) analysis of exemplars of category membership, and the notion that there are both strong exemplars of categories (e.g. 'bus' in the category 'vehicle') and weak exemplars (e.g. 'wheelchair' in the category 'vehicle'). We expected that, especially for the weak exemplars, participants in the conflict expectation condition would rate the exemplars as lesser members of the categories than those in the control conditions (cf. Isen & Daubman, 1984).

The procedure was identical to that described earlier, except that participants were given a categorization task (Rosch, 1975) in place of the problem solving task, and they were actually exposed to another's first offer in the negotiation that was either cooperative or contentious. The participants conducted two offer exchanges with the ostensible buyer in the negotiation. Each offer exchange involved them first receiving a written message and offer from the buyer, which was hand-delivered by the experimenter, after which they sent a response. In the cooperation condition, the buyer's offers were quite favourable and included a note about the importance of reaching a cooperative solution that gave them, together, the highest profits. In the conflict condition, the buyer's offers were unfavourable and included a note about the importance of the participant capitulating. After two offer exchanges, the experimenter interrupted the negotiation, and administered the categorization task.

Participants were asked to rate each of nine exemplars of four categories identified by Rosch (1975): vehicle, furniture, vegetable, and clothing. Three of the exemplars were pre-selected as weak (e.g. camel), three as moderate (e.g. airplane), and three as strong exemplars (e.g. bus), in terms of how well they fit into the four categories (e.g. vehicle). The participants were asked to rate each exemplar on a ten-point scale, from 'Not a member at all' to 'A very good example'.

The data indicated that, in all conditions, the participants rated the strong exemplars as very good members of the categories, the moderate exemplars less so, and the weak exemplars the least. More importantly, as predicted, participants in the conflict expectation condition rated the weak exemplars as poorer members of the categories than participants in the control or cooperation expectation conditions, although the difference between the cooperation expectation condition and the control condition was only marginally different (control = 5.15; cooperation = 5.91; and conflict, 3.75).

The data thus suggested that cooperation and conflict can affect the cognitive variable of categorization, and the tendency to make black–white categorizations, i.e. to respond extremely. A person in a conflict state tends to view fringe exemplars of categories less as members of the categories or as similar to category members than do persons in a control condition. We interpret these results as evidence of a change in cognitive organization or in the perceived relationships among stimuli under conditions of social conflict.

Social values in cooperative and competitive situations

As we have shown, cooperative and competitive expectations or experiences of negotiation can affect the cognitive variables of problem solving ability and categorization. However, recall that the purpose of this chapter is to present the reader with some good news about competitive people. Therefore, Carnevale and Probst (1997, experiment 4) extended the analysis of the impact of cooperative and competitive situations on cognition, described above, to the possible moderating effects of social value orientation. There were two main research questions: 1. In general, do cooperators, individualists and competitors differ in cognitive rigidity? and 2. Do cooperators, individualists and competitors react differently to cooperative and competitive situations?

The experiment was a 3 × 3 completely crossed between factorial. Participants were classified as either cooperative, competitive or individualistic. They were then randomly assigned to either a cooperation, competition or no expectation control condition.

Individual differences in social values were determined using the decomposed game procedure employed in past work (Messick & McClintock, 1968). Participants are presented three choices in a matrix game, such that each choice specifies a particular payoff to the participant and to an unknown other. On each trial participants were presented a three by two matrix similar to the one shown in Table 9.1 that specifies own and other's outcomes for each of three choices (A, B and C).

Table 9.1   *A triple-dominance decomposed game (choice 'A' maximizes cooperation; choice 'B' maximizes competition; choice 'C' maximizes individualism)*

		Choice		
		A	B	C
Payoff to	Self	5	4	6
	Other	5	0	3

As can be seen in Table 9.1, a choice of A by participant 1 would give her five points and participant 2 five points. If participant 2 chooses B, this gives participant 1 no points and participant 2 four points. Participant 1's total points would be five, whereas participant 2 would receive nine points. (Note that Participant 1 is 'self' in her own decision, but 'other' in Participant 2's decision.) Total outcomes were determined by the sum of the number of points allocated as a consequence of their choice and the choice of the unknown other. Thus, in the example, the cooperative choice is exemplified by A because it maximizes joint gain. Choice B is the competitive choice since it maximizes relative gain. And choice C is the individualist choice since it maximizes own gain regardless of the other's. A minimum of seven consistent responses out of the twelve trials was required for classification of an individual as either cooperative, individualistic or competitive. This measure of social value orientation has good test-retest reliability and is predictive of behaviour over time (see Liebrand et al., 1986; Liebrand & Van Run, 1985; Van Lange & Kuhlman, 1994).

In a similar fashion to experiments 1 and 2, the participants were led to expect either a cooperative or a competitive negotiation, or were told nothing about a negotiation. Then they were given the Rosch (1975) categorization task, described earlier, consisting of ten categories (e.g. toy, clothing, furniture). In each category (e.g. vehicle), there were two words: a strong exemplar (e.g. car) and a weak exemplar (e.g. sled). As in experiment 2, participants were asked to rate on a ten-point scale ranging from 'Not a member at all' to 'A very good example' the goodness of each of the two exemplars in terms of how well they fit into the category.

Of the 203 participants, 86% ($N = 174$) were classifiable using the decomposed games task. Of these, 47% ($N = 81$) were individualist; 20% ($N = 34$) were competitive; 34% ($N = 59$) were cooperative. Table 9.2 presents the mean ratings of the exemplar ratings as a function of the cooperation, competition and control conditions for each of the three motivational dispositions (individualist, cooperator, competitor).

As predicted, an interaction between social values and conflict expectation was found. As can be seen in Table 9.2, in the control condition, the cooperative participants' ratings for the exemplars were highest, suggesting that cooperators, in general, had the most flexible categories. Upon introducing a competitive or cooperative expectation, however, the cognitive flexibility of the *competitive* participants was influenced by the social context. When expecting competition, competitors rated the exemplars as particularly poor representatives of their category. But, when they expected cooperation, the competitors rated the exemplars as particularly good representatives of their category.

In other words, the results supported the hypothesis that expectations of cooperation or competition and an individual's social value orientation can interact to affect categorization and the tendency to respond extremely to exemplars of a given category. When anticipating competition, the competitive participants were much more likely to reject weak exemplars (e.g. 'chess' in the category 'sport') than cooperative or individualist participants. This

Table 9.2 *Mean goodness of fit of weak exemplars by cooperators and competitors, as a function of expecting cooperation, conflict or no expectations (Ns range from 12 to 27)*

| | Situation expectation | | |
	No expectation	Competitive	Cooperative
Cooperators	6.68	5.96	6.19
Competitors	5.92	5.00	6.89
Individualists	5.73	6.16	5.64

Source: Partial data from Carnevale and Probst, 1997

suggests that 'rigid' or 'black and white thinking' is most likely to occur among competitive people in competitive situations. This is the bad news.

The good news is that the competitive participants exhibited the most cognitive flexibility in the cooperative expectation condition. Recall that this cooperation condition involved the participants working together, cooperatively, to do better than another group (see description of experiment 1). Thus, the incentive was to compete, but as a group rather than as an individual. As an individual, the incentive was to cooperate with the other person. In other words, the cooperative situation had features in common with intergroup competition, as defined by Bornstein and Erev (1994; see their chapter in this book).

Bornstein and Erev reported that intergroup competition motivates an increase in intragroup cooperation. The data of the present study suggest that the effect of intergroup competition on intragroup cooperation may be even stronger with competitive individuals. Here, the competitive individuals showed the greatest flexibility of thinking when they were faced with a need to cooperate with a partner in a competition against other groups.

Culture and cooperation in single group and intergroup dilemma situations

Individual differences in cooperativeness and competitiveness are related to culture. This point was made in the classic study by Kelley et al. (1970), where it was discovered that regions of the world vary in terms of the salience of cooperative and competitive perceptions. Studies of culture also focus on issues of cooperation and competition, with the bulk of the work related to collectivism and individualism. As mentioned earlier, people identified as 'vertical individualists' are singularly competitive (Singelis et al., 1995).

Following Triandis (1994, 1995), culture is defined here as the 'human-made part of the environment', and it is seen as having a subjective component, i.e. the shared perceptions of the social environment. According to Triandis (1995), the subjective aspect of culture results in automatic processing of information, because it specifies the things that are noticed, and provides a language for labelling experience. Culture also specifies how things are to be evaluated, and what behaviours are desirable or prescribed for members of the culture (norms), for individuals in the social structure (roles), as well as the important goals and principles in social life (values).

Collectivism and individualism

Individualism–collectivism and related constructs have been discussed in many contexts in the social sciences, in the areas of values, social systems, morality, religion, cognitive differentiation, economic development and others (Triandis, 1995). Hofstede's (1980) work drew early attention to the constructs. Corresponding to the individualism and collectivism concepts, at the cultural level, are processes at the psychological level. There are numerous defining attributes (Triandis, 1994, 1995). For collectivists, the group is the basic unit of social perception; the self is defined in terms of ingroup relationships; ingroup goals have primacy or overlap with personal goals; ingroup harmony is valued; and social behaviour tends to be very different when the other person belongs to an ingroup vs. an outgroup. For individualists the individual is the basic unit of social perception; the self is an independent entity; personal goals have primacy over ingroup goals; ingroup confrontation is acceptable; and social behaviour is not so different when the other person belongs to an ingroup vs. an outgroup.

Triandis (1989, 1995) proposed a theory of the self in relation to culture. In individualistic cultures, the organizing theme is the centrality of the autonomous individual, with members whose selves include more private elements (e.g. 'I am kind'; 'my strengths are many'). In collectivist cultures it is the centrality of the collective – family, tribe, ethnic group – and the self has more collectivist elements (e.g. 'my family expects me to be kind'; 'my co-workers believe that I have many strengths'). Members of individualistic cultures also have public selves with more individualistic elements (e.g. 'people in general expect me to be kind') while those in collectivist cultures have public selves with more collectivist elements ('people in general expect me to be a good family man'). The most important cognitions for individualists are 'I', 'me', 'mine'; for collectivists they are 'us,' 'we', 'ours' vs. 'they' and 'them' (Triandis, 1995). Since there are more elements in the private, collective or public selves in some cultures than in others, the probability that different types of elements will be sampled differs across different cultures (Markus & Kitayama, 1991).

Vertical and horizontal individualism and collectivism

Recent theory has claimed that it is important to distinguish between vertical and horizontal elements of individualism and collectivism (Singelis et al., 1995; Triandis, 1995). *Vertical individualism* (V-I) is a cultural pattern in which the individual views the self as autonomous, and expects inequality. Doing well in competition is an important aspect of this pattern.

Vertical collectivism (V-C) is a cultural pattern in which individuals view the self as an aspect of the group, the self concept is closely tied and interdependent with others of the ingroup, but the members of the ingroup differ from one another, particularly with regard to social status. Inequality is accepted, and people do not see each other as the same. Sacrificing for the good of the group is a salient feature of this pattern (Singelis et al., 1995). *Horizontal collectivism* (H-C) is the cultural pattern in which the individual sees the self as an aspect of the group, where the self concept is seen as closely tied and interdependent with others of the ingroup, who are seen as similar; equality among group members is a value. *Horizontal individualism* (H-I) is a cultural pattern characterized by a self concept that is autonomous, but the individual is seen as equal in status to others; self-reliance is especially stressed. Each of these patterns corresponds to cultural patterns identified by Fiske (1990,

1992), who developed a framework for types of universal social relationships that pertain to how societies distribute resources (Singelis et al., 1995).

We (Carnevale, Probst, Hsueh & Triandis, 1997) extended prior analyses of cooperation by examining the relationships between vertical and horizontal individualism and collectivism and social value orientations, and by examining the relationship between the cultural patterns and behaviour in single-group and intergroup social dilemmas (Bornstein, 1992; Bornstein & Ben-Yossef, 1994; Bornstein & Erev, 1994).

Single-group and intergroup social dilemmas

A social dilemma is a situation where people are interdependent and face a choice between cooperative (i.e. collective) interests and selfish interests. Examples can be found in virtually every domain of social behaviour, from work and family settings to international relations. In social dilemmas, if everyone behaves in a manner that maximizes personal gain, everyone is worse off than if everyone behaves in a manner that maximizes collective gain (Dawes, 1980; Messick & Brewer, 1983).

An interesting aspect of social dilemmas is that they often occur in the context of intergroup conflicts, and the intergroup conflict produces a social dilemma within each of the competing groups. Dawes (1980) described this in lucid terms: 'Soldiers who fight in a large battle can reasonably conclude that no matter what their comrades do they personally are better off taking no chances; yet if no one takes chances, the result will be rout and slaughter worse for all the soldiers than is taking chances' (p. 170). The intragroup problem contained in this example incorporates the two defining characteristics of a social dilemma: individual group members are better off not cooperating with their group, yet they are rewarded more if they all cooperate rather than if they all do not.

Bornstein and Erev (1994) reported that people were nearly twice as likely to cooperate in an Intergroup Prisoner's Dilemma (IPD) game than in a standard single-group Prisoner's Dilemma game (PD), even though the cost of cooperation for the individual group member was the same in the two games and the external gain to the individual's groups ensuing from a cooperative choice was also the same. The difference between the two games was the presence of an outgroup. They concluded that intergroup conflict serves as a unit-forming factor that enhances group identification (Campbell, 1965; Rabbie, Schot & Visser, 1989), and that group identification leads to a blurring of the distinction between self-interest and group interest (Brewer & Kramer, 1985).

The present study followed Bornstein's design but examined individual differences in competitiveness, as defined by vertical and horizontal dimensions of individualism and collectivism. We expected a replication of the Bornstein and Erev (1994) results, that the intergroup dilemma would produce greater cooperation than the single-group dilemma. But we also expected that this effect would vary as a function of cultural characteristics.

We expected that vertical individualists, due to the value that they place on competition, would be the least cooperative, especially in the single-group dilemma. We expected that they would show greater cooperation in the inter-group dilemma, primarily because, in that context, cooperation with the three-person group is a way of maximizing personal outcomes in the competition with the opposing three-person group. We also expected that vertical collectivists, due to their greater emphasis on sacrificing for their ingroup (Singelis et al., 1995), would be more cooperative with each other than any of the other types, especially in the intergroup dilemma if they defined their three-person group as an ingroup. We expected that the horizontal collectivists and individualists would exhibit a moderate level of cooperation, due to the greater emphasis that they place on equality.

Participants and design

Undergraduate students at the University of Illinois participated in the study. Most were native speakers of English, but about a third were non-native speakers of English and were mostly from Asian countries. The design involved a comparison of cooperative behaviour in either the single-group or the intergroup dilemma, and four categories of individuals as defined by vertical and horizontal dimensions of individualism and collectivism.

The measures of culture

Vertical and horizontal individualism and collectivism was assessed by means of the INDCOL 32-item scale developed by Singelis et al. (1995). The scale consists of four a priori groups of items written to measure the four dimensions. The dimensionality of the items was re-assessed in the present sample. Maximum likelihood factor analysis was performed and the results were submitted to an oblique rotation, as previous analyses suggest these are not orthogonal dimensions (Singelis et al., 1995). A four-factor solution corresponding to the four cultural dimensions was obtained, accounting for 25.9% of the variance. Based on the factor analysis, the five or six items with the highest factor loadings for each factor were selected to measure horizontal and vertical individualism and collectivism, and were summed and averaged, producing four indexes, one for each culture factor.

The four indices were converted to standard scores. Participants were then categorized on the basis of their predominant culture characteristic, either H-I, V-I, H-C or V-C. On the standardized index, if their score on V-I was highest, they were categorized as vertical individualist; and so on for each of the four indices.

Procedure and dilemma tasks

The procedure and task was identical to that reported in Bornstein and Erev (1994; see their chapter in this book). What follows is an abbreviated description:

When participants first arrived, they were randomly assigned to a group with two other participants. Each group was seated in a private room and partitions were used so that participants could not interact with one another. The game instructions were neutral and were stated in terms of the individual's payoffs as a function of his/her decision to invest or not invest, the decisions of the members of his/her group, and the decisions of the other group (for the IPD condition).

The IPD game is a competition between two groups where the intragroup payoff structure is a social dilemma, regardless of the outgroup's decisions. The IPD game was compared with a structurally identical (single-group) social dilemma (PD) game. In both the IPD and PD games, a set of six participants is split into two groups of three each. Each participant is given an endowment of $1.05 and has to decide whether to keep the money or contribute it for the team's benefit. In the IPD game, each participant's payoff is a function of his/her decision to contribute or not contribute his/her endowment, the decisions of his/her group members, and the decisions of the members of the other group. In the PD game, each participant's payoff is a function of his/her decisions and the decisions of his/her group members.

In the IPD game, if two people in group A invest their endowment and only one person in group B invests their money, group A has one more investor than group B. The two investors in group A each receive $2.00 and the noninvestor receives $3.05; the total group payoff is $7.05. The investor in group B receives $1.00 and the two noninvestors each receive $2.05; the total group payoff is $5.10. If all three members of both group A and group B invest their money, everyone receives $1.50. The total group payoff for each group is $4.50. If no one from the two groups invest their money, then each person receives $2.55 and the total group payoff for each group is $7.65.

In the PD game, if two people in a group invest their endowment, each investor receives $1.00 and the noninvestor receives $2.05. The group earns a total of $4.05. If everyone in the group invests their money, each person receives $1.50 and the total group payoff is $4.50. If no one in the group invests, then each person keeps their $1.05 endowment and the total group payoff is $3.15.

Participants made ten consecutive decisions whether to contribute or not contribute their endowment. Each decision was recorded on a separate page in a booklet. The pages were numbered from 1 to 10 and participants were told that at the end of the study, one page would be randomly chosen and their payoffs would be calculated using the decisions made by the six members of the set (in the IPD condition) or the three members of the group (in the PD condition) on that particular page. Participants had no opportunity to communicate, and feedback was not given between decisions.

Participants also completed Messick and McClintock's (1968) measure of cooperative and competitive social motivation. This entailed making choices in twelve decomposed triple-dominance games.

The data

The frequency with which the participants decided to contribute across the ten trials of the social dilemma was analysed by a 4 x 2 ANOVA, with culture (H-C, V-C, H-I, V-I) as the four-level factor, and type of dilemma (PD vs. IPD) as the two-level factor. No main effect for type of dilemma was obtained, and only a marginal main effect for culture was obtained. But a significant two-way interaction was obtained. The two-way interaction pattern is shown in Figure 9.1. The interaction pattern was consistent with our expectations that culture characteristics interact with features of the situation.

As can be seen in Figure 9.1, the vertical individualists were especially noncooperative in the single-group dilemma, but they were particularly cooperative in the intergroup dilemma ($p < 0.05$). Moreover, the vertical collectivists were most cooperative in the single-group dilemma, but were less cooperative in the intergroup dilemma ($p < 0.05$). The levels of cooperation for horizontal individualists and collectivists did not significantly differ from each other, nor did they differ across dilemma conditions.

This interpretation suggests that the participants in the Bornstein studies were mostly vertical individualists, or perhaps they were all highly competitive. Support for this interpretation is shown in Table 9.3, which reports the correlations between the four culture scales and Messick and McClintock's (1968) measures of cooperative and competitive social motivation.

As can be seen in Table 9.3, the vertical-individualism scale was positively correlated with Messick and McClintock's measure of competitive social

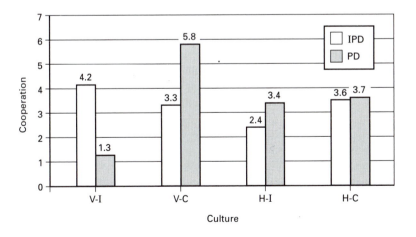

Figure 9.1 *Mean cooperation on ten trials as a function of type of dilemma: IPD (Intergroup Prisoner's Dilemma) or PD (three-person Prisoner's Dilemma), and culture: V-I (vertical individualist), V-C (vertical collectivist), H-I (horizontal individualist) and H-C (horizontal collectivist) (Data from Carnevale et al., 1997)*

Table 9.3 *Correlations between Singelis et al.'s (1995) measures of horizontal and vertical individualism and collectivism, and Messick and McClintock's (1968) measures of cooperative and competitive social motivation (N = 165)*

	V-I	V-C	H-I	H-C
Competitive	0.15**	–0.10	0.11	–0.03
Cooperative	–0.13*	0.19**	–0.09	0.17**

* $p < 0.10$.
** $p < 0.05$.
Source: Data from Carnevale et al., 1997

motivation. It is important to note that the key feature of vertical individualism is competition. All of the INDCOL items for vertical individualism relate to competition (e.g. agreement with the statements 'Competition is the law of nature'; 'Winning is everything'). In other words, the vertical individualists fit the definition of people with a competitive orientation, and indeed they behaved like competitive people in the social dilemma. For competitive people, the goal is to do better than others, i.e. to win, and this means, in a single-group dilemma, that the goal is achieved through noncooperation with others in the group. But, in the intergroup dilemma, the goal of winning is achieved by cooperating with one's own group in order to win the competition with the outgroup. In the intergroup dilemma, cooperation with one's own group meant one's group received a higher payoff than the other group. So, the vertical individualists may have cooperated with their team in order to beat the other team. For vertical individualists, competition is a particularly salient feature of life, and this explains why they were more cooperative in the intergroup dilemma than in the group dilemma.

Moreover, the collectivists, in particular the vertical collectivists, may have been more interested than individualists in maximizing group outcomes, as opposed to individual outcomes. For vertical collectivists, the defining characteristics relate to sacrificing one's own interests for the interests of the group (e.g. agreement with the statements 'I usually sacrifice my self-interest for the benefit of my group' and 'I hate to disagree with others in my group'). In the single-group dilemma, it was clearly in the group's best interest if everyone contributed their endowment and, in this condition, vertical collectivists showed the highest level of cooperation. But, in the intergroup dilemma, the vertical collectivists may have defined *all six people* as the group. Indeed, they had no reason to think that the other two people in their room were any different from the three in the other room, since they all were separated by partitions, had not met, had no conversation, and had no expectations of future interaction. In the intergroup dilemma, the payoff structure is such that all six people are better off if they do not cooperate.

Perhaps the collectivists had a general cooperative orientation to all five others in the dilemma. Support for this can also be seen in Table 9.3, which shows the correlations with Messick and McClintock's (1968) measures of cooperative and competitive social motivation. The horizontal and vertical collectivism scales were both positively correlated with Messick and McClintock's measure of cooperative social motivation.

The horizontal individualists and collectivists showed an intermediate level of cooperation and, for both types, there were no differences in cooperation between the single-group and intergroup dilemmas. It may be that their predominant characteristic, equality matching (i.e. resources should be divided equally; cf. Fiske, 1990), guided their behaviour in both social dilemmas.

Conclusions

We began this chapter with the observation that competitive people, compared to cooperative people, get a lot of bad press. We listed some of the bad news: e.g. competitive people are likely to take a greater share of a common resource; competitive people carry angry facial expressions. In this chapter, we argued, and showed in several laboratory studies, that the news is not all bad. The good news includes the following two items:

1 Competitive people, compared to cooperative people, are especially flexible in their thinking when they must work cooperatively with others in their own group in a competition with an outgroup.
2 Competitive people, compared to cooperative people, are especially cooperative with their own group members when their group is in a competition with an outgroup.

These points apply to competitive persons as defined by Messick and McClintock (1968), and to vertical individualists as defined by Triandis (1995; see also Singelis et al., 1995). There are probably many important differences between competitive people identified via the Messick/McClintock procedure and vertical individualists. However, the significant (albeit modest 0.15) correlation between the two measures, as well as the parallel findings for the measures of categorization and reactions to intergroup competition, suggest that competitiveness is a meaningful component of vertical individualism.

Earlier we mentioned that competitive people have angry facial expressions even when they talk about positive life events (Kuhlman & Carnevale, 1984). The results of the studies described here suggest several interesting extensions of this finding. It might be interesting to see if vertical individualists also show angry facial expressions, since competitiveness is a strong component of this construct.

It might also be interesting to examine the implications for team composition in organizations. In teams, people often communicate and interact. But competitive people, with angry facial expressions, may find it difficult to interact in a positive manner. However, we might speculate that competitive people are especially happy when in a group that is competing with an outgroup, and would demonstrate this in their facial expressions. In other words, competitive people, who generally are characterized as having angry facial expressions, might display the most happiness to other members of their own group when their group is in intergroup competition.

We might further speculate that competitive people, when in a losing group effort in intergroup conflict, would be especially angry and especially prone to leave the group in favour of a more successful group.

It is interesting to note that competitive people, when dealing with an ingroup member in intergroup conflict, may be especially flexible and cooperative. But, when dealing with outgroup members, competitive people may become especially inflexible and contentious. In other words, competitive people, unlike their cooperative counterparts, have an ability to shift their manner of thinking in reaction to properties of the social context.

The results of the studies described here suggest that there may be an important mediating role of cognitive rigidity in the resolution of social conflict. The interaction of dispositions and situations best predicts cognitive functioning and behaviour in social conflict. The results further suggest that competitive people may be particularly effective in group contexts that entail conflict with an outgroup. Competitive people can enhance the likelihood of ingroup goal-attainment and ingroup survival in intergroup situations. From an evolutionary perspective, competitive people can serve an adaptive function in ingroup behaviour: it may be beneficial for groups to attract and maintain competitive people as group members for purposes of fostering ingroup cooperation in intergroup competition. The paradox is that ingroup cooperation in the service of intergroup conflict can in some cases produce poor intergroup relations and even disastrous intergroup outcomes.

Note

This material is based upon work supported by the National Science Foundation under Grants BNS-8809263 and DBS-9210536.

References

Adamson, R.E. and Taylor, D.W. (1954). Functional fixedness as related to elapsed time and to set. *Journal of Experimental Psychology, 47*, 122–6.

Bornstein, G. (1992). The free rider problem in intergroup conflicts over step-level and continuous public goods. *Journal of Personality and Social Psychology, 62,* 597–606.

Bornstein, G. and Ben-Yossef, M. (1994). Cooperation in intergroup and single-group social dilemmas. *Journal of Experimental Social Psychology, 30*, 52–67.

Bornstein, G. and Erev, I. (1994). The enhancing effect of intergroup competition on group performance. *The International Journal of Conflict Management, 5*, 271–83.

Brewer, M.B. and Kramer, R.M. (1985). The psychology of intergroup attitudes and behavior. *Annual Review of Psychology, 36*, 219–43.

Campbell, D.T. (1965). Ethnocentric and other altruistic motives, in D. Levine (ed.), *Nebraska symposium of motivation*. Lincoln: University of Nebraska Press, pp. 289–311.

Carnevale, P.J. and Isen, A.M. (1986). The influence of positive affect and visual access on the discovery of integrative solutions in bilateral negotiation. *Organizational Behavior and Human Decision Processes, 37,* 1–13.

Carnevale, P.J. and Probst, T.M. (1997). 'Social values and social conflict in creative problem solving and categorization'. Manuscript submitted for publication.

Carnevale, P.J., Probst, T.M., Hsueh, E. and Triandis, H.C. (1997). 'Cooperation and culture in intergroup and single-group social dilemmas'. Manuscript submitted for publication.

Carnevale, P.J. and Pruitt, D.G. (1992). Negotiation and mediation. *Annual Review of Psychology, 43,* 531–82.

Dawes, R.M. (1980). Social dilemmas. *Annual Review of Psychology, 31,* 169–93.

De Dreu, C.K.W. and Van Lange, P.A.M. (1995). Impact of social value orientation on negotiator cognition and behavior. *Personality and Social Psychology Bulletin, 21,* 778–89.

Deutsch, M. (1969). Conflicts: Productive and destructive. *Journal of Social Issues, 25,* 7–41.

Deutsch, M. (1994). Constructive conflict resolution: Principles, training, and research. *Journal of Social Issues, 50,* 13–32.

Duncker, K. (1945). On problem-solving. *Psychological Monographs, 58.* (Whole No. 5).

Fiske, A.P. (1990). *Structures of social life: the four elementary forms of human relations.* New York: Free Press.

Fiske, A.P. (1992). The four elementary forms of sociality: Framework for a unified theory of social relations. *Psychological Review, 99,* 689–723.

Glucksberg, S. and Danks, J. (1968). Effects of discriminative labels and of nonsense labels upon availability of a novel function. *Journal of Verbal Learning and Verbal Behavior, 7,* 72–6.

Hofstede, G. (1980). *Culture's consequences.* Beverly Hills, CA: Sage.

Isen, A.M. and Daubman, K.A. (1984). The influence of affect on categorization. *Journal of Personality and Social Psychology, 47,* 1206–17.

Jervis, R. (1976). *Perception and misperception in international politics.* Princeton, NJ: Princeton University Press.

Judd, C.M. (1978). Cognitive effects of attitude conflict resolution. *Journal of Conflict Resolution, 22,* 483–98.

Kagitcibasi, C. and Berry, J.W. (1989). Cross-cultural psychology: Current research and trends. *Annual Review of Psychology, 40,* 493–532.

Kelley, H.H. and Stahelski, A.J. (1970a). Social interaction basis of cooperators' and competitors' beliefs about others. *Journal of Personality and Social Psychology, 16,* 66–91.

Kelley, H.H. and Stahelski, A.J. (1970b). Errors in perception of intentions in mixed-motive games. *Journal of Experimental Social Psychology, 6,* 379–400.

Kelley, H.H., Sure, G.H., Deutsch, M., Faucheux, C., Lanzetta, J.T., Moscovici, S., Nuttin, J.M. and Rabbie, J.M. (1970). A comparative study of negotiation behavior. *Journal of Personality and Social Psychology, 16,* 411–38.

Knight, G.P. and Dubro, A.F. (1984). Cooperative, competitive, and individualistic social values: an individualized regression and clustering approach. *Journal of Personality and Social Psychology, 46,* 98–105.

Kramer, R.M., McClintock, C.G. and Messick, D.M. (1986). Social values and cooperative response to a simulated resource conservation crisis. *Journal of Personality, 54,* 576–92.

Kuhlman, D.M. and Carnevale, P.J. (1984). *Nonverbal affective style of cooperators, competitors, and individualists.* Paper presented at the annual meeting of the American Psychological Association, Washington, DC.

Kuhlman, D.M. and Marshello, A. (1975). Individual differences in game motivation as moderators of preprogrammed strategy effects in prisoner's dilemma games. *Journal of Personality and Social Psychology, 32,* 922–31.

Kuhlman, D.M. and Wimberly, D.M. (1976). Expectations of choice behavior held by cooperators, competitors, and individualists across four classes of experimental games. *Journal of Personality and Social Psychology, 34,* 69–81.

Lanzetta, J.T. and Englis, B.G. (1989). Expectations of cooperation and competition and their effects on observers' vicarious emotional responses. *Journal of Personality and Social Psychology, 56,* 543–54.

Liebrand, W.G.B., Jansen, R., Rijken, V.M. and Suhre, C. (1986). Might over morality: the interaction between social values and the interpretation of decision making in experimental games. *Journal of Experimental Social Psychology, 22*, 203–15.

Liebrand, W.G.B. and Van Run, G.J. (1985). The effects of social motivation across two cultures on behavior in social dilemmas. *Journal of Experimental Social Psychology, 21*, 86–102.

MacCrimmon, K.R. and Messick, D.M. (1976). A framework for social motives. *Behavioral Science, 21*, 86–100.

Markus, H. & Kitayama, S. (1991). Culture and self: Implications for cognition, emotion, and motivation. *Psychological Review, 98*, 224–53.

McClintock, C.G. and Allison, S.T. (1989). Social value orientation and helping behavior. *Journal of Applied Social Psychology, 19*, 353–62.

McClintock, C.G. and Liebrand, W.B.G. (1988). Role of interdependence, individual orientation, and another's strategy in social decision making: a transformational analysis. *Journal of Personality and Social Psychology, 55*, 396–409.

McClintock, C.G., Messick, D.M., Kuhlman, D.M. and Campos, F.T. (1973). Motivational bases of choice in three-choice decomposed games. *Journal of Experimental Social Psychology, 9*, 572–90.

Messick, D.M. and Brewer, M.B. (1983). Solving social dilemmas: a review, in L. Wheeler & P. Shaver (eds), *Review of personality and social psychology.* Beverly Hills, CA: Sage, Vol. 4, pp. 11–44.

Messick, D.M. and McClintock, C.G. (1968). Motivational basis of choice in experimental games. *Journal of Experimental Social Psychology, 4*, 1–25.

Olekalns, M., Smith, P.L. and Kibby, R. (1996). Social value orientations and negotiator outcomes. *European Journal of Social Psychology. 26*, 299–314.

Pruitt, D.G. (1981). *Negotiation behavior.* New York: Academic Press.

Rabbie, J.M., Schot, J.C. and Visser, L. (1989). Social identity theory: a conceptual and empirical critique from the perspective of behavioral interaction model. *European Journal of Social Psychology, 19*, 171–202.

Rosch, E. (1975). Cognitive representations of semantic categories. *Journal of Experimental Psychology: General, 104*, 192–233.

Schwartz, S.H. (1990). Individualism–collectivism: Critique and proposed refinements. *Journal of Cross-Cultural Psychology, 21*, 139–57.

Singelis, T.M., Triandis, H.C., Bhawuk, D.P.S. and Gelfand, M.J. (1995). Horizontal and vertical dimensions of individualism and collectivism: a theoretical and measurement refinement. *Cross-Cultural Research, 29*, 240–75.

Steigleder, M.K., Weiss, R.F., Balling, S.S., Wenninger, V.L. and Lombardo, J.P. (1980). Drivelike motivational properties of competitive behavior. *Journal of Personality and Social Psychology, 38*, 93–104.

Suedfeld, P. and Tetlock, P. (1977). Integrative complexity of communications in international crises. *Journal of Conflict Resolution, 21*, 169–79.

Triandis, H.C. (1989). Self and social behavior in differing cultural contexts. *Psychological Review, 96*, 269–89.

Triandis, H.C. (1994). *Culture and social behavior.* New York: McGraw-Hill.

Triandis, H.C. (1995). *Individualism and collectivism.* Boulder, CO: Westview.

Van Lange, P.A.M. and Kuhlman, D.M. (1994). Social value orientations and impressions of partner's honesty and intelligence: a test of the might versus morality effect. *Journal of Personality and Social Psychology, 67*, 126–41.

White, R.K. (1984). *Fearful warriors: a psychological profile of US–Soviet relations.* New York: Free Press.

10

Productive Conflict: Negotiation as Implicit Coordination

Linda L. Putnam

Organizational conflict is often treated as a dreaded disease or as a disruptive, even deviant activity. Managers frequently shun disagreements with fellow supervisors; employees gloss over differences with co-workers and their bosses; and executives often cover up disputes that arise in the workplace (Robbins, 1978). This dread of conflict may stem from the tense emotional climate that accompanies these situations. Although conflict theorists argue that disagreements are essential to the formation and maintenance of organizational life, managers and scholars continue to highlight the detriments of disputes.

The recognition that conflict is productive is not new. Theorists of the 1950s and 1960s address the functional and the productive side of conflict (Coser, 1956; Deutsch, 1969). Specifically, they contend that conflict in organizations balances power relationships, promotes flexibility and adaptiveness, and prevents stagnation of work units (Bacharach & Lawler, 1981; Coser, 1956; Pfeffer, 1981). Conflict also enhances adaptation, growth and stability of organizations; it guards against groupthink; and it facilitates effective decision making through challenging complacency and illusions of invincibility. Conflict is defined in this chapter as 'an expressed struggle between at least two interdependent parties who perceive incompatible goals, scarce rewards, and [potential] interference from the other party in achieving their goals' (Hocker & Wilmot, 1985, p. 23).

This chapter suggests that conflict and cooperation are part of the many pairs of opposing tendencies that characterize organizational life. Weick (1979), among other theorists, has noted how organizational systems engender and even thrive in the midst of these polar opposites such as integration and differentiation, risk taking and risk avoiding, structure and anarchy, dynamic and static.

As Pondy (1989) notes:

> if there were no active conflicts within these pairs, then one of the polar extremes would gradually become dominant. In each case, the diversity of behavioral repertoires available to the organization would diminish, the organization would lose its capacity for adaptation in the face of environmental change, and it would run a high risk of eventual failure . . . conflict is not only functional for the organization, it is essential to its very existence. (p. 96)

Thus, conflict is not simply inevitable; it is the nature of complex organizations. To talk about productive aspects of conflict suggests that conflict is a
malfunction or a disruption in the harmony of the system. Perhaps we should
treat 'an organization as a means for internalizing conflicts, for bringing
them within a bounded structure so they can be confronted' (Pondy, 1989, p.
94). Conflict is not a breakdown of a cooperative, purposeful system. Rather
conflict is central to what an organization is.

One of the most productive aspects of conflict is its contribution to the
durability of organizations. Indeed, the longest lasting organizations, primarily legislative bodies and universities, are known for open conflict among
diverse organizational employees. 'The 66 oldest institutions in Western civ-
ilization consist of four parliaments and 62 universities' (Pondy, 1989, p. 96),
organizations in which conflict is frequent, spontaneous, and managed within
the routine processes of deliberative problem solving.

One arena in which conflict is often viewed as a destructive force in organizational life is intergroup disputes. Intergroup conflict typically surfaces
through coalitions or interest groups that unify under a common set of issues,
beliefs or values. As conflict develops, within-group loyalty grows, members
solidify around ingroup positions, and employees exaggerate the differences
between groups. These patterns often lead to rigid stereotypes and ill-will
between groups.

Traditional studies that focus on the destructive patterns of intergroup disputes, however, overlook the way in which conflict contributes to balancing
power, improving communication, and enhancing adaptation and growth of
both units. Intergroup conflict is often characterized by an increased flow in
communication between and within groups (Coser, 1956; Deutsch, 1969;
Putnam & Poole, 1987). Through engaging in a controversy with another
group, both groups can enhance their understanding of complex problems,
broaden their perspectives on organizational life, and develop a foundation to
manage differences.

Small group decision theorists have argued that conflict expands the range
of judgments, spawns creative ideas, leads to a re-examination of goals,
increases calculated risks, and fosters acceptance of group decisions (Folger,
Poole & Stutman, 1993; Hall & Williams, 1966). To stimulate conflict and
avoid groupthink, strategic management theorists have examined the effects
of dialectical inquiry and devil's advocacy as methods of dealing with ill-
structured organizational problems (Cosier, 1978; Mason & Mitroff, 1981;
Schweiger, Sandberg & Ragan, 1986). Both methods introduce controversy
into group decision making procedures.

This chapter provides a case study of intergroup conflict through collective
bargaining in the public sector. It examines the way in which clashing on
issues, disagreeing on courses of action and enacting disputes aids in consti-
tuting group and organizational identities. It questions how ritualized conflict
management becomes productive and beneficial, not only through obtaining
particular goals, but through promoting effective communication and building relationships from the on-going struggle between intergroup forces. This

struggle extends beyond the traditional boundaries of collective bargaining to coalitions between members of opposing groups, alliances with external ties, and interdependent organizational linkages that give symbolic meaning to this event.

Research on teachers' negotiation

This research consists of naturalistic studies of two different teachers' negotiations. The study employs a multiple-case design with the bargaining events of two different school districts as the units of analysis. Specific analyses centre on the type of interaction that takes place between bargainers, between negotiators and team members, and between teams and their constituents about the bargaining events. These case analyses address the following exploratory questions: 1. What functions does collective bargaining serve and how are they enacted in the negotiation? 2. What types of relationships form among negotiation participants, constituents and audiences? How do these relationships contribute to the productive side of conflict? 3. What was the symbolic significance of bargaining? How do these meanings contribute to the benefits of negotiation?

Participants and school districts

Two different school districts were included in this study. Both districts had engaged in collective bargaining for seven years. Under the state law that governed public sector bargaining, management must negotiate issues of salary, hours, fringe benefits and grievances. Management must discuss either in collective bargaining or in alternative meetings the issues of working conditions, curriculum, class size, pupil–teacher ratio, reduction in force and budget appropriations, but they were not required to include these items in the contract. However, once they appeared in the contract, these items were negotiable. If a settlement was not reached in the bargaining, the parties could employ fact finding or mediation. Binding arbitration was not included in the contract of either district nor in the state law; strikes were unlawful in this state. The state ranked 48th in its aid to public education; hence teachers' salaries had been considerably below the national average for several years.

The first district, comprising 155 teachers, 6 schools and 3,300 students, was located in a small farming community of 11,500 people. The teachers' team consisted of eleven teachers and a professional negotiator from the state teachers' association. The board's team was represented by five elected school board members, two principals, a superintendent and a hired professional negotiator. Negotiations consisted of two pre-negotiation meetings for each side, two eight-minute sessions at the table, four two-hour caucus meetings and three thirty-minute private meetings (side-bars) between the two negotiators, and settled in ten hours.

The second district exemplified a more traditional bargaining process. This district, comprising 485 teachers, 10 schools and 8,055 students, was represented by six teachers and six administrators. No elected board members served on the administrators' negotiating team. This district was located in a large metropolitan area of approximately 750,000 people. The two sides met on nine separate days and bargained for thirty hours with an additional twenty-five hours of caucus and pre-negotiation sessions. The chief negotiator for the teachers' team was the current president of the local teachers' association; the assistant superintendent bargained for the administrators; hence, neither side hired professional negotiators.

Data collection

The data for this study was collected through participant observation, interviews, analysis of documents and survey questionnaires. In the participant observation method, the researcher and three assistants took short-hand notes of verbatim talk during the negotiations. These sessions were transcribed into approximately 2,800 pages of field notes.

In addition, the researchers conducted 38 one-hour, focused interviews with chief negotiators, members of both teams, teachers who were active in past negotiations, and members of central administration. The interviews employed open-ended questions on perceptions of conflict issues in the organization, discussions of conflict management activities in the organization, questions on the history and development of collective bargaining in the district and in the state, stories of pre- and post-bargaining activities, perceptions of the relationships among multiple parties involved in the process (namely the bargainers, the teams, the constituents, the parents, the community and the state legislator); questions about the philosophies of the bargainers; and queries about the meaning or significance of the bargaining process.

Documents included past contracts, initial proposals, counterproposals, final settlements, memoranda sent to constituents, agendas of meetings and press releases. The survey included items on the functions of bargaining; the processing of information with constituents before, during and after the bargaining; general and comparative satisfaction with the settlement; perceptions of bargainer effectiveness; and background information on each respondent.

Data analysis

This study entails two stages of analysis: assessment of responses to survey items on the functions of bargaining and insights on the benefits of conflict from participant observation and interviews. In the first stage, the researcher examined the results of seven rank-ordered items in District 1 and eight seven-point Likert items for District 2. The seven rank-ordered items were: 'Rank order the most important functions that bargaining performs in your district by placing a 1 for the most important and a 7 for the least important'. The seven items were: settle critical differences; exchange information between the board and the teachers; clarify misunderstandings between the sides; make decisions about on-going, daily operations; legitimate the rights of teachers; obtain an equitable settlement for salary and fringe benefits; and provide a means for keeping the school board from restricting the rights of teachers. The eight Likert items for District 2 asked teachers, 'To what extent does bargaining in your district perform the following functions?' These were: (1) settle differences between teachers and administrators; (2) provide a means of information exchange between teachers and administrators on current problems; (3) provide a means of signalling potential problem areas to the other side; (4) clarify misunderstandings and misinterpretations on important issues; (5) make decisions about on-going, daily operations; (6) provide a way of maintaining the legitimate rights of teachers; (7) provide a way of getting equitable salary and fringe benefits for teachers; and (8) influence administrative decisions on policy issues and teacher working conditions. Teachers responded on a seven-point scale from 1 = not at all to 7 = to a great extent for each statement. Scores on each statement were grouped into categories of high, moderate and low. Only those scores in the high category are reported in this study. Scores on each statement were also correlated with three satisfaction items, which were: (1) To what extent were you satisfied with the contract this year? (2) How does your satisfaction with this year's overall contract compare with your satisfaction with previous contracts? and (3) To what extent did this year's settlement exceed your expectations? I calculated scores for each of the three items and correlated each item with each of the eight functions of bargaining.

Survey data provided markers for the second stage of analysis: synthesizing case material collected through interviews, participant observation and ethnographic analysis. Responses to Questions 2 and 3 were addressed through qualitative analyses. That is, the qualitative analysis was used to determine how conflict contributed to relationship patterns and what was the symbolic significance of negotiation. Notes were taken on the interpretations or consensual meanings of the bargaining event and on descriptions of relationships between and among negotiators, teams, constituents and audiences.

Results and discussion

For the first district, 75 of the 155 teachers returned the survey, representing a response rate of 51%. Of those who responded to these items on the survey, 76% or 57 respondents were highly or moderately satisfied with the contract. Compared with previous years 40% or 30 of the respondents were more satisfied than in the past while 48% or 45 of them felt their satisfaction was about the same. For the metropolitan school district, 128 of the 200 randomly sampled teachers returned the survey, yielding a response rate of 63%. In this sample 83% or 106 of the respondents were highly or moderately satisfied with the contract; 61% or 78 respondents were more satisfied than they were with past agreements, and 52% or 67 teachers saw the settlement as greatly exceeding their expectations. As a whole, then, the two districts were generally pleased with the settlements that they reached.

Functions and task benefits of negotiation

To address Question 1, what functions did collective bargaining serve and how are they enacted in the negotiation, I calculated the mean ranks for the seven survey items in District 1 and determined a new rank order based on these means. Teachers indicated that bargaining served (1) to get equitable salary and fringe benefits ($m=2.15$); (2) to establish the legitimate rights of teachers ($m=3.11$); (3) to settle critical differences between the teachers and the school board ($m=3.23$); (4) to clarify misunderstandings ($m=3.86$); (5) to exchange information with board members ($m=4.12$); (6) to provide a means for keeping the school board from restricting the rights of teachers ($m=5.79$); and (7) to facilitate decisions about on-going, daily operations ($m=6.18$). In these results, the primary benefits of negotiation were obtaining benefits and maintaining the legitimate rights of the teachers. Even though the top-ranked functions focused primarily on rights, the teachers also felt that bargaining helped them resolve differences between the sides, helped clarify misunder-standings and aided in the exchange of information. Survey data, then, indicated that improving communication between the parties was an impor-tant outcome of negotiation.

This side-effect of conflict management also surfaced in District 2 in responses to the survey. Respondents indicated that bargaining functions to a great extent by helping teachers get salary and fringe benefits (78%, $n=100$); maintaining teachers' rights (74%, $n=95$); signalling potential problems (72%, $n=92$); clarifying misunderstandings (64%, $n=82$); exchanging information (59%, $n=76$); influencing administrative decisions (40%, $n=51$); and making decisions about daily operations (31%, $n=40$). Hence, the primary benefits of bargaining were similar to the rank order in District 1. Bargaining was a means of obtaining salary and fringe benefits as well as protecting teacher rights. However, other valuable functions that negotiation performed were signalling problems, clarifying misunderstandings and exchanging informa-tion.

To determine which functions contributed to bargaining satisfaction, I correlated responses on the eight benefits items with those on the bargaining satisfaction items. Exchanging information and reaching common under-standings of events accounted for 29% of the variance in predicting satisfaction with the contract and 22% of the variance in predicting satisfac-tion compared with previous contracts. Correlation of the eight benefit items with satisfaction with the contract compared to previous years and degree to which the settlement exceeded expectations revealed differences between these functions. Since these analyses entailed running multiple correlations and incurring potential error, only coefficients at 0.33 or higher ($p < 0.001$) were incorporated into these results.

Interestingly, high satisfaction in comparison with previous contracts was tied to gains in salary and fringe benefits (r =0.45, n=126) and to receiving settlements that maintained teachers' rights (r =0.42, n=123). But, for a negotiated settlement to exceed expectations, it must serve as a means for exchanging information (r =0.36, n=123), signalling potential problems (r =0.33, n=122), clarifying misunderstandings (r =0.37, n=122) and influencing administrators' decisions (r =0.35, n=122). Interviews and surveys converged in their emphasis on the communication benefit of bargaining, a function that extends beyond the labour relations benefit of gaining rights and resources (Dunlap, 1985). Hence, exchanging information, clarifying misunderstandings and signalling potential problems contributed both to the productive nature of organizational conflict and to satisfaction with the settlement. An examination of the ethnographic data reveals subtleties in the way that bargaining performed these functions.

Gaining information and reaching mutual understanding   Bargaining functioned as a catalyst for identifying and defining problems and reaching understanding by enabling members to negotiate the meanings of organizational events. As Susie, the negotiator for District 2, stated: 'I think bargaining is primarily a medium for exchange of ideas. Many issues cannot be solved between labor and management except at the bargaining table because they have two separate philosophies . . . Issues are not solved because of blank walls between them . . . The trick is getting them to hear something that they never really heard before. Their purposes for doing something may have never been known to you before. Through this exchange you get feedback going that widens the understanding of the problem.'

Ironically, a close examination of the bargaining transcripts suggested that negotiators engaged primarily in arguments for and against their positions. Arguments centred on the rationale for changing the status quo, workability of alternative proposals and disadvantages of these proposals (Putnam, 1990; Putnam & Wilson, 1989). When information was exchanged in an explicit manner, it served as evidence for a bargainer's contention. Information sharing, then, was ambiguous, cryptic and guarded rather than open and honest as some proponents of integrative bargaining would suggest (Pruitt & Lewis, 1975; Walton & McKersie, 1965). Both sides revealed their knowledge of activities, events and organizational circumstances through the subtle use of examples, causal explanations and analogies (Putnam & Geist, 1985). For example, in discussing the problem of placing reprimand notes in a teacher's file, negotiators discovered that both sides were using different definitions of a file. Sharing examples and providing analogies helped participants understand the other side's definition of the problem. If bargaining facilitates clarifying misunderstandings, exchanging information and reaching common understandings, these functions are achieved indirectly rather than explicitly.

An example of exchanging information and sharing interpretations occurred in deliberations about a proposed preparation period for faculty who were assigned four or more 'preps' in one term. The administration opposed the teacher's proposal because it was too costly, but the teachers argued firmly against the inequities of the current system. A lengthy debate on this issue led to discussions about the scheduling process. The scheduling process, then, became a vehicle for reframing the proposal on teacher preparation time. In effect, if changes were made in the scheduling system to reduce the number of different preparations that teachers were assigned, then the need for a designated preparation period would be reduced.

Through confronting one another on initial proposals, both sides uncovered problems with scheduling that impinged directly on the proposed preparation period. Conflict between the sides provided a forum for discovering related problems. In this instance, knowledge or mutual understanding accrued from a heated conflict that led to reframing of the problem. Although information was exchanged on the number of teachers with four or more preparations, on the harmfulness of this situation, on the costs of additional preparation periods and on the scheduling process, it served as an attack on the opponent's position or a defence of each party's stance. In effect, the ritualistic activities of exchanging offers, attacking and defending positions, and cooperating by competing, imparted information through signals, hints and ambiguities. Information exchange, then, functioned as a sharing of insights or a basis for 'seeing the other person's point of view' that evolved from the act of bargaining.

Facilitating decision making   Although opinions varied as to whether bargaining improved decision making, most respondents saw negotiation as a way of clarifying problems and providing input on decisions. In District 1 respondents ranked making policy decisions in day-to-day operations as the least beneficial function of negotiation. In District 2 bargaining settlements exceeded expectations if participants influenced decision making, but only 24% ($n=31$) of the respondents thought that negotiations produced effective decisions.

Effectiveness of the settlements was limited by the reliance on past formulas to reach bargaining settlements; the use of packaging, logrolling or other compromise alternatives to get agreements; and the employment of pressure tactics to persuade opponents and team members to accept proposals. For example, in District 1, participants employed a ritual of reaching decisions by trading contract language items for money issues. Thus, the participants failed to engage in effective decision making on issues of teacher evaluation, academic freedom and binding arbitration. Bargainers reached less than an optimal settlement on salary through logrolling pay on extracurricular salaries into regular salaries. Thus, coaches received only a 5% increment for extracurricular pay while teachers were given a 6% overall salary boost. In both districts, pressure tactics prevent participants from engaging in effective problem solving on issues of grievance and binding arbitration.

Moreover, bargaining research revealed that bias and faulty judgment processes moderated the effects of conflict on bargaining decisions (Bazerman, 1983; Neale & Bazerman, 1985). That is, given a negotiator's tendency to engage in systematic bias and overconfidence, bargaining might not be a forum for effective decision making.

However, negotiation contributed to effective problem identification. For example, in District 1, both sides began the negotiation by defining the problem with insurance as one of rising premiums. The teachers wanted the board to pay additional rates and match the percentage that they paid for administrator premiums. The board claimed that they could not afford the teachers' proposal. After extensive confrontation on the insurance rates, participants began to raise issues of the insurance carrier and the extensiveness of the coverage in their plans. The problem then switched from one of insurance rates to the number of 'extras' included in the insurance coverage.

Even though this conflict transformed the insurance problem, participants could not reach agreement on an effective solution. Thus, they referred the item to a committee. As a whole, this study indicated that bargaining was not a forum for vigilant decision making. Rather, negotiation facilitated effective problem identification and provided inputs for future policy deliberations.

Relationship benefits among negotiators, teams and constituents

The items listed on the survey questionnaire probed the ways that bargaining contributed to instrumental or task-related benefits. Conflict in negotiation, however, also facilitated the building of relationships, coalitions and alliances. Question 2 of the research, how does negotiation form webs of relationships among constituents and audiences, was analysed through interview and participant observation data. Specifically, the multi-group nature of negotiation made it a medium for redefining coalitions within groups, for forming alliances between members of opposing groups, and for tightening or loosening ties with constituents and publics. These interlocking networks furthered efforts to reaching a mutually satisfactory outcome by introducing variation into the system and by de-escalating conflict. That is, this complex web of relationships fostered the productive side of conflict by promoting friendships across groups, facilitating intergroup understanding and reducing reliance on rigid stereotypes.

Participants in the bargaining were intertwined in intergroup networks. Board members as elected officials of the community were concerned with managing the tax dollar; yet these individuals were often parents who were active in the school system. Seven administrators on the bargaining teams were former teachers in the district and had been active in the local union at one time. Two of the teachers involved in the bargaining aspired to be administrators. The professional negotiator for District 1 worked for the state and national teachers' union. These linkages provided both sides with frames of reference that extended outside their team. Members of each unit were able to make arguments for the other side, comment on the legitimacy of the opponent's arguments and place the issues in a broad spectrum.

In interviews and interactions during caucus sessions, participants made references to the linkages among and between bargainers, team members, constituents and audiences (Lewicki & Litterer, 1985). These linkages revealed shared differences in task and socio-emotional ties as Friedman and Podolny (1992) found in their study of boundary spanning patterns between negotiators and constituents. That is, certain linkages specialized in role functions. Three types of intergroup linkages surfaced in this analysis: common enemies, coalitions between opponents and alliances with audiences.

In both districts, the opposing teams developed common enemies. These were often shared through stories and references to past practices. In District 1 both sides recalled with disdain the lawyer who controlled the board's rigidity and the teachers' bargainer who was militant and hostile. They were unified in a goal to exclude such participants from the bargaining process. Moreover, the teachers and several board members shared reservations about the superintendent – particularly concerning his ability to communicate with the teachers and the students. In District 2 both sides shared common enemies in the desire to exclude outside intervention – 'no fact finding and mediation for us. We want a settlement without the interference of lawyers and outsiders.' Moreover, both sides had difficulty dealing with John, the accountant who held the purse strings to the corporation. As one teacher explained, 'Nobody understands John. He has a way of complicating an already complex budget by using 18-month fiscal reports for a 12-month time frame. No one, not even the administrators, trusts the accountant.' These common enemies not only unified the sides with superordinate goals, but provided scepticism that promoted commitment to the process and flexibility of action. The sides were unified in their shared enemies. They remained flexible and committed to reaching a satisfactory settlement through their shared desire to keep outsiders, e.g. fact finders and mediators, away from the bargaining process.

Opposing groups were also united through symbolic and actual coalitions. Symbolic coalitions formed as one or two teachers took the administrators' position in deliberating with their team members and as administrators and board members reminded their constituents of the plight of teaching. One board member commented, 'Why are we hassling over ½%? Give them the money. Teachers make less than UPS drivers.'

Coalitions also formed when members of each team had informal exchanges outside the bargaining. One of the administrators in District 2 even attended a party in which several teachers talked with him about negotiation issues. He was typically sympathetic with the teachers' position on issues. The two professional negotiators in District 1 were friends, bargained against each other in other districts, and had coffee together after the negotiations. Two of the board members in District 1 worked with several teachers on programmes for improving the middle school's math curriculum. One of them had opposed the principal's stand on this innovative programme. Hence, symbolic and actual coalitions across groups reduced the bipolar nature of disputes and revealed intergroup tensions among individuals on the same team. These intergroup tensions promoted diversity and guarded against groupthink within each team.

Finally, in the past both districts had turned to parents, the public and the local community for support in advocating their positions. Although these alliances had pressured one side or the other to concede on key points, they had also constrained the bargaining process. Hence, in both districts, alliances with audiences that were not directly involved in the process were measures of last resort. Teachers and administrators in both districts shared stories about the detrimental effects of 'going public with the dispute'. Past contacts with external groups served the symbolic function of pressuring for agreements with statements like, 'We don't want them to go back to the shopping centres and hand out leaflets about the district', and 'This issue is hardly worth having the parents call the board members every night to appeal for a settlement.' Thus, both sides concurred that the teams should strive for joint agreement without appealing to external audiences. Alliances with external audiences, then, functioned like common enemies to form an implicit pact between opposing groups. In effect, webs of contact systems and relationships among the parties and stakeholders to the process provided common ground for the two sides, de-escalated volatile arguments and introduced flexibility and variety into the system. These factors, in turn, facilitated understanding and the commitment to reach a mutual agreement.

The symbolic significance of bargaining

In addition to the instrumental and task-related benefits of negotiation, bargaining helps to make sense of organizational identities and to address power relationships among groups – in other words, it takes on a symbolic significance (see Question 3 of the research). Trice and Beyer (1984) see bargaining as a type of worker participation that helps nullify hostile and dissatisfied groups. Negotiation then symbolizes the willingness of authorities to cope with problems, to listen and to pay attention to the complaints of participants. Moreover, it minimizes status differences and emphasizes equality.

The administrators and board members in this study treated bargaining as a necessary rite, like 'going to church on Sunday morning'. They claimed that it was not the settlement nor the details of the final agreement that made a difference. It was the symbolic process of producing a contract, sharing unsolved problems and collaborating to release tensions and to manage recurring differences. It was a tradition that kept people thinking that everything was normal.

The teachers, in contrast, viewed the rite as a communication forum for raising issues that administrators had ignored or handled poorly throughout the year and for identifying problems that would become major issues if they were not addressed. One teacher described bargaining as a tennis match in which the ball got bigger as it went back and forth between the sides. Neither side really had a firm grasp on it, but both tried to shape and control it.

Another teacher noted that bargaining was really not a power play – only the state legislature had the power. Ironically, most participants in this study felt powerless in exerting any real control over resource distribution.

Administrators felt constrained by board members; board members saw their authority as restricted by public sentiment, the law and the legislature; teachers were repressed by administrators and the board; and the union was handicapped by the law. Each group felt that the ultimate authority resided outside of their control and often outside of the immediate bargaining context. As a direct resource to the bargaining, power was not a central element.

However, each of the groups had varying degrees of power over the outcomes of the dispute. Within the limitations of the system, bargaining contributed to the balance of power between administrators and teachers regarding decisions about reduction in force, teacher evaluation, sabbatical and personal leaves, and assignments to extra-curricular duties. Negotiation, then, seemed to balance expert, referent and informational bases of power, but not monetary rewards and punishments nor legitimate power. Bargaining also served as a form of symbolic power – a rite for demonstrating that two opposing parties can sit down together and work things out.

These comments indicated that one of the most beneficial aspects of the bargaining rite was to manage the forces that constrained action and the practical problems that called for resolution (Cassirer, 1946). School districts could not raise taxes to increase funds for improving curriculum, purchasing classroom computers or remodelling buildings. In effect, bargaining helped both sides deal with their feelings of powerlessness in raising levy limitations for school districts, controlling state allocations to education and recovering the status once associated with the position of an educator.

Conclusion

This study suggests that as a form of conflict management in organizations, bargaining can be productive, but not for the reasons put forward by some conflict theorists. In this study bargaining functions as a forum for discovering problems and for revealing the opponent's perspective on issues. This function, rather than emanating from explicit information exchanges, stems from implicit learning gleaned through engaging in the dispute. Bargaining also serves to manage differences of opinion and recurring disagreements, but rarely does it deal with the underlying conflicts of interest that form the basis of the dispute. Although bargaining helps in decision making, its value may lie with identifying and signalling problems rather than reaching the best solution. As Trice & Beyer (1984) note, the bargaining rite signifies participatory decision making, but only in realms that both parties can control. In this public sector setting, bargaining may be a means of coping rather than sharing power.

Finally, the productive nature of bargaining seems to hinge on relationships among and between members of intra- and inter-organizational groups. These relationships promote diversity and perpetuate conflicts within and among teams, constituents and publics. Both the enactment and the symbolic significance of this on-going struggle aids in perpetuating conflicts. What keeps the struggle from escalating and destroying the organization is its reliance on overlapping and intergroup relationships that make bargaining not simply a confrontation between labour and management, but an event in which multiple groups interact prior to, during and after the negotiation.

An additional factor that promotes 'flexible stability' of intergroup conflict is crossovers among members of various groups that are party to the bargaining. Hence, negotiators and team members in the conflict develop formal and informal allegiances which lead to divided loyalties across groups and which aid in diffusing polarized conflict (Friedman, 1992). This diversity, in turn, may contribute to flexibility and to innovation in the organization.

The findings of this study have implications for practice, ones rooted in using negotiation to further implicit coordination. These implications centre on shaping expectations about the process and training negotiators to focus on the subtle cues that shape the relational and identity aspects of bargaining. Negotiators need to be trained to use controversy and argumentation to discover problems, to reveal different frames of references, and to understand codes and signals. Telling stories or providing analogies can build common bonds, save the opponent's face, and provide indirect ways of signalling needs and interests. Bargainers need to stay committed to the pursuit of a settlement and to follow new directions that broaden or redefine the nature of a problem. Finally, negotiation teams need to foster diversity within groups and build unity between groups through overlapping experiences, cross memberships and indirect alliances. Although bargaining is not panacea for organizational ills, it provides an intriguing model of productive conflict – one rooted in implicit coordination.

Note

This text first appeared as an article in *International Journal of Conflict Management*, 1994, 5(3), at 285 to 299.

References

Bacharach, S. B. and Lawler, E.J. (1981). *Bargaining: Power, tactics, and outcomes*. San Francisco: Jossey-Bass.

Bazerman, M.H. (1983). Negotiator judgment. *American Behavioral Scientist, 27*, 211–28.

Cassirer, E. (1946). *Myth of the state*. New Haven, CT: Yale University Press.

Coser, L.A. (1956). *The functions of social conflict*. New York: Free Press.

Cosier, R.A. (1978). The effects of three potential aids for making strategic decisions on prediction accuracy. *Organizational Behavior and Human Performance, 22*, 295–306.

Deutsch, M. (1969). Conflicts: Productive and destructive. *Journal of Social Issues, 25*, 7–41.

Dunlap, J.T. (1985). *Industrial relations systems*. New York: Holt, Rinehart & Winston.

Folger, J.P., Poole, M.S. and Stutman, R.K. (1993). *Working through conflict* (2nd edn). New York: Harper Collins.

Friedman, R.A. (1992). The culture of mediation: Private understandings in the context of public conflict, in D.M. Kolb and J.M. Bartunek (eds), *Hidden conflict in organizations*. Newbury Park, CA: Sage, pp. 143–64.

Friedman, R.A. and Podolny, J. (1992). Differentiation of boundary spanning roles: Labor negotiations and implications for role conflict. *Administrative Science Quarterly*, *37*, 28–47.

Hall, J. and Williams, M.S. (1966). A comparison of decision making performances in established and ad hoc groups. *Journal of Personality and Social Psychology*, *23*, 214–22.

Hocker, J.L. and Wilmot, W.W. (1985). *Interpersonal conflict* (2nd edn). Dubuque, IA: William C. Brown.

Lewicki, R.J. & Litterer, J.A. (1985). *Negotiation*. Homewood, IL: Richard D. Irwin.

Mason, R.O. and Mitroff, I.I. (1981). *Challenging strategic planning assumptions*. New York: Wiley-Interscience.

Neale, M.A. and Bazerman, M.H. (1985). The effects of framing and negotiator overconfidence on bargaining behaviors and outcomes. *Academy of Management Journal*, *28*, 34–49.

Pfeffer, J. (1981). *Power in organizations*. Marshfield, MA: Pitman.

Pondy, L.R. (1989). Reflections on organizational conflict. *Journal of Organizational Change Management*, *2*, 94–8.

Pruitt, D.G. and Lewis, S.A. (1975). Development of integrative solutions in bilateral negotiations. *Journal of Personality and Social Psychology*, *31*, 621–33.

Putnam, L.L. (1990). Reframing integrative and distributive bargaining: a process perspective, in B.H. Sheppard, M.H. Bazerman and R.J. Lewicki (eds), *Research on negotiation in organizations*. Greenwich, CT: JAI Press, Vol. 2, pp. 3–30.

Putnam, L.L. and Geist, P. (1985). Argument in bargaining: an analysis of the reasoning process. *The Southern Speech Communication Journal*, *50*, 225–45.

Putnam, L.L. and Poole, M.S. (1987). Conflict and negotiation, in F.M. Jablin, L.L. Putnam, K.H. Roberts and L.W. Porter (eds), *Handbook of Organizational Communication*. Beverly Hills, CA: Sage, pp. 549–99.

Putnam, L.L. and Wilson, S.R. (1989). Argumentation and bargaining strategies as discriminators of integrative outcomes, in M.A. Rahim (ed.), *Managing conflict: an interdisciplinary approach*. New York: Praeger, pp. 121–41.

Robbins, S.P. (1978). 'Conflict management' and 'conflict resolution' are not synonymous terms. *California Management Review*, *21*, 67–75.

Schweiger, D.M., Sandberg, W.R. and Ragan, J.W. (1986). Group approaches for improving strategic decision making: a comparative analysis of dialectical inquiry, devil's advocacy, and consensus. *Academy of Management Journal*, *29*, 51–71.

Trice, H.M. and Beyer, J.M. (1984). Studying organizational cultures through rites and ceremonials. *Academy of Management Review*, *9*, 653–69.

Walton, R. E. and McKersie, R.B. (1965). *A behavioral theory of labor negotiations: an analysis of a social interaction system*. New York: McGraw-Hill.

Weick, K.E. (1979). *The social psychology of organizing* (2nd edn). Reading, MA: Addison-Wesley.

11

Constructive for Whom? The Fate of Diversity Disputes in Organizations

Anne Donnellon and Deborah M. Kolb

A junior faculty member complains to his university ombudsman that one of the senior faculty members has been making unwanted sexual advances to him. The senior faculty member denies the allegations. In confidential consultations with both parties, the ombudsman works out an agreement that the senior faculty member will exempt himself from any role in decisions affecting the junior person's career, specifically tenure. The agreement satisfies both parties. Two years later, the junior faculty member is denied tenure and sues the University claiming that there is a systematic pattern of homophobia within the department that has a chilling effect on many junior faculty members. The school prides itself on valuing diversity.

The partners of a franchised distributorship, one African-American and the other white American, are working to turn around the performance of their franchise. Faced with declining market share and a drop off in sales, they try to introduce a new distribution system. The new system brings to light performance problems among the salesforce but it also divides the company along functional and racial lines. The salesforce, predominantly African-American reports to the African-American partner, and the finance and operations people, mostly white Americans, report to the white partner. The white partner's proposal to terminate poor performers in sales is met with an accusation of racism and discrimination by the African-American partner. (Thomas, 1992)

After the birth of her second child, a five-year associate negotiates with her managers a part-time work schedule in the accounting firm where she works. A consistently high performer, she anticipates making partner at the usual time. However, she is turned down when the committee decides that she does not have the breadth of experience required of a partner. She complains to the managing partner and he agrees to look into the matter. Recent hiring data shows that the firm is having trouble attracting women.

Managers and dispute resolution professionals increasingly find themselves involved in conflicts like these, which can have significant legal and performance implications. Organizations are investing heavily to enhance the capacity of their members to deal with conflict – through restructuring, training and the design of dispute resolution systems. These practices of constructive conflict management have been used to resolve significant organizational disputes successfully. The problem, however, is that the practices of constructive conflict management leave the type of dispute represented above either essentially unaddressed or resolved in a way that is not constructive for all parties. The type of disputes that are problematic are those arising out of, or complicated by, social diversity.

As new social groups enter the workforce and move up in organizations, conflicts rooted in class, gender, race and ethnicity have become more prominent. Existing definitions of what it means to manage conflict constructively fail to take account of the fact that the workforce is more heterogeneous than it has been at any time in the past. Furthermore, this is happening at the same time as organizations, faced with new competitive challenges, are instituting new structures that make conflict more prevalent.

In new organizational forms, that have variously been described as networks, clusters and/or post-bureaucracies, the established lines of authority and formalized rules and procedures are gone. The requirements for getting work done reside less in the exercise of authority and more in the ability to communicate and negotiate with a wide variety of members of an organization. Conflict is the essence of these organizations, inherent in the very fabric of their designs. As a result, there is a great deal of interest on the part of organizations and their members in finding new ways to deal with conflict constructively.

To deal with conflict constructively, however, is complicated by the changing character of the workforce. Changing demography and demand for labour has resulted in a workforce that is considerably more diverse than its cohort even ten years ago. This diversity inside the organization's walls imports and creates social conflict. As society's conflicts get played out on the organizational stage, they become intertwined with individual performance, career development and other critical human resource issues. Although this is not itself a new phenomenon, the current intersection of changing demography and new organizational forms has exacerbated these tendencies.

Our purpose here is to explore the ways that organizations can learn to deal *constructively* with conflicts that have their bases in social diversity. In order to do that, we need to consider how these issues are talked about, understood and managed within existing theories and practices of dispute resolution, i.e. the discourses of organizational conflict. There are three discourses of organizational conflict management, which we discuss in the following section. No discourse exists for disputes arising from diversity. There are a number of explanations for the suppression of these conflicts; we discuss these in the second section. The consequences of suppressing diversity are discussed in a third section. In the concluding section, we consider what possibilities exist for managing conflict in a more inclusive and constructive manner, using the introductory vignettes.

Discourses of organizational conflict management

Groups of people, and organizations in particular, develop discourses for everything they do. By discourse, we mean the accepted ways of thinking, talking and acting in specific arenas (Scott, 1988). What is important about discourses is that over time, they come to be seen as natural and are, therefore, unquestioned. Because they are taken for granted, they exert powerful influence on action. For example, for many years the discourse on child care has gone by the label of 'mothering'. One effect of this discourse was that concerns about work and family were seen and treated as a women's issue. Ways of thinking and acting in the child care arena are beginning to change, partially as a result of a new discourse of 'parenting', that includes not only discussions of fathers as primary caregivers, but also emergent organizational policies on flexible schedules and release time for parents of either gender.

There are three dominant discourses on the constructive management of organizational conflict. There is a structural discourse that says: organizations can deal with conflict by changing their structure (Kolb, 1986; Miles, 1980). There is a process discourse that says: organizations can help people negotiate their differences (Bazerman & Lewicki, 1983). Finally, there is a complaint or grievance discourse that says: organizations can pursue conflicts via a formal dispute resolution system (Ewing, 1989; Ury, Brett & Goldberg, 1988).

The structural discourse of organizational conflict focuses on the necessity for increasing functional specialization, the inevitable conflict that results from such structural arrangements, and the kinds of structural changes needed to deal with conflicts that arise between organizational entities (Lawrence & Lorsch, 1967; Thompson, 1967; Walton & Dutton, 1969). These changes include the creation of specialized roles and lateral groups such as task forces and teams that are superimposed on existing functional structures (Donnellon, 1983; Galbraith, 1977; Lawrence & Lorsch, 1967). The purpose of these structural changes is to reduce the conflicts that occur between members with diverse organizational interests. To the degree that gender, race or ethnicity are factors in conflict, they are masked within an organizational group focus (Alderfer, 1986).

The process discourse has developed as new, less hierarchical, organizational forms have become more prevalent. In the decision making of such organizations, groups (and individuals) with relatively equivalent power but different interests and resources need negotiation skills in order to establish their influence and control and secure what they need to do their work (Bazerman & Lewicki, 1983; Lax & Sebenius, 1986). Here the assumption is that individuals need to, and can, acquire the skills necessary to deal constructively with conflicts as they arise in the normal course of doing the work. In these negotiations, power and influence are derived from organizational and transorganizational dependencies and strategic orientation (Pfeffer & Salancik, 1978; Zucker, 1977). The issues to be negotiated are those that cover more or less routine issues in the workplace such as task responsibilities, resource allocation, performance evaluations and schedules. In the discourse of negotiation, individuals speak for themselves or their group seeking to resolve the inevitable differences that occur in the process of doing business. To the degree that these routine issues intersect with matters of race, gender, class and ethnicity, social group concerns tend to be downplayed or ignored.[1,2]

The third form of discourse concerns constructive conflict in formal dispute systems. While grievance procedures have long been a fixture in union–management agreements, more recently a wide array of organizations have installed complaint systems that are intended to give employees voice in the expression of their grievances (Edelman, 1990; Ewing, 1977; Hirschman, 1970; Rowe, 1987; Ury et al., 1988; Westin & Feliu, 1988; Ziegenfuss, 1988). The promise of an 'open door', the availability of an ombudsman, a peer complaint board and/or a multi-step grievance procedure are often instituted as means of addressing conflicts within the organization. Indeed, in apparent contradiction to our claim here that organizations prefer to suppress social conflict, this avenue is seen as a primary way for members of an organization to pursue complaints that have gender or racial significance.

In fact, a certain number of disputes that have their roots in gender and race relations in organizations do find their way into dispute systems, e.g. sexual and other forms of harassment, disparate treatment, etc. However, as a vehicle for organizations to deal with conflicts arising from diversity, the dispute system approach is problematic. First, the few studies that have looked into how these procedures are used find that relatively few disputes find their way into the formal channels and that negative consequences (performance evaluations and promotions) attend their use (Kolb, 1987; Lewin, 1987). The effect is exaggerated for women who are more reluctant than other groups to pursue complaints through formal channels because they fear the consequences (Gwartney-Gibbs & Lach, 1991). This is not surprising. Given existing power structures in contemporary organizations and the norms against public claiming (in the absence of unions), it is unlikely that these formal channels constitute a location where social conflict and grievances are to be worked out (Kolb, 1987).

Second, complaint systems by design are intended to handle individual problems. Individuals grieve over specific incidents. Indeed, people often experience bias as an individual problem. Racist remarks and sexist treatment are typically seen by the victims as the conscious or unconscious action of individuals (Kolb & Silbey, 1990). By trying to resolve these issues at the place where they occur – by mediating between a woman and her boss, for example – the problem remains an individual and isolated one. To the degree that the problem is more systemic and widespread, complaint systems are often ill-equipped to deal with them. Further, the confidentiality pledge that marks most procedures means that even if more widespread patterns do exist, the evidence to document these patterns is unlikely to accumulate (Kolb, 1987). Ironically, the presence of these procedures may act as a safety valve and keep disputes in check at the same time as they mask more pervasive problems. Finally, the burden is placed on individuals to resolve their differences without similar pressure on the organization to change its culture and practices that make disputes of the gender and racial sort more likely in the first place.

In these discourses, the management of conflict is assumed to be central to the smooth and integrated functioning of organizations. Whether conflict is managed through structures and rules (Lawrence & Lorsch, 1967), by learning more expert negotiation strategies (Bazerman & Neale, 1983; Lax & Sebenius, 1986) or by channelling disputes to complaint handling systems (Kolb, 1987; Ury et al., 1988), the implications are similar. Constructive conflict management means keeping disputes under control. It is in the interests of management to ensure that conflicts and disputes do not threaten the existing social order.

There is also a pervasive fear that disputes over race and gender, if aired, will be unpredictable, potentially explosive, and hard to contain. As a result, organizations and individuals employ discourses that seek to control these forces and have the effect of suppressing alternative discourses. Our perspective is, however, that such thinking is shortsighted. It fails to recognize that workforce diversity is inevitable, that this diversity infuses all aspects of organizational life, and that it holds enormous potential for creativity and learning in the organization. Such learning will not come without conflict. In order to respond to the challenges of the new organization and its demands for commitment and collaboration (Donnellon & Scully, 1992), members of organizations must learn not merely how to resolve diversity disputes, but also how to learn from them.

We are not yet there. There are good reasons for those who lead organizations to deal with conflicts in ways that deny their systemic social group basis. We turn next to a consideration of why issues arising from diversity are suppressed in the existing discourse of constructive conflict management and some of the consequences of doing so.

Suppressing diversity discourse in organizations

It is hard to get diversity into the discourse of organizations. When explanations for organizational conflict other than social diversity can be found, they tend to be asserted with such alacrity that those who would explore other causes are typically silenced. In effect, diversity as anything other than an abstract value or a rhetorical response to social concerns is still generally not discussed. In this section, we open up the discourse, by discussing four reasons for this suppression of the diversity explanation: the implicit challenge to the distribution of power, the ideology of individual merit, the absence of collective identity on the part of minorities, and the irresolvability of social conflict.

Social diversity and the distribution of power

Differences among people who are working together in a coordinated effort – whether these are differences of opinion, interest or social group membership – are threatening. Because social diversity entails a diversity of experience and interest, it challenges convention and working agreements. It creates ambiguity. Maybe new criteria for performance evaluation will be required and these may be difficult to define. Old timers may have to change their ways.

Barnard (1938), recognizing the potentially higher transaction costs that diverse groups incur, made the first, and perhaps only, written recommendation that executives should avoid such costs by hiring people of similar types:

> The general method of maintaining an informal executive organization is so to operate and to select and promote executives that a general condition of compatibility of personnel is maintained. Perhaps often and certainly occasionally men cannot be promoted or selected, or even must be relieved, because they cannot function, because they 'do not fit,' where there is no question of formal competence. This question of 'fitness' involves such matters as education, experience, age, sex, personal distinctions, prestige, race, nationality, faith, politics, sectional antecedents; and such very specific personal traits as manners, speech and personal appearance, etc. (p. 224)

Whether they heeded Barnard's advice, or had some intuitive understanding of the dynamics he described, or followed their tribal instinct, the managerial elite ruling US corporations has always been, and remains today, an essentially homogeneous group of white men. This is less true of the ranks below the executive, which are characterized by considerable demographic diversity. As such, we observe that power and diversity are in inverse relation: the more powerful the group, the less diverse it is likely to be.

Acknowledging or legitimizing diversity thus questions the prevailing order. Often such questions are feared as preliminaries to demands for redistribution of some sort. Self-interest may thus lead those in power to interpret demands for recognition of the impact of social diversity on organizational dynamics as an implicit (and illegitimate) challenge to their governance. Those in power generally favour peaceable resolution to conflict; those without power do not fear disruption so much (Sheppard, Lewicki & Minton, 1992).

People in power exercise control over most decisions that are made within the organization by controlling the premises under which decision making occurs (March & Simon, 1958). Thus, the powerful are able to preserve their positions, prerogatives (Michels, 1962) and even their own interpretations of experience (Gray, Donnellon & Bougon, 1985). The less powerful – most of whom tend to be people with less social status – are denied voice (Hirschman, 1970), the opportunity to assert one's own interpretations (Gray et al., 1985), except when it is channelled into formal dispute systems. Powerlessness thus persists, allowing the powerful people not just to retain their own power and privileges, but also to perpetuate the self-delusions that power is reasonably distributed and that privilege is based on merit (McIntosh, 1988).

The ideology of individual merit

One major obstacle in the progress towards legitimation of social diversity in organizations is the ideology of individual meritocracy (Scully, 1992). Meritocracy is governance by the people with the greatest merit (Young, 1958). The allocation of responsibility within an organization on the basis of merit is arguably the most cherished tenet of the bureaucratic form of organization (Donnellon & Scully, 1992). To this day, the belief that organizational power is allocated according to individual merit, rather than privilege or social rank, is a major motivational force binding employees to their organizations and in silencing challenges to the existing order. In the egalitarian US culture, the belief that everyone can achieve his or her goals through unstinting individual effort is so profound that it shapes all of the major institutions of US society, from educational design to healthcare practices to government policy.

But this ideology of meritocracy is problematic for diversity and dispute resolution. Individual merit is becoming harder to assess, as work becomes more complex and tasks create more interdependencies (Donnellon & Scully, 1992). This means that assessment, as it becomes more subjective, is becoming more susceptible to self-serving bias (Gioia & Sims, 1985; Miller & Ross, 1975; Rand & Wexley, 1975). Performance assessors, likely to be from the dominant group (or to have internalized the values of that group), are apt to perceive differences in performance (often merely stylistic) as deficiencies (Kanter, 1977; Murphy & Cleveland, 1991). Through this typically tacit process, 'performance deficiencies' become 'correlated with' the observable differences in gender, race or ethnic origin. Thus, the vicious cycle of diversity, perceptual bias and disparate outcomes is likely to reinforce the existing social order.

The use of objective metrics to qualify candidates for certain roles was, of course, one of the major legitimizations of bureaucracy. The majority of people continue to believe that, on balance, such measures produce fair treatment. As they decry the ineffectiveness of bureaucracies, they continue to subscribe to the myth of the meritocracy that most people get what they deserve. Thus, people are ideologically more likely to prefer explanations that are based on individual differences and less likely to look for additional, and perhaps more significant, factors such as social bias.

The absence of collective identity

The ideology of individual merit is so deeply ingrained that individuals tend to ignore their collective identities, resist group memberships and deny that collective identities influence what happens to them. They prefer to strive for individual distinction, for reasons both positive and negative. Thus, they consciously or unconsciously ignore what collective bases for conflict may exist and so close out some avenues of conflict resolution.

As Kanter (1977) pointed out, people who are in the minority in organizations have higher visibility than majority group members. In these times of increased corporate sensitivity to public image with regard to social diversity, individuals who are of a minority type and who excel may be offered unusual opportunities. While these opportunities may be due as much to their minority group membership as to their own merit, individuals are likely to find it more congruent with their sense of self to attribute their position to their own meritorious performance. Thus, they may hope to avoid marginalization or tokenism by the majority and may be surprised when their fellow minority group members seek coalitions or assistance from them.

Without a collective identity, the only course open is individual complaint. But here because current practice in performance assessment is consistent with the ideology of meritocracy, disputes that are claimed to have arisen from social diversity are likely to be treated by organizational representatives as self-interested individual manipulations of larger societal issues. Those who press their claims on the grounds of social diversity are marginalized as malcontents, troublemakers or social activists.

Anticipating such interpretations and treatment, people learn not to press their claims through the formal complaints system. As a result, the data do not accumulate that could document systemic patterns of discrimination against certain groups of people. Thus, patterns in the differential outcomes are masked as objective differences in performance. This in turn reinforces the view that people who claim social diversity as an explanation for conflict are trying to exploit their minority status and manipulate the system.

All of these factors contribute to the absence of collective identities in organizations, particularly at the level of professional and managerial employees where variable benefits accrue to individuals. Collective action, therefore, except for certain organized groups such as unions, is an underdeveloped mechanism for dealing constructively with conflict.

The irresolvability of social conflict

The final reason that social diversity is suppressed in the discourse of organizational conflict is that the organization can deal only with its symptoms and manifestations. These disputes are rooted in society. Therefore relative to other forms of conflict, disputes over diversity can never be ultimately resolved by organizations. Therefore, it is risky and costly to open up the diversity discourse.

Because issues of social diversity are central to identity and rights, the exploration of such conflicts is likely to be emotional for all parties concerned.[3] It takes longer to process such conflict thoroughly, assuming that it can be brought to some mutually satisfactory closure. It also requires considerable expertise to handle emotional issues. This time and talent are costly.

There is also a cost in diverting the attention and energy of organizational members from their work. Issues involving one's identity and rights are not just important to the individuals involved; they also attract the attention of others. When disputes involve parties of different social groups and this becomes widely known, other members of the same groups are likely to pay attention to the resolution process for cues as to their own futures. More conflict may surface as a result.

There are additional psychic costs to minority group members in opening up the diversity discourse. Resolution of diversity-based conflicts can result in stereotypes and labels that can have a negative impact on work relationships and performance (Carter, 1992). Again, other conflicts may be caused by the original resolution.

It is also sometimes claimed that organizations may, in the interest of closing down a dispute and restoring order, make concessions that would make the organization subsequently less effective. For example, urban police departments have sued in disputes over promotions, claiming that affirmative action quotas make organizations less effective because they are staffed by less competent people.

It is not surprising therefore that organizations and the majority of their managers and employees would prefer to ignore or to suppress the social basis of some conflicts. However, the realities of human nature and the world mean that such avoidance will have certain consequences.

Consequences of suppressing diversity

There are three important consequences of suppressing the social diversity explanation for certain organizational conflicts. First, as mentioned above, the underlying social conflict does not disappear when it is ignored or treated as an individual or organizational factor. The antagonism seeks and finds occasions or opportunities to be expressed in conflicts that are organizationally more acceptable (Smith, 1989). For example, Thomas (1991) found that unsuspected racial tensions accounted for the persistence and intensity of a labour dispute. Burroway (1979) argued that conflicts between workers over the use of new technology, resulting in lower production and quality, could be traced to class differences between the management and the employees.

Second, as implied by the two examples above, social conflicts create organizational costs whether they are addressed, ignored or attached to other conflicts. From this one might conclude, as Chester Barnard proposed, that it would be preferable to reduce the amount of social diversity that exists in the organization. However, as is now widely recognized, this would not only be difficult, it would actually be impossible for organizations to accomplish. Changes in demography and in the labour supply inevitably lead to a more diverse workforce.

A third consequence is that competitive benefits that diversity could provide are not realized. As organizational environments and marketplaces becomes more global, they become more diverse. To compete more effectively in such contexts, organizations require the kinds of creativity and new ways of thinking that a diverse workforce can bring to solving problems and developing new products and services. Realizing these advantages from diversity will require an enhanced capacity on the part of organizations to deal constructively with conflicts that accompany such diversity.

Managing diversity disputes

Practically speaking, the issue of social diversity within organizations illuminates some important problems with the dominant approaches to dispute resolution. In the interest of problem solving, complaints that go to dispute resolutions systems are individualized. Perversely, this approach prevents organizations from recognizing and addressing the institutional implications of such complaints. Further, the existence of these systems legitimates the expression of certain disputes and marginalizes others. Injunctions to negotiate differences also take place within an existing organizational reality that promises more of the status quo than change. Organizational rearrangements typically fail to address underlying issues (Kolb, 1989). There are, however, several approaches that have enabled organizations to deal constructively, for all parties, with diversity disputes. In this section, we propose four approaches: increasing the diagnosis of organizational conflicts, legitimizing the diversity lens, building support for collective action, and anticipating the consequences for the distribution of power.

Increase the scope of diagnosis

Disputes can be phrased in many ways. While the structure of formal dispute resolution systems encourages individual complaints, it is possible to help dispute resolution professionals think about redefining the problem in more institutional and group terms. Consider the university case we described at the beginning of this chapter. The ombudsman has a number of choices in dealing with a charge of sexual harassment. In one case we know of, the ombudsman treated the charge as a symptom that the school might be creating a hostile environment for gays and lesbians in both overt and subtle ways. Based on this hunch, the ombudsman collected and then analysed data that suggested a host of issues affecting junior faculty who were gay – few cohorts, demands on their time for committee work and student counselling, and exclusion from high visibility projects, among others. Armed with this systemic understanding of the problem, the ombudsman was able to work with the entire department to design a set of interventions that enabled them to air and discuss these issues and to set up a process for situations that might arise in the future. A potential benefit to the organization arising from this diagnosis and the resulting solutions could be a larger pool from which high performing students and faculty could be selected. A more tolerant environment might attract more gays and lesbians.

There are always obstacles to extending the role of the dispute resolution professional in the terms we describe here. First, there are norms of confidentiality that empower complainants to bring problems to an ombudsman. Opening up the dispute obviously requires that the complainant concur. Relatedly, some dispute resolvers claim to leave choice of how a conflict will be dealt with up to the individual (Rowe, 1990). It is our contention that dispute resolution professionals need to weigh these choices against potential organizational costs from keeping these matters hidden.

Legitimate the diversity lens

For diversity to offer the potential for transformation, it must be legitimized. There must be a mindset among those at the top of the organization (and those who are assigned to address disputes) that values and seeks out a diversity of perspective on organizational phenomena. If one of the first reactions to a dispute, as proposed above, is 'Could this be a function of social differences?' then the questions and actions that follow are likely to legitimate diversity as a source of both conflict and potential benefit. This can be accomplished in a number of ways.

Organizational diagnosis, when conducted by insiders, is often quite narrow and avoids conclusions that might stress the system (Kolb, 1986). All managerial employees need to be taught to expand their purview when it comes to analysis and to include questions that ask, 'Could this dispute be a function of social differences?' Being taught how to assess the full set of influences on organizational dynamics and outcomes, including social differences, would not only develop managers' ability to recognize the impact of such diversity, but it would also signal the importance being attached to it as a factor in organizational conflicts. Such programmes legitimate the diversity lens and communicate to managers that it is not apart from organizational functioning but an integral part of it and must not be marginalized.

The hiring of outside consultants, until internal capacity is acquired, can also be an effective means of legitimizing the diversity lens. In the franchise distribution case, failure to see how race intersects with the organization's structure and performance standards was costly. An outside consultant openly explored the diversity explanation. With this legitimation, and after some resistance, he was able to help the partners see how race infused not only their own relationship, but also the functional areas they managed, and their ability to deal with performance problems. As a result of the intervention, the partners recognized the intricate interweaving of race relations and organizational systems and structures as causes of their conflict. Only then were they able to deal with the salesforce problems, and they ultimately turned around the company's performance. Had the conflict resolution effort been focused solely on structural arrangements or on the individual behaviour of the alleged racist, it is likely that not only would performance have suffered, but race relations in the firm would have deteriorated considerably.

Support collective action

It is possible, although often quite difficult, for individuals who are connected by their minority status to band together as a coalition for change. Collective action can be initiated at many levels in the organization and can force an organization to deal openly with conflicts that arise from social diversity. In the accounting firm described, the women partners convened a meeting to explore their interest in forming a network, whose purpose would be to advocate for change in the career track and management of women in the organization. In a culture of professionals, where individuals rarely work together, helping the group to bring its conflicts to the surface and find a basis for collective action is difficult (Morrill, 1992). However, once the network was established, its members acted together to bring gender issues to the attention of senior management and to have a process installed whereby it would be possible to be a part-time partner (see also Loveman, 1990).

Getting beyond the individual resistance to collective action is necessary but not sufficient. Once formed, minority coalitions also require the support of senior management. This is a critical antecedent to the effective management of social diversity because the phenomenon is group-orientated and there is a general tendency within an organization to be suspicious of collectivities, especially where the established order can be threatened. David Kearns, former Xerox chief executive officer, played the role of catalyst in developing tolerant, eventually positive, attitudes among senior managers of Xerox in 1970s when black professionals began to form a caucus. Sent to investigate the concerns that brought the group together, Kearns learned that the group not only had legitimate grievances but also that there were numerous organizational benefits to be realized in supporting the black caucus (Friedman, 1991).

We are not proposing here a top-down model of change in which the organization or senior managers create social groups. Collective identity cannot nor should it be imposed on people. Its benefits to individuals and organizations depend on the voluntary association of people who identify with one another. Rather, we are proposing that managers prepare themselves to avoid negative interpretations of collective action and defensive responses when collective action is taken.

Anticipate the consequences for power distribution

People with power act to retain it. As discussed earlier, managers and other organizational members may interpret pressure to explore the diversity explanation for some organizational conflicts as a threat to their power and privilege in the organization. To manage such conflicts constructively for all parties may indeed entail some redistribution of power. By anticipating the consequences for those in power, it may be possible to offset some of the natural resistance to any redistribution. Linking a loss of personal power to an improvement in organizational well-being is useful. For example, the accounting firm could communicate to all partners that increasing the number of part-time professionals may help the firm continue to attract the best and the brightest, half of whom might otherwise choose to join competitor firms offering such benefits.

McIntosh (1988) makes an interesting, counterintuitive argument about the negative consequences that privilege has *for the privileged*. Asserting that privilege amounts essentially to unearned advantage and conferred dominance, she points out that

> those who do not depend on conferred dominance have traits and qualities which may never develop in those who do . . . the 'underprivileged' people of color who are the world's majority have survived their oppression and lived survivors' lives from which the white global minority can and must learn . . . Members of the so-called privileged groups can seem foolish, ridiculous, infantile or dangerous by contrast. (p. 13)

McIntosh thus implies that privilege may deprive a person of valuable developmental experiences. There are two organizational implications of this notion. The first is that organizations may derive enhanced benefit from their 'underprivileged' members if they are willing and able to expand the definition of value. For example, minority-group managers may be better able to conduct delicate cross-cultural negotiations due to their experience in straddling multiple identities. The second organizational implication is that those who seek such changes must help the privileged recognize that there will be personal benefits – not merely costs – in altering the current practices. Developing one's own skill base through learning from others and increasing the size of the organizational pie through the fuller utilization of minority members' skills are compelling arguments for learning how to address diversity conflicts constructively for all parties – despite the consequences for power distribution.

Conclusion

The argument that we have tried to develop is that the concept of constructive conflict is not an absolute. As practised, it has proved constructive for some, under some circumstances, but not for all parties to organizational conflicts. In order for organizations to rise to new challenges and become hospitable to all, the role of social group diversity in organizational conflict must be recognized, legitimated and incorporated into processes of conflict management and dispute resolution. To achieve these outcomes, the discourse of diversity must be opened up and enriched.

Summary

Managers and dispute resolution professionals find themselves increasingly involved in the management of conflicts that have significant legal and performance implications for their organizations. In this context, constructive conflict management practices have gained considerable currency. There is, however, one kind of dispute that these practices leave unaddressed: disputes that arise out of, or are complicated by, social diversity. As new social groups enter the workforce and move up in organizations, conflicts rooted in class, gender, race and ethnicity have become more prominent. Existing discourses of organizational conflict management mask such conflicts, dealing with them in ways that are not constructive for all parties considered. An ideology of meritocracy in organizations based on privileging individual success (perhaps at the expense of others), an absence of collective identity by groups and differential access to power and influence keep disputes that arise from diversity from being heard properly. Some approaches are suggested to help organizations deal constructively – for all involved – with conflicts that have their bases in social diversity.

Notes

This chapter is reprinted with permission from the original article by Anne Donnellon and Deborah Kolb in the *Journal of Social Issues*, 1994, *50*, 139–55.

1. This is not to say that collective entities do not exist; indeed, blacks, women, ethnic minorities and other interest groups may cluster into support groups, caucuses and networks (Friedman, 1991). However, these groups generally lack the kind of voice and clout of groups that have formal power and influence such as unions. Thus we cannot understand diversity issues without attending to how disparities of power in organizations and structure and culture defuse certain kinds of political influence and enable some groups to control and dominate others (Braverman, 1974; Burrell & Morgan, 1979; Burroway, 1979; Edwards, 1979; Goldman & Van Houten, 1977; Kunda, 1992).

2. Those who feel their lack of power often deal with conflict in the few ways that remain open to them. These include working behind the scenes and pursuing complaints through some form of grievance procedure. In the former, members keep their disputes out of public view and use private spaces to air complaints and seek support (Kolb & Bartunek, 1992). Given the limited possibilities to air conflicts that arise from gender and race, it is quite likely that members of minority groups make extensive use of these spaces to network and commiserate about problems they share in common. While these possibilities may be individually gratifying, unless they get introduced into the public discourse, they have the effect of perpetuating existing practices that give rise to problems in the first place.

3. It bears mentioning here that such costs are not absent when conflicts arising from social diversity are treated in the typical ways that suppress that reality. They are simply experienced and borne by one party, rather than both.

References

Alderfer, C.P. (1986). An intergroup perspective on group dynamics, in J. Lorsch (ed.), *Handbook of organizational behavior*. Englewood Cliffs, NJ: Prentice-Hall, pp. 190–222.

Barnard, C. (1938). *Function of the executive*. Cambridge, MA: Harvard University Press.

Bazerman, M. and Lewicki, R. (1983). *Negotiating in organizations*. Newbury Park, CA: Sage.

Bazerman, M. and Neale, M. (1983). Heuristics in negotiation, in M. Bazerman & R. Lewicki (eds), *Negotiating in organizations*. Newbury Park, CA: Sage, pp. 51–67.

Braverman, H. (1974). *Labor and monopoly capital*. New York: Monthly Review Press.

Burrell, G. and Morgan, G. (1979). *Sociological paradigms and organizational analysis*. Portsmouth, NH: Heineman Educational Books.

Burroway, M. (1979). *Manufacturing consent*. Chicago: University of Chicago Press.

Carter, S. (1992). *Reflections of an affirmative action baby*. New York: Basic Books.

Donnellon, A. (1993). Crossfunctional teams in product development: Accommodating the structure to the process. *Journal of Product Innovation Management, 10*, 571–89.

Donnellon, A. and Scully, M. (1992). Teams, performance and rewards: Will the post-bureaucratic organization be post-meritocratic? Working paper.

Edelman, L. (1990). Legal environments and organizational governance. *American Journal of Sociology, 95*, 1401–41.

Edwards, R. (1979). *Contested terrain*. New York: Basic Books.

Ewing, D.W. (1977). What does business think about employee rights? *Harvard Business Review, 53*, September/October, 81–94.

Ewing, D. W. (1989). *Justice on the job: Resolving grievances in the nonunion workplace*. Cambridge, MA.: Harvard Business School Press.

Friedman, R.A. (1991). Black caucus groups at Xerox Corporation. (Harvard Business School Case, 5-491-109.) Boston, MA: Harvard Business School Publishing Division.

Galbraith, J. (1977). *Organization design*. Reading, MA: Addison-Wesley.

Gioia, D.T. and Sims, H.P. (1985). Self-serving bias and actor-observer differences in organizations: an empirical analysis. *Journal of Applied Social Psychology, 15*, 547–63.

Goldman, P. and Van Houten, D. (1977). Managerial strategies and the worker: a marxist analysis of bureaucracy. *Sociological Quarterly*, *18*, 108–25.

Gray, B., Donnellon, A. and Bougon, M.B. (1985). Organizations as constructions and destructions of meaning. *Journal of Management*, *11*, 77–92.

Gwartney-Gibbs, P. and Lach, D.H. (1991). Workplace dispute resolution and gender inequality. *Negotiation Journal*, *7*(2), 187–99.

Hirschman, A. (1970). *Exit, voice and loyalty*. Cambridge, MA: Harvard University Press.

Kanter, R.M. (1977). *Men and women of the corporation*. New York: Basic Books.

Kolb, D.M. (1986). Who are organization third parties and what do they do? in R. Lewicki, B. Sheppard and M. Bazerman (eds), *Research on negotiation in organizations*. Greenwich, CT: JAI Press, pp. 207–28.

Kolb, D.M. (1987). Corporate ombudsman and organization conflict resolution. *Journal of Conflict Resolution*, *31*, 673–91.

Kolb, D.M. (1989). Labor mediators, managers, and ombudsmen: Roles mediators play in different contexts, in K. Kressel and D. Pruitt (eds), *Mediation research*. San Francisco: Jossey-Bass, pp. 91–114.

Kolb, D. and Bartunek, J. (eds) (1992). *Hidden conflict in organizations: Uncovering behind the scenes disputes*. Newbury Park, CA: Sage.

Kolb, D.M. and Silbey, S.S. (1990). Enhancing the capacity of organizations to deal with difference, in J.W. Breslin and J.Z. Rubin (eds), *Negotiation theory and practice*. Cambridge, MA: Harvard Law School, Program on Negotiation, pp. 315–22.

Kunda, G. (1992). *Engineering culture: Culture and control in a high-tech organization*. Philadelphia: Temple University Press.

Lawrence, P.R. and Lorsch, J.W. (1967). *Organization & environment*. Homewood, IL: Richard D. Irwin.

Lax, D. and Sebenius, J. (1986). *The Manager as negotiator*. New York: Free Press.

Lewin, D. (1987). Dispute resolution in the non-union firm: a theoretical and empirical analysis. *Journal of Conflict Resolution*, *31*(3), 465–502.

Loveman, G. (1990). The case of the part-time partner. *Harvard Business Review*, reprint No. 90507. Boston, MA: Harvard Business School Publishing Division.

March, J.G. and Simon, H. (1958). *Organizations*. New York: John Wiley & Sons.

McIntosh, P. (1988). White privilege and male privilege: a personal account of coming to see correspondences through work in women's studies. Working paper No. 189. Wellesley, MA: Wellesley College Center for Research on Women.

Michels, R. (1962) *Political parties*. Glencoe, IL: Free Press.

Miles, R. (1980). *Macro organizational behavior*. Santa Monica, CA: Goodyear.

Miller, D.T. and Ross, M. (1975). Self-serving biases in the attribution of causality: Fact or fiction? *Psychological Bulletin*, *82*, 213–25.

Morrill, C. (1992). The private ordering of professional relations, in D. Kolb & J. Bartunek (eds), *Hidden conflict in organizations: Uncovering behind the scenes disputes*. Newbury Park, CA: Sage, pp. 92–115.

Murphy, K.R. and Cleveland, J.N. (1991). *Performance appraisal*. Boston, MA: Allyn & Bacon.

Pfeffer, J. and Salancik, G. (1978). *The external control of organizations*. New York: Harper & Row.

Rand, T.M. and Wexley, K.N. (1975). A demonstration of the Byrnes similarity hypothesis in simulated employment interviews. *Psychological Reports*, *36*, 535–44.

Rowe, M. (1987). The corporate ombudsman. *Negotiation Journal*, *3*(2), 127–40.

Rowe, M. (1990). People who feel harassed need a complaint system with both formal and informal options. *Negotiation Journal*, *6*(2), 161–72.

Scott, J.W. (1988). Deconstructing equality-versus-difference: Or the uses of poststructuralist theory for feminism. *Feminist Studies*, *14*, 33–50.

Scully, M. (1992). Meritocratic ideology and the imperfect legitimation of inequality in internal labor markets. Unpublished manuscript. Graduate School of Business, Stanford University.

Sheppard, B., Lewicki, R.J. and Minton, J.W. (1992). *Organizational justice: the search for fairness in the workplace*. New York: Lexington Books.

Silbey, S. and Sarat, A. (1988). Dispute processing in law and legal scholarship: From institutional critique to the reconstitution of the judicial subject. Working paper. University of Wisconsin Law School, Institute for Legal Studies.

Smith, K.K. (1989). The movement of conflict in organizations: the joint dynamics of splitting and triangulation. *Administrative Science Quarterly*, *34*, 1–21.

Thomas, D. (1991). Role of organization – environment relations in diagnosis. Working paper. Harvard Business School.

Thomas, D. (1992). Star Distributors, Inc. (A). (Harvard Business School Case, 9-493-015.) Boston, MA: Harvard Business School Publishing Division.

Thompson, J. (1967). *Organizations in action*. New York: McGraw-Hill.

Ury, W., Brett, J. and Goldberg, S. (1988). *Getting disputes resolved*. San Francisco: Jossey-Bass.

Walton, R.E. and Dutton, J.M. (1969). The management of interdepartmental conflict: a model and review. *Administrative Science Quarterly*, *14*, 73–84.

Westin, A.F. and Feliu, A.G. (1988). *Resolving employment disputes without litigation*. Washington, DC: BNA.

Young, M. (1958). *The rise of meritocracy*. New York: Penguin Books.

Ziegenfuss, J.T. (1988). *Organizational troubleshooters: Resolving problems with customers and employees*. San Francisco: Jossey-Bass.

Zucker, L. (1977). The role of institutionalization in cultural persistence. *American Sociological Review*, *42*, October, 726–43.

PART IV

DESIGNING INTERVENTIONS: TOWARDS APPLICATIONS

12

Positive Effects of Conflict: Insights from Social Cognition

Robert A. Baron

In 1989, Mitsubishi Estate, a subsidiary of the giant Japanese company Mitsubishi, purchased an 80 percent interest in a famous piece of real estate: the renowned Rockefeller Center in New York City. Mitsubishi bought this interest from the Rockefeller Trusts, an organization whose sole function is that of overseeing trusts that benefit more than one hundred descendants of the legendary John D. Rockefeller. When Mitsubishi bought the property, it was profitable, but within a few years, the real estate market in New York was shaken to its core. Prices tumbled, and for the first time in many years, prime rental space became vacant – and stayed vacant – as many corporations fled the city and its serious problems. Rockefeller Center was no exception to these trends, and soon, Mitsubishi Estate found itself facing large shortfalls in cash flow, and huge paper losses in the value of its property. At this point, it sought help from the Rockefeller Trusts, which had retained an interest in Rockefeller Center. The response was quick in coming: No way! Top executives at Mitsubishi were stunned and angered by this reply. They felt that they had been humiliated by the Rockefellers, who had charged them far too much for the property and 'gotten out' at precisely the right moment – just before the crash in New York real estate. They wanted a concession from the Rockefellers to help them save face and regain their image as a savvy real estate investor. The refusal of Rockefeller Trusts to offer such a face-saving gesture generated so much ill-will and conflict that Mitsubishi decided to push the property into bankruptcy rather than give in and sink more funds into this deal-gone-sour. As one observer put it: 'Above all else, it seems, Mitsubishi's executives are determined to prevent the Rockefellers from regaining control of the property. To that end, they are likely to pour out large sums and to cut deals with creditors.' (Hylton, 1995)

This situation offers a classic example of *conflict* – a situation in which both parties perceive a sharp divergence in their interests, coupled with the belief that their goals and those of their opponent cannot both be achieved simultaneously (Rubin, Pruitt & Kim, 1994). Moreover, it illustrates the often devastating negative effects that can – and often do – result from unresolved conflicts. Mistubishi has already experienced both financial and psychological losses (its 'image' has been severely tarnished), while the Rockefeller Trusts have failed to regain control of the property – probably one of their major goals all along. Even worse, they may now have to watch as the famous centre, named after the Trusts' founder, slides into bankruptcy. In fact, it appears that events have reached the stage at which each side is *more concerned with inflicting further harm on its opponent than on its own bottom-line results*. Could these outcomes have been prevented? Almost certainly. A large body of evidence suggests numerous ways in which this conflict could have been resolved to the mutual satisfaction, and gain, of both parties (Tjosvold, 1991).

Why, then, did this not happen? Why, in short, did the conflict not result in positive outcomes? Given the magnitude of the stakes involved, such results might reasonably have been expected, and could well have included such benefits as placing the Center on a sound financial basis, reducing financial and psychological losses to both sides, and improved communication between Mitsubishi and the Rockefeller Trusts (Baron, 1991). Many factors probably played a role in preventing such positive outcomes from occurring. However, it is suggested here that important insights into this and many other conflict situations can be gained by adopting a *cognitive perspective*.

In conflict situations, as in all others, the persons involved are not passive participants; nor do they respond to the situation or their opponents' actions in an 'automatic' manner reflecting past conditioning. On the contrary, they are *active* participants, and this involves strenuous efforts to understand many aspects of the situation – the options available to them, the potential gains and losses that may result from these, the intentions and actions of their opponents, whether these persons' statements are to be trusted, and so on. The ways in which parties to a conflict situation think about this situation, the information they notice and remember, the conclusions and judgments they reach – all these cognitive processes play a powerful role in their behaviour and, therefore, in the ultimate outcomes experienced by both sides. The important role of such processes in conflict has been recognized by many investigators (e.g. Thomas, 1992; Thompson & Hastie, 1990). To date, however, there has been no systematic attempt to relate various aspects of cognition to the potential effects of conflict – to the question of how the likelihood of positive effects can be maximized and the probability of negative effects minimized. Research on cognition, and especially on *social cognition* – the ways in which we notice, store and use social information – has accelerated greatly in recent years, and has provided many new insights into the nature of these processes (e.g. Fiske, 1993). Since conflict situations generally involve direct or indirect contact between the parties involved, it seems appropriate to apply this expanding body of knowledge to such situations.

Consistent with these suggestions, the present chapter will focus on two major tasks. First, it will review several aspects of cognition – and especially social cognition – that can play a potentially important role in conflict situations and in determining whether conflict produces mainly positive or negative effects. Second, it will examine potential techniques for modifying conflict situations so as to tip the balance in favour of positive, rather than negative, effects.

Cognitive factors in conflict: their nature and potential impact

As has been noted, parties to a conflict generally interact with one another either directly, in face-to-face meetings, or indirectly (e.g. through third parties such as mediators or arbitrators; Lewicki, Weiss & Lewin, 1992). During the course of these contacts, they engage in vigorous efforts to understand many aspects of the conflict situation. Several different cognitive processes are involved in such activities, and can, potentially, exert strong effects on the course and outcomes of conflict.

Attributions: efforts to understand the causes of others' behaviour

When we interact with others, we usually want to know more than simply *what* they have said or done. We generally also want to know *why* they have engaged in various actions. Such information is often extremely useful from the point of view of predicting their future behaviour. For example, if we can conclude that others' actions stemmed from stable aspects of their personality or from their important long-term goals and motives, we can be reasonably certain that they will act in the same manner on future occasions. If, in contrast, we conclude that their actions stemmed from temporary causes or factors beyond their control, we have less confidence in the stability of their actions over time and across situations (Kenny, 1994).

The same basic principles apply to conflict situations. When individuals discover that their interests have been or may soon be thwarted by another person, they generally try to determine why this person acted in the way he or she did. Was it malevolence – a desire to harm them or give them a hard time? Or did the opponent's actions stem from factors beyond his or her control? A growing body of evidence suggests that when people reach the former conclusion, anger and subsequent conflict are more likely and more intense than when they reach the latter conclusion. For example, in several studies on this issue, the present author (Baron, 1985, 1988) had students engage in simulated negotiations with another person (actually an accomplice). Both individuals played the role of executives representing different departments within a large organization; they bargained over the division of $1,000,000 in surplus funds between their respective departments. The accomplice adopted a very confrontational stance, demanding fully $800,000 out of the $1,000,000 for his or her own department, and offered only two small concessions during the negotiations.

As the bargaining proceeded, the accomplice made several statements that provided insight into *why* he or she was acting in this manner. In one condition, the accomplice stated that this was the result of orders from his or her supervisor; thus, the accomplice had no choice but to act in this manner. In another condition, in contrast, the accomplice stated that he or she was simply 'this kind of person' – one who likes to win and defeat opponents. In this case, of course, the accomplice's confrontational actions stemmed primarily from internal causes. As predicted, participants reported more negative reactions to the accomplice, and stronger tendencies to avoid and compete with this person on future occasions, in the latter condition than in the former. Moreover, this difference was especially pronounced when participants received additional information indicating that the accomplice's claims about 'orders' were accurate.

These findings, and those of related studies (e.g. Shapiro, Buttner & Barry, 1994) suggest that attributions often influence the effects of conflict, determining whether these are positive or negative in nature. Additional research indicates that such attributions, in turn, are often strongly influenced by personal dispositions. In many situations, including ones involving conflict, interpreting others' actions is not a simple task: their behaviour is ambiguous, and we cannot easily determine the intentions behind their actions. Does a current offer stem from a genuine desire to resolve the conflict? Or is it part of a calculated strategy to mislead, and hence, defeat us? Frequently, it is difficult even for skilled and highly practised negotiators to solve this puzzle. It is precisely in situations involving such uncertainty that a personal characteristic known as *hostile attributional bias* becomes relevant. This factor refers to the tendency to perceive hostile intentions or motives behind others' actions when these behaviours are ambiguous. In other words, persons high in hostile attributional bias rarely give others the benefit of the doubt: they simply assume that any seemingly provocative actions by these others are intentional, and stem from conscious plans and strategies (Dodge, Murphy & Buchsbaum, 1984).

Many studies offer support for the potentially harmful effects of this 'tilt' in attributions. For example, in one investigation on this topic, Dodge, Price, Bacharowski and Newman (1990) examined the relationship between hostile attributional bias and aggression among a group of male adolescents confined to a maximum security prison for juvenile offenders. These young men had been convicted of a wide range of violent crimes, including murder, sexual assault, kidnapping and armed robbery. The researchers hypothesized that hostile attributional bias among these men would be related to the number of violent crimes they had committed, as well as to trained observers' ratings of the prisoners' tendencies to engage in aggression in response to provocation from others. Results offered support for both predictions. While there is no intention here of equating direct physical aggression with conflict, it seems possible that the cognitive tendency to perceive malice or hostility in others' actions can strongly influence attributions – one important aspect of social cognition.

Stereotypes and stereotype-driven thinking

It is a sad fact of life that the things people want and value most – good jobs, high income, nice homes, status – are always in short supply. The result is inevitable: individuals and groups often find themselves in competition for these scarce, valued resources. One result of such conflicts, it appears, is a strong tendency to view one's opponents in an increasingly negative manner. Such persons or groups are seen as 'enemies', who are markedly different from oneself or one's own group. In other words, they are perceived as the 'outgroup', which is, by definition, inferior to one's own 'ingroup' in many ways (e.g. Tajfel, 1982). Put in other terms, conflict sometimes leads to various forms of prejudice, and to the tendency to *stereotype* one's adversaries. This latter tendency, in turn, can play an important role in determining the outcomes of conflict situations.

In modern research, *stereotypes* are defined as cognitive frameworks consisting of knowledge and beliefs about specific social groups. As noted by Judd, Ryan and Park (1991), they involve generalizations about the typical or 'modal' characteristics of members of various groups. In other words, stereotypes suggest that all members of such groups possess certain traits, at least to a degree.

Like other cognitive frameworks, stereotypes exert strong effects on the processing of social information. Information relevant to an active stereotype is processed more quickly than information unrelated to it (e.g. Dovidio, Evans & Tyler, 1986). Similarly, stereotypes lead persons holding them to pay attention to specific types of information – usually information consistent with the stereotypes. And when information inconsistent with stereotypes does manage to enter consciousness, it may be actively refuted or even simply denied (Bardach & Park, 1996; O'Sullivan & Durso, 1984). For example, recent findings indicate that when individuals encounter persons who behave in ways contrary to stereotypes they hold, they tend to perceive these persons as a new 'subtype', and so avoid altering their existing stereotype, which is still viewed as basically accurate (Kunda & Oleson, 1995). Additional, recent evidence about stereotypes suggests that they also involve a strong emotional or affective component (Jussim, Nelson, Manis & Soffin, 1995). Thus, when they are activated, they not only influence various aspects of cognition (beliefs, expectancies, etc.), but also influence affective reactions. The role of this affective component of stereotypes in shaping the outcomes of conflicts will be considered below, in a more general discussion of the role of affect in conflict. For the moment, however, it should be emphasized that stereotypes exert powerful effects on our thinking about others, and on the judgments and decisions we make about them.

Clearly, stereotypes are relevant to many situations involving conflict. Once they are activated, they lead the individuals involved to perceive their opponents in negative terms – to make negative attributions about them and their intentions, to perceive them as enemies who have many undesirable traits, and who, undoubtedly, are up to no good! Clearly, to the extent such stereotype-driven thought develops, the possibilities of positive outcomes are diminished. Discouragingly, merely attempting to suppress stereotypes through conscious efforts to avoid such thoughts does not appear to be a useful means for reducing their impact. While such suppression may at first succeed, recent findings indicate that it is often followed by a strong 'rebound effect', in which stereotypic thinking actually increases in likelihood (Macrae, Milne & Bodenhausen, 1994). However, there do appear to be other techniques for combating the deleterious effects of stereotypes, and these will be described in a later section.

The potential costs of thinking too much

Conflict situations often involve issues of great importance to the parties involved. Indeed, if the issues at hand are trivial to both sides, conflicts may never develop, or will be very short-lived in nature (Thomas, 1992). For this reason, conflicts are one social context in which individuals often try very hard to overcome the human tendency to do as little work – physical or cognitive – as possible. Instead of avoiding the effort involved in careful, systematic thought, persons involved in such situations do try to be as rational and systematic as possible. Only by doing so, they believe, can they protect their interests while at the same time identifying various effective, integrative solutions (Rubin et al., 1994). However, a growing body of evidence indicates that sometimes this extra cognitive effort does not pay off. On the contrary, if carried to extremes, it can actually lead to less effective rather than more effective strategies and decisions (see Wilson & Schooler, 1991). Anyone who has ever thought long and deep about a problem or decision, to the point at which they found themselves becoming more and more confused, has had first-hand experience with such effects. Direct evidence for their occurrence has also been obtained in several recent studies.

For example, in one ingenious investigation, Wilson and Schooler (1991) asked college students to sample and rate several different strawberry jams. Half of the students were simply asked to taste the jams and rate them; the others were asked to analyse their reactions – to indicate why they felt the way they did about each product. When the students' judgments were compared with those of a group of experts who rate such products on a regular basis, it was found that the students who merely rated the jams did better than those who tried to describe the reasons behind these ratings. The ratings by those in the former group were significantly more similar to the ratings provided by the experts. Corresponding findings have been obtained in several other contexts, including ones that are considerably more important than choosing a brand of jam (e.g. selecting college courses). Thus, it appears that sometimes thinking too deeply can interfere with our ability to make good decisions or accurate judgments.

Can such effects occur in conflict situations? While no direct evidence on this issue is known to the present author, there appear to be no strong grounds for ruling out such effects. Indeed, the fact that participants in negotiations often overlook workable strategies that could resolve the conflict quickly in a manner acceptable to both sides is consistent with the view that they 'cannot see the wood for the trees'. It seems possible that one reason why this happens is – paradoxically – that they are thinking so deeply about it. Such effort may lead them into what I would call mental ruts – characteristic modes of thought about a given situation or class of situations. And such ruts, in turn, may be so deep that the parties to a conflict have little chance of escape without the intervention of outside agents.

Affect, emotion and conflict

Psychologists currently draw a distinction between *affect* and *emotion*. The term affect refers to temporary, and generally mild, fluctuations in current feelings (Isen & Baron, 1991). In other words, it refers to the extent to which individuals are currently experiencing what most would describe as a good or bad mood. In contrast, the term emotion refers to stronger reactions, involving physiological responses, subjective cognitive states, and observable expressive behaviours (Izard, 1992). Joy, despair, rage, passion – these are the kind of words we use to describe the stronger experiences viewed as emotions. Potential links between certain emotions and conflict seem obvious (e.g. between anger and conflict). In addition, however, recent findings indicate that conflict may also be influenced by milder affective states. These will be considered first, after which attention will be shifted to connections between various emotions and conflict.

Affect and cognition: how feelings shape thought and thought shapes feelings

A large and growing body of evidence indicates that even relatively mild shifts in current moods can exert strong effects on important aspects of cognition. The first, and perhaps most important, of these effects is known as the *mood-congruent judgment* effect. It refers to the fact that our current moods often tend to influence the way we think and our social judgments (e.g. Clore, Schwarz & Conway, 1993). Thus, when we are in a positive mood, we tend to think happy thoughts, to retrieve happy ideas and experiences from memory, and to evaluate many aspects of the social world – including other persons – in a relatively favourable manner. In contrast, when we are in a negative mood, the opposite tends to be true (Seta, Hayes & Seta, 1994). Such effects have been observed in many different studies, and appear to be both robust and general in nature (e.g. Baron, 1993a; Seta et al., 1994). For example, consider a recent study by Mayer and Hanson (1995): These researchers attempted to determine whether changes in mood over time are related to shifts in thinking about other persons, and especially to judgments about them. To gather evidence on this important issue, they asked students at a large university to complete measures of their current moods and of their current social thought. The measure of social cognition included estimates of the likelihood of positive and negative events (e.g. 'What is the likelihood of a nuclear war?' 'What is the probability that a 30-year-old will be involved in a happy, loving romance?') and items relating to categorical judgments. For instance, in the latter section of the questionnaire, participants chose one of several words (conscientious, lazy, honest) to describe 'the typical worker'. Participants completed these measures once, and then again a week later. The major prediction was that individuals' judgments would change with their shifting moods. Thus, their moods on the first occasion would predict their judgments at that time, but would not accurately predict their thoughts and judgments one week later. However, their mood on the second occasion would predict their thoughts and judgments at this later time. Results offered strongly support these hypotheses. In other words, changes in participants' moods over time were indeed closely linked to changes in their social cognition.

The mood-congruent judgment effect is not the only way in which affect influences cognition, however. For example, it has been found that being in a happy mood can sometimes increase creativity – perhaps because being in a good mood activates a wider range of ideas or associations, and creativity involves combining these into new patterns (e.g. Estrada, Isen & Young, 1995). In addition, current moods have been found to influence performance on many tasks, the tendency to make risky decisions, and several other aspects of cognition (see, e.g. Isen & Baron, 1991).

One additional effect of current moods on cognition was mentioned briefly above: the impact of affective states on stereotype-driven thinking. Common sense suggests that being in a good mood might tend to reduce the impact of stereotypes. After all, if one is feeling happy or content, the tendency to attribute negative traits to members of various 'outgroups' might be reduced. In fact, however, research findings point to the opposite conclusion: when individuals are in a good mood, they are actually more likely to engage in stereotypic thinking (Mackie & Worth, 1989). The reason for this surprising finding seems clear: when individuals are in a pleasant mood they do not wish to engage in any activities that will tend to disrupt these feelings. Thinking clearly about others or making judgments about them on the basis of current information is definitely hard work. Thus, individuals in a good mood fall back on stereotypes, which offer less effortful, if error-prone, 'short-cuts' to making judgments about others. The result: When individuals are in a good mood, they are more likely to engage in stereotype-driven thinking than when they are in a more neutral mood. This pattern has been observed in several recent studies (e.g. Macrae et al., 1994), so it appears to be a real, if somewhat unsettling, fact of social thought.

There is definitely another side to the coin where the interface between affect and cognition is concerned. While feelings influence several aspects of cognition, other findings suggest that cognition can influence current moods. For example, expectancies have been found to exert powerful effects on affective reactions to new events or stimuli. If people expect that they will dislike a new food, for instance, they often show visible signs of displeasure even before they taste it. Conversely, when they expect to enjoy a film, or to like a stranger, they are very likely to do so even if they would have had weaker positive reactions in the absence of such expectations. Indeed, some evidence suggests that expectations can even shape our memories of events so that we recall them as more (or less) pleasant than they actually were, in line with expectations (Wilson & Klaaren, 1992).

In addition, our interpretation of and thoughts about various affect-inducing events can mediate the impact of these events. For instance, apologies or clear causal accounts (explanations) for seemingly provocative actions can often reduce anger and other negative reactions to these events (Ohbuchi, Kameda & Agarie, 1989). Conversely, the positive reactions that often follow praise can be mitigated if individuals interpret such comments as mere flattery, delivered for ulterior purposes (Zillmann, 1993).

Emotion and cognition

There is an old saying to the effect that 'When emotions run high, reason flies out the window.' And a growing body of empirical evidence suggests that it contains a considerable grain of truth. When individuals experience strong emotional arousal, they often appear to suffer what Zillmann terms a cognitive deficit – reduced ability to formulate rational plans of action, or to evaluate the potential outcomes of various behaviours (Zillmann, 1994). One result of such deficits may be an impulsive 'lashing out' at others, even under conditions where the probability that they will retaliate in kind is high. With respect to conflict, cognitive deficits may play a role in the all-too-familiar script in which individuals or groups become more concerned with harming their opponents than with their own outcomes. Such cases often involve a strong desire for revenge – efforts to 'even the score' for past real or imagined wrongs or slights. The situation described at the start of this chapter appears to provide an example of such reactions. In this particular case, the top managers of a large corporation (Mitsubishi) feel that they have been treated unfairly by an opponent (the Rockefeller Trusts), and made to lose face in their dealings with this adversary. The result: They are prepared to accept large financial losses and the possible bankruptcy of a world-famous property rather than back down and experience additional loss of face (Hylton, 1995). Fortunately, several techniques for preventing or reducing such cognitive deficits exist; these will be reviewed in a later section.

In sum, it is clear that both mild shifts in affective states and the more powerful affective reactions described as emotions can exert potentially important effects on several aspects of cognition and, hence, on the outcomes and effects of many conflict situations.

Overcoming cognitive barriers: some potential techniques for enhancing the likelihood that conflict will yield positive effects

If recent research on human cognition points to one firm conclusion, it is this: As human beings, we are definitely not perfect information-processing devices. On the contrary, our capacity to notice, store and process information is severely limited (Wyer & Srull, 1994). Moreover, in our efforts to make sense out of the complex world around us, we make use of many mental short-cuts that succeed in reducing cognitive effort, but only at the cost of decreased accuracy in our social judgments and conclusions (Fiske & Taylor, 1991). It is also clear that some of these factors influence our behaviour in conflict situations. Indeed, several of the shortcomings and biases discussed above appear to tip the balance towards negative rather than positive effects and outcomes in conflict situations. Can anything be done to counter such effects, and therefore to maximize the probability that conflict will yield the positive effects it is capable of producing? The answer appears to be 'yes', and in this section several techniques that may prove useful in attaining this important goal will be described.

Countering the tendency to attribute malice to others

With respect to attribution, the key issue seems to be that of preventing individuals from jumping to the conclusion that others are 'out to get them' when this is not actually the case. While it may be difficult to prevent some individuals (those high in the hostile attributional bias) from reaching such conclusions, several steps appear to be useful. Among the most important of these would appear to be (1) avoiding insincerity and (2) providing opponents with explanations for seemingly confrontational actions.

Turning to the first of these factors, a number of recent studies (e.g. Shapiro et al., 1994) indicate that many persons react very negatively to evidence of insincerity on the part of their opponents. Faced with an opponent who says one thing while doing another, or who misrepresents his or her position, most individuals seem to give up hope of reaching an integrative resolution, and concentrate, instead, on maximizing their own outcomes. Clearly, then, such 'two-faced' behaviour should be avoided if conflict is to have an opportunity of providing positive effects.

The importance of providing one's opponents with clear explanations for seemingly confrontational actions is equally important. Without such explanations, parties to a conflict situation often assume the worst: they attribute all actions by their adversary to selfishness and malevolence. These tendencies overlook the fact that on some occasions, at least, seemingly confrontational actions do not stem from such causes. Indeed, they may, occasionally, stem from motives that actually transcend purely selfish goals. For example, when a manager rejects a project proposed by a subordinate this may primarily reflect a desire to protect the organization's resources, and not a desire to block the aspirations or interests of the subordinate. Yet, the subordinate may jump to the latter conclusion, thus assuring negative effects for the future working relationship of the manager and subordinate. If the manager took the time and trouble to explain the reasons behind the rejection, however, the subordinate's tendency to formulate such attributions might well be reduced.

A clear illustration of the benefits of providing such explanations is provided by a field study conducted by Greenberg (1990): In this investigation, Greenberg arranged for information about a pay cut to be presented to employees in two different plants of a single company in strikingly different ways. In one plant the reasons for the pay cut were carefully explained, and the announcement was made with repeated expressions of remorse over the hardships this would produce. In the other plant, in contrast, limited information was supplied about the reasons for the pay cut, and no effort was made to 'soften the blow'. Over the next few months, the amount of employee theft at the two plants was recorded. As predicted, theft was much higher in the plant where no effort had been made to provide employees with an explanation for the pay cut. Similar results have been obtained in other studies (Bies, Shapiro & Cummings, 1988). Together these findings suggest that providing opponents with a clear and carefully-worded explanation for confrontational actions (ones that reduce their outcomes) may be very valuable in tipping the balance towards positive rather than negative effects and outcomes.

Countering the impact of stereotypes

As conflicts proceed, the tendency for both sides to engage in stereotype-driven thinking tends to increase. To the extent that it does, the likelihood of positive outcomes is reduced. For example, descriptions of the conflict between Mitsubishi Estate and the Rockefeller Trusts (described at the start of this chapter) suggest that both sides engaged in stereotypic thinking. Persons representing the Rockefeller Trusts, in particular, seemed to view their Japanese opponents in negative terms as crafty, grasping persons who had taken enough profit from the USA and needed to be taught a lesson. Such thinking may well have been one factor in the intransigent position adopted by the Rockefeller Trusts.

How can such thinking be prevented or at least reduced? Research findings point to several potentially useful techniques. First, the impact of stereotypes can be reduced by encouraging individuals to think carefully about others – to pay careful attention to their unique characteristics rather than their membership in various groups. Such attribute-driven processing, as it is sometimes termed, can be encouraged by such simple procedures as reminding the persons involved that their own outcomes or rewards are affected by the actions of their opponents, or by stating that it is very important to be accurate in forming impressions and judgments of others. Under these conditions, it appears, the tendency to rely on stereotypes can be reduced (e.g. Neuberg, 1989).

Another technique for reducing reliance on stereotype-driven thinking is suggested by the finding that individuals are more likely to engage in such thought when in a good mood than in a more neutral one (e.g. Macrae et al., 1994). This suggests, for instance, that prompting parties to a conflict to consider the 'downside' of the situation may serve to counter any tendencies to take the 'easy way out' by relying on stereotypes and stereotype-driven thinking. Similarly, it suggests that efforts to put negotiators in a good mood – a common practice in many settings – can sometimes backfire, and should be avoided except where high levels of tension or annoyance dictate the necessity of such interventions.

Countering the confusion that can result from thinking too much

In many conflict situations, the stakes are high: money, power, influence and many other desirable outcomes are involved. Thus, it is not at all surprising that the persons involved in such situations often think long, hard and deep about them. As noted earlier, such thought is useful – but only up to a point. Growing evidence suggests that thinking too much or too deeply can lead to distorted and erroneous judgments (e.g. Wilson & Schooler, 1991).

What does this imply with respect to conflict? That participants should be encouraged to think about the situation – to consider a wide range of possible resolutions, and various techniques for reaching integrative solutions. However, they should also be discouraged from agonizing over them: from engaging in meticulous efforts to analyse their opponents' motives or strategies; from attempting to make precise predictions about every conceivable outcome; from focusing too deeply on their own motives and preferences. Beyond some point, such cognitive activity is more likely to generate confusion and error than new insights and increased flexibility. In sum, where conflict-related cognition is concerned, moderation – not excess – appears to be the preferred approach.

Countering the cognitive deficits produced by strong emotions

Strong emotions appear to interfere with many aspects of cognition. With respect to conflict, they may be linked to strong desires for revenge or 'evening the score' that decrease the likelihood of positive outcomes. Such feelings may well have played some role in the decision by representatives of the Rockefeller Trusts to adopt positions that caused their opponent, Mitsubishi, to lose considerable face. How can such effects be reduced? One technique involves what has been termed pre-attribution – attributing confrontational actions by others to unintentional causes before these actions occur (Zillmann, 1993). If parties to a conflict are reminded that the actions of their opponents are not necessarily a reflection of their personal preferences, and that, in fact, they may stem from other, unintentional causes, the levels of anger generated by such actions, when they occur, is reduced. Precisely such effects have been demonstrated in several studies (see Zillmann, 1993), so while this technique may seem somewhat counterintuitive, it appears to be quite effective.

Another technique for preventing the detrimental effects of strong emotions on conflict involves what has been described as the induction of incompatible responses (e.g. Baron, 1993b). In this procedure, individuals who have been subjected to anger-provoking events are exposed to other events or stimuli designed to induce emotional states incompatible with anger. A wide range of stimuli have been found to be effective in this regard – everything from providing participants with a small gift, through exposing them to humorous materials (e.g. Baron, 1984). Also effective are activities that are merely attention-absorbing. While these do not induce emotional states incompatible with anger, they offer a 'cooling off period' during which anger can dissipate and cognitive control of behaviour can be re-established (Zillmann, 1993, 1994). The basic principle is simply this: strong emotions such as anger should be dampened or reduced insofar as possible in conflict situations, for they lead to reduced cognitive efficiency, and therefore to reduced likelihood of positive outcomes.

Summary

That cognitive processes play an important role in conflict is well established (e.g. Pinkley & Northcraft, 1994). However, the possibility that several aspects of cognition influence the effects of conflict, and whether these effects are predominantly positive or negative, has not been systematically investigated. In this chapter, several aspects of cognition that may play an important role in this respect are examined. These include *attributions, stereotypes* and *stereotype-driven thinking*, the potential effects of *thinking too much*, relatively mild *affective states*, and strong negative *emotions*. This list is not meant to be exhaustive; on the contrary, it seems likely that several other aspects of cognition also influence the course and outcomes of conflict. While all of these factors can, and often do, tip the balance in conflict situations away from positive effects and towards negative ones, basic research points to various techniques for countering such effects. Careful use of such procedures may well be effective in increasing the likelihood that conflict yields the positive effects it is capable of producing.

References

Bardach, L. and Park, B. (1996). The effect of in-group/out-group status on memory for consistent and inconsistent behavior of an individual. *Personality and Social Psychology Bulletin, 22*, 169–78.

Baron, R.A. (1984). Reducing organizational conflict: an incompatible response approach. *Journal of Applied Psychology, 69*, 272–9.

Baron, R.A. (1985). Reducing organizational conflict: the role of attributions. *Journal of Applied Psychology, 70*, 434–41.

Baron, R.A. (1988). Attributions and organizational conflict: the mediating role of apparent sincerity. *Organizational Behavior and Human Decision Processes, 41*, 111–27.

Baron, R.A. (1991). Positive effects of conflict: a cognitive perspective. *Employee Rights and Responsibilities Journal, 4*, 25–36.

Baron, R.A. (1993a). Interviewer's moods and evaluations of job applicants: the role of applicant qualifications. *Journal of Applied Social Psychology, 23*, 254–71.

Baron, R.A. (1993b). Affect and organizational behavior: When – and why – feeling good (or bad) really matters, in J. K. Murnighan (ed.), *Social psychology in organizations*. Englewood Cliffs, NJ: Prentice-Hall, pp. 63–88.

Bies, R.J., Shapiro, D.L. and Cummings, L.L. (1988). Causal accounts and managing organizational conflict: Is it enough to say it's not my fault? *Communication Research, 15*, 381–99.

Clore, G.L., Schwarz, N. and Conway, M. (1993). Affective causes and consequences of social information processing, in R.S. Wyer and T.K. Srull (eds.), *Handbook of social cognition*, (2nd edn). Hillsdale, NJ: Erlbaum.

Dodge, K.A., Murphy, R.R. and Buchsbaum, K. (1984). The assessment of intention-cue detection skills in children: Implications for development psychopathology. *Child Development, 55*, 163–73.

Dodge, K.A., Price, J.M., Bacharowski, J.A. and Newman, J.P. (1990). Hostile attributional biases in severely aggressive adolescent males. *Journal of Abnormal Psychology, 99*, 385–92.

Dovidio, J.H., Evans, N. and Tyler, R.B. (1986). Racial stereotypes: the contents of their cognitive representations. *Journal of Experimental Social Psychology, 22*, 22–37.

Estrada, C.A., Isen, A.M. and Young, M.J. (1995). Positive affect improves creative problem solving and influences reported source of practice satisfaction in physicians. *Motivation and Emotion, 18*, 285–300.

Fiske, S.T. (1993). Social cognition and social perception. *Annual Review of Psychology, 44*, 155–94.

Fiske, S.T. and Taylor, S.E. (1991). *Social cognition*. New York: McGraw-Hill.

Greenberg, J. (1990). Employee theft as a reaction to underpayment inequity: the hidden cost of pay cuts. *Journal of Applied Psychology, 75*, 561–8.

Hylton, R.D. (1995). Behind the fall of Rockefeller Center. *Fortune*, July 10, 82–5.

Isen, A.M. and Baron, R.A. (1991). Affect and organizational behavior, in B.M. Staw and L.L. Cummings (eds), *Research in organizational behavior*. Greenwich, CT: JAI Press, Vol. 15, pp. 1–53.

Izard, C. (1992). Basic emotions, relations among emotions, and emotion-cognition relations. *Psychological Review, 99*, 561–5.

Judd, C.M., Ryan, C.S. and Park, B. (1991). Accuracy in the judgment of in-group and out-group variability. *Journal of Personality and Social Psychology, 61*, 366–79.

Jussim, L., Nelson, T.E., Manis, M. and Soffin, S. (1995). Prejudice, stereotypes, and labeling effects: Source of bias in person perception. *Journal of Personality and Social Psychology, 68*, 228–46.

Kenny, D.A. (1994). *Interpersonal perception: a social relations analysis*. New York: Guilford.

Kunda, Z. and Oleson, K.C. (1995). Maintaining stereotypes in the face of disconfirmation: Constructing grounds for subtyping deviants. *Journal of Personality and Social Psychology, 68*, 565–79.

Lewicki, R.J., Weiss, S.E. and Lewin, D. (1992). Models of conflict, negotiation, and third party intervention: a review and synthesis. *Journal of Organizational Behavior, 13*, 209–52.

Mackie, D.M. and Worth, L.T. (1989). Processing deficits and the mediation of positive affect in persuasion. *Journal of Personality and Social Psychology, 57*, 27–40.

Macrae, C.N., Milne, A.B. and Bodenhausen, G.V. (1994). Stereotypes as energy-saving devices: a peek inside the cognitive toolbox. *Journal of Personality and Social Psychology, 66*, 37–47.

Mayer, J.D. and Hanson, E. (1995) Mood-congruent judgment over time. *Personality and Social Psychology Bulletin, 21*, 237–44.

Neuberg, S.L. (1989). The goal of forming accurate impressions during social interactions: Attenuating the impact of negative expectancies. *Journal of Personality and Social Psychology, 56*, 374–86.

O'Sullivan, C.S. and Durso, F.T. (1984). Effects of schema-incongruent information on memory for stereotypical attributes. *Journal of Personality and Social Psychology, 47*, 55–70.

Ohbuchi, K.I., Kameda, M. and Agarie, N. (1989). Apology as aggression control: its role in mediating appraisal of and response to harm. *Journal of Personality and Social Psychology, 56*, 219–27.

Pinkley, R.L. and Northcraft, G.B. (1994). Conflict frames of reference: Implications for dispute processes and outcomes. *Academy of Management Journal, 37*, 193–205.

Rubin, J.Z., Pruitt, D.G. and Kim, T. (1994). *Social conflict: Escalation, stalemate and settlement*. New York: McGraw-Hill.

Seta, C.E., Hayes, N.S. and Seta, J.J. (1994). Mood, memory, and vigilance: the influence of distraction on recall and impression formation. *Personality and Social Psychology Bulletin, 20*, 170–7.

Shapiro, D.L., Buttner, E.H. and Barry, B. (1994). Explanations: What factors enhance their perceived adequacy? *Organizational Behavior and Human Decision Processes, 58*, 346–68.

Tajfel, H. (1982). *Social identity and intergroup relations*. Cambridge: Cambridge University Press.

Thomas, K.W. (1992). Conflict and conflict management: Reflections and update. *Journal of Organizational Behavior, 13*, 265–74.

Thompson, L. and Hastie, R. (1990). Social perception in negotiation. *Organizational Behavior and Human Decision Processes, 47*, 98–123.

Tjosvold, D. (1991). *The conflict-positive organization*. Reading, MA: Addison-Wesley.

Wilson, T.D. and Klaaren, K.J. (1992). 'Expectations whirl me round': the role of affective expectations affective experience, in M.S. Clark (ed.), *Emotion and social behavior*. Newbury Park, CA: Sage, pp. 1–31.

Wilson, T.D. and Schooler, J. (1991). Thinking too much: Introspection can reduce the quality of preferences and decisions. *Journal of Personality and Social Psychology, 60*, 181–92.

Wyer, Jr., R.S. and Srull, T.K. (eds) (1994). *Handbook of social cognition* (2nd edn). Hillsdale, NJ: Erlbaum, Vol. 1.

Zillmann, D. (1993). Mental control of angry aggression, in D.M. Wegner & J.W. Pennebaker (eds), *Handbook of mental control*. Englewood Cliffs, NJ: Prentice-Hall.

Zillmann, D. (1994). Cognition-excitation interdependencies in the escalation of anger and angry aggression, in M. Potegal and J.F. Knutson (eds), *The dynamics of aggression*. Hillsdale, NJ: Erlbaum.

13

Third Party Consultation as the Controlled Stimulation of Conflict

Ronald J. Fisher

The constructive management of conflict in organizational settings appears to have been initially prescribed by Mary Parker Follett, a political scientist who also turned her attention to the field of business administration (Follett, 1924; Metcalf & Urwick, 1940). Follett identified three ways of dealing with conflict – domination, compromise and integration – and maintained that the first two are unsatisfactory and essentially futile, particularly in the longer term. Integration, however, builds on past understanding to create solutions in which both sets of interests find expression and in which neither side has sacrificed something essential, thus inducing stability in the relationship. Integration does not magically appear, but requires persistence and ingenuity. First, the parties must bring their issues into the open and differentiate their opposing demands in order to determine what each other really wants. Then a direct confrontation of interests can lead to a revaluing process that induces flexibility, and finally, according to Follett, a mutual process of creative integration can occur in which both parties' interests are satisfied.

The developing fields of management and organizational psychology have by and large adopted Follett's prescriptions, although her pioneering work is not always directly acknowledged. Schmidt and Tannenbaum (1960), for example, provide a set of guidelines for the constructive management of conflict by organizational leaders. They suggest first diagnosing the differences in terms of their nature, source, underlying factors and stage of the dispute. The manager should then select an approach from the following options: avoidance, repression, sharpening and transformation into problem solving. While all approaches are appropriate in certain situations, Schmidt and Tannenbaum appear to favour turning differences into creative problem solving whenever possible. Nonetheless, they also legitimate the stimulation of conflict as a useful option for the clarification of positions and the education of the parties about organizational realities. The downside of sharpening conflict is the cost in energy and the risk of destroying relationships and harming future effectiveness. Thus, enriched problem solving which both manages differences and builds relationships is given more attention by Schmidt and Tannenbaum and by most other past and contemporary theorists in the field. The general position is that effective conflict management through some form of problem solving achieves positive changes and enhances organizational performance.

An approach and rationale that runs counter to the singular focus on problem solving is offered by Robbins (1974), who elevates conflict stimulation to a level equal with conflict resolution. In his model of conflict management, Robbins (1974) includes numerous stimulation techniques for increasing the intensity of interpersonal and intergroup conflict in order to achieve organizational goals. The challenge for the manager is to manipulate conflict to an optimal level of intensity. In Robbins's model, conflict is seen as a function of communication, structure and personal-behaviour factors; thus, both resolution and stimulation must work with variables in these areas. For example, to stimulate conflict the manager could exclude someone from a communication loop, could repress information thus redistributing power, or could send out ambiguous information. Similarly, changes in structural factors, such as size, leadership or membership, can stimulate conflict by altering the distribution of resources and power. Finally, leaders can be selected on the basis of personality characteristics that are likely to stimulate useful intra-unit conflict.

The overall goal of Robbins's model is to keep the intensity of conflict at a functional level, above apathy but below destructiveness, so that a high degree of performance is achieved. As Robbins himself acknowledges, his approach with its emphasis on stimulation 'represents a radical departure from previous treatises on conflict management' (1974, p. 88). Moreover, one must question the ethical propriety of the extent of deception and manipulation that are proposed in some cases to stimulate conflict among unknowing subordinates. At the same time, this work raises the useful question of how conflict intensity might be increased in order to engender functional interaction among the parties. This is an issue that has been largely ignored in the conflict resolution field.

This chapter will address this issue by first considering how third party interventions are sometimes useful to escalate conflict to an optimal level for adequate diagnosis and productive confrontation. In particular, the approach of third party consultation will be examined for its utility in stimulating escalation, in terms of the relationship between the consultant and the parties, and the design and implementation of the overall intervention. A number of illustrative applications will be briefly described to demonstrate the utility of stimulating conflict to increase organizational performance. It will be concluded that third party consultation offers a mechanism for stimulating conflict when necessary to optimize its constructive use in organizational settings.

Third party intervention as conflict stimulation

Turning to the role of outside intervenors in conflict resolution, we also find an emphasis on management, de-escalation and problem solving. At the intergroup level in organizational settings, the pioneering work was carried out in the 1960s by Robert Blake, Jane Mouton and their colleagues (Blake & Mouton, 1961; Blake, Mouton & Sloma, 1965; Blake, Shepard & Mouton, 1964). Coming from a human relations training base and at the forefront of innovations in organization development, these scholar-practitioners developed a variety of interventions for turning destructive and dysfunctional intergroup relations into productive and satisfying ones. Working with union–management, headquarters–field and merger conflicts, Blake and Mouton developed techniques for creating and sharing images of own and other group, of ideal vs. actual relationships and of the issues in the conflict, all within the context of an intergroup problem solving process. The overall sequence was from the diagnosis of difficulties to the creation of action steps to move the relationship in constructive and collaborative directions.

At the interpersonal level, the seminal work on third party consultation is provided by Walton (1969) who facilitated confrontations between organizational executives engaged in dysfunctional conflict. Walton provides not only a theory of practice in terms of the third party attributes, role, functions and tactics, but also a theory of understanding in the form of a diagnostic model of interpersonal conflict. The overall flow of an intervention moves from preliminary interviews with the antagonists, to structuring the context for the confrontation, to intervening in the confrontation, and finally to planning for future dialogue. Critical to Walton's model is the concept of confrontation, i.e. 'the process in which the parties directly engage each other and focus on the conflict between them' (1969, p. 95). This central interaction includes exploration and clarification of the issues in dispute, the underlying needs of the parties, and the current feelings engendered by the conflict. Most importantly, the confrontation must move through two distinct phases – differentiation and integration – in order to achieve mutual understanding and to develop mechanisms for control or resolution. The differentiation phase involves each party describing issues and ventilating feelings, with an indication that the other party understands these. The integration phase involves each party acknowledging similarities and commonalities, expressing respect and warmth, and engaging in constructive actions to manage the conflict.

Walton's (1969, 1987) work is based on the premise that a moderate level of conflict has a variety of positive consequences for the organization, including increased motivation and innovativeness. Walton also maintains that an optimum level of tension, i.e. a moderate degree of stress, is necessary for productive confrontation, since it induces a sense of urgency and related problem solving behaviours. He therefore outlines some third party interventions that are useful to escalate the conflict, such as sharpening the issues between the parties or exchanging emotional reactions between them. An important implication is that conflict sometimes needs to be stimulated or intensified before it can be adequately managed or resolved.

Fisher (1972) developed a generic model of third party consultation based on the pioneering initiatives of Walton, Blake and Mouton, and other creative scholar-practitioners including Burton (1969) and Doob (1970). The typical design in this approach involves a workshop format in which the parties, or influential representatives of the parties, come together with a third party team for an extended amount of uninterrupted, private, low-risk discussion, usually lasting a few days. The model emphasizes the facilitative and diagnostic functions of a knowledgeable, skilled and impartial third party in helping the antagonists to directly confront the issues dividing them. Conflict analysis is engendered by fostering an open, nonadversarial and nonargumentative form of discussion, and by the third party's suggestions of concepts and processes that may apply to the dispute in question. In addition to diagnosing the conflict, improving communication and inducing motivation for problem solving, an important third party function is that of regulating the interaction. This involves two elements. The first is the obvious one of controlling the interaction and maintaining the problem solving atmosphere so that disruptive behaviours do not derail and inflame the discussions. The second requirement is to pace the phases of the confrontation from differentiation to integration. Here, Fisher (1972) acknowledges Walton's suggestion that at times the parties will require assistance to confront the issues and engage each other directly. Thus, the consultation model includes an element of conflict stimulation in the sense that the third party will at times identify thorny issues or contentious behaviours and invite the parties to address these. This creates a crucible in which intense interactions occur in a more respectful and productive manner than has been happening in the on-going relationship. Thus, the third party is inducing escalation in order to increase mutual understanding and ultimately the capacity of the parties to jointly address difficult matters in a constructive way.

The clearest statement prescribing escalative interventions by consultants in conflicts between or within groups is provided by Van de Vliert (1985), who notes that such interventions are extremely rare in the professional literature as compared to those designed to de-escalate conflicts. Van de Vliert makes a call for limited escalation in certain situations, e.g. to help change a conflict's course, or to provide a clearer understanding of it, or to stimulate a search for alternate behaviours. From the literature on conflict management, Van de Vliert is able to identify eight potential objectives of escalative interventions, four of which relate intrinsically to the process of the conflict itself. In this vein, conflict stimulation can be very useful for aiding in the diagnosis of the conflict, since it will lead the parties to engage more in the contentious behaviours that constitute their approach to it. Secondly, an escalative intervention can raise tension to a more constructive level whereby the parties are more motivated and energized to deal with the conflict. Escalative interventions, since they involve direct confrontation, also discourage avoidance behaviour by the antagonists which is usually counterproductive. Finally, Van de Vliert acknowledges the importance of adequate differentiation prior to integration, and notes that limited escalation facilitates this, thus preventing premature and inadequate attempts at resolution. External to the conflict, Van de Vliert identifies the objectives of bringing about radical change, increasing group cohesiveness, improving effectiveness, and learning to fight fairly.

In order to identify different types of escalative interventions, Van de Vliert (1985) draws on both structural and process models of conflict to produce five core elements that can serve as the foci of interventions: antecedent conditions, conflict issues, parties, behaviours and consequences. Thus, stimulating the conflict can be achieved by bringing attention to a conflict antecedent, such as a structural inequality or an underlying condition such as suspicion. Extending the conflict issues may be operationalized by drawing attention to differences the parties are unaware of or by linking a fresh issue to longstanding concerns, in both cases creating an increase in frustration. Constructive escalation sometimes occurs by increasing the number or size of parties through coalition formation or by siding first with one party and then the other. In addition, the third party can directly prescribe or provoke contentious and escalative behaviours, e.g. by calling for a ventilation of feelings or a direct confrontation on antecedent conditions or issues. Finally, the escalative consequences of contentious behaviour (e.g. the negative effects on the other) can be stressed by the consultant as another way of increasing conflict intensity. Van de Vliert thus provides a wide array of possible interventions that can be used by consultants to facilitate the controlled stimulation of conflict. However, he expresses a preference for interventions which focus on behaviours or consequences, since these allow more for escalation by degrees and also allow for more control by the parties.

Third party consultation: facilitating controlled stimulation

The model of third party consultation provides a conceptual base for understanding how interpersonal and intergroup conflict can be stimulated and escalated in a controlled fashion towards optimal functioning and productivity. The components of the model (Fisher, 1972, 1976; Fisher & Keashly, 1990) focus on the identity and relationship of the consultant with the antagonists, the situation (i.e. the setting and agenda for the discussions), and the third party role, functions and tactics for achieving the objectives within an overall programme of consultation. In order to understand how the method can be successfully used to stimulate and then resolve conflict, it is essential to look at three elements: the relationship the consultant establishes with the parties, the design of the intervention and the implementation of the intervention.

Before proceeding with this analysis, it is important to identify the levels of interaction that are being considered in relation to a programme of consultation. At the interpersonal level, the parties to the conflict are individuals, and it is they who must be involved in the confrontation. Walton's (1969) work typifies this type of intervention in organizational settings. At the intergroup level, the picture becomes more complicated. In conflicts involving subgroups within a work team or department, or involving small intact units, it is possible to engage all members of the two parties in the intervention. Consultation typically requires a meeting or a series of meetings in a workshop format which involves the members of each party in intra- and intergroup interactions. The design follows a small group format and the number of participants would generally be no more than twenty and rarely more than thirty. Thus, when larger groups are involved in conflict, such as departments or divisions within a large organization, or union and management, it is not possible to accommodate all members of the two parties in the intervention. It then becomes necessary to work with the leadership of the two parties, such as the union executive and the company's top management team. This form of intervention is illustrated, for example, in the early work of Blake et al. (1964) on union–management conflict.

Regardless of whether the participants are the complete memberships or the representatives of the parties, the preparation and implementation of the intervention will be similar. However, an important distinction must be made in relation to the processes of conflict stimulation and escalation. When the intervention involves all members of the parties, the stimulation and controlled escalation of the conflict is complete within the intervention. The identification of issues, the analysis of causes, and any positive directions that emerge are coterminous with the total expression and management of the conflict. In contrast, when the intervention deals with representatives, the interaction is only a partial stimulation and controlled escalation of the complete conflict. The conflict as represented in the minds and behaviour of the members not present is not affected in the short term, and remains at whatever level of escalation exists. Thus, in this case, attention will need to be given to the transfer of any positive outcomes from the intervention to the wider relationship between the parties involving all members. It is important to note that members of the parties not included in the intervention will not have experienced the controlled escalation that may be necessary for the ultimate management or resolution of the conflict.

The consulting relationship

In all cases, a trusting and respectful relationship between the consultant and each of the two parties is essential if they are to enter willingly and constructively into the crucible of conflict interaction. Such a positive consulting relationship is built in the first instance on the identity of the third party. He or she (or they as is common in intergroup interventions) must be seen as knowledgeable, skilled and impartial by both sides – not an easy task in situations of intense and protracted conflict. The professional and personal expertise of the consultant to manage the intervention and to facilitate productive confrontation usually lies in a combination of scholarly education in the social sciences and professional training in human relations and organization development. In short, the intervenor requires expertise in both conflict analysis and group processes.

At the same time, the consultants either must have or should develop a moderate knowledge of the parties and their conflict, so that they can intervene appropriately around the content of the conflict and yet without the preconceived judgments that a high degree of knowledge often brings. As this is a noncoercive role, the third party must bring a fair amount of expert and referent power in order to have influence with the parties. Furthermore, the consultant must continuously demonstrate impartiality – in attitudes, in behaviour and in design choices – towards the two parties. The culmination of these qualities, as they are expressed in interactions with the parties, is that the two sides will develop confidence in the integrity and the ability of the consultant to design and manage an intervention that will indeed stimulate and potentially escalate the conflict between them. Building a relationship in which the antagonists trust the third party to do this is a considerable challenge, as is the maintenance of credibility and impartiality.

The design of the intervention

In designing interventions, the setting for the confrontation must be carefully considered by the third party. Congruent with the informal nature of the work, a physical setting that is less formal and more private than the work setting is usually prescribed. It is also useful to choose a neutral setting that is not identified with either party in order to reinforce impartiality and balance situational power. When the intervention consists of a workshop over some number of days, a secluded yet accessible setting, such as a residential training or conference centre is ideal. The rationale for the choice of setting is to have an environment in which distractions will be minimized and participants are motivated and supported to engage in focusing directly on the conflict.

Prior to and at the beginning of the sessions, the third party must prescribe certain ground rules that will help build the norms of productive confrontation, including conflict stimulation. These ground rules typically call for an analytical approach to the conflict rather than an adversarial one, and seek certain assurances from participants regarding confidentiality of proceedings and nonattribution of statements. The participants are influenced not to slip into the debating, arguing or blaming style that is characteristic of conflict interactions, but to work to understand the other party adequately before analysing together the sources and escalation processes of the conflict. To encourage freedom of expression, participants are asked and must agree not to attribute statements made by individuals in the workshop after the sessions are over. In addition, the parties should agree what content of the discussions will be reported back to the organizational setting or the public following the workshop and how this will be done. These ground rules thus allow individuals to speak frankly about their perceptions of the dynamics of the conflict, so that it is possible to engage the issues in an intense and yet constructive manner.

The agenda for the confrontation, whether a single session or an extended workshop, is also geared to stimulate conflict in a controlled manner. Typically there will be some initial discussion of the major issues of the conflict – what each party thinks the conflict is about. In Van de Vliert's (1985) terms, the parties will, with third party support, identify antecedent conditions that they are dissatisfied with, and their behaviour will often reinforce a trigger for the other party. Concurrently, the third party's involvement will have lowered many of the barriers to engaging the conflict directly. The outcome is an escalation of behaviour within the confrontation which is both an expression of the conflict and an opportunity for learning. Often when the participants see that they have slipped into characteristic adversarial and destructive interaction, they are then in a position to consider more constructive alternatives.

Issues may be added to the agenda by the third party, thus contributing to escalation. Prior to the confrontation, the consultant almost invariably meets with each party separately in order better to understand their perspective and to build trust and credibility. This enables the consultant to see issues that the parties are not mutually aware of, in terms of such items as competition for additional resources, latent role conflict or hidden power conflict. As Van de Vliert (1985) points out, these items can be injected into the situation, thus increasing the overall level of frustration and escalation. On the positive side, the consultant is making a judgment that these issues must be faced and dealt with if the conflict is to be resolved.

The initial confrontation of issues can hopefully be used by the third party to increase both the understanding of the differing perspectives of the two parties and the negative dynamics of the conflict. A common next step in agenda formation is a deeper analysis, informed by theories of conflict etiology, wherein the parties are invited to go beneath the surface issues and mutually probe underlying forces. A typical focus is to examine in some fashion the interests, needs, values or fears that underlie the positions of the two parties. Issues are typically stated in terms of the positions which include demands on the other that are unacceptable. Beneath the position is an interest or initial reason that helps explain why the position is taken. Beneath the interest is often a deeper need, whose frustration threatens the identity or existence of the party, and a deeper fear of the consequences of not addressing the need. For example, an older and smaller plant in a multi-plant operation may take the position of demanding a larger budget allocation over a five-year period in order to retool and update its production capacity. The interest is to cut production costs and remain competitive, based on a value of efficiency and profit. However, the deeper drivers are an underlying need for security and a fear that no change will mean the death of the plant and the loss of jobs. An agenda which allows for the exploration of these underlying concerns in a direct and intense manner will initially increase the stakes and the intensity of the conflict, but also pave the way for its resolution.

Following the attention to conflict analysis, confrontation agendas typically provide for the parties to talk about what they want in the situation. Here the third party can at one point support one side (legitimately so) and then the other (equally legitimately) in terms of what are understandable motives. In Van de Vliert's (1985) terms, this provides an opportunity for the third party to induce productive escalation by temporarily extending the parties in the conflict. Addressing wants may involve looking at the characteristics of an ideal relationship that the parties desire, or jointly constructing a future vision of the department or organization. In interpersonal conflict, it may be as simple as asking each person how they want to be treated by the other. While this agenda item may escalate the interaction by challenging the parties to contribute more to the relationship, it also has the potential of increasing their mutual motivation to do precisely that.

The analysis of issues, underlying concerns and wants generally coincides with the differentiation phase of the confrontation, and can be augmented by considering other elements such as the effects of external actors on the conflict. This is the phase where the controlled stimulation and escalation of conflict is predominant, and the consultant must make a critical judgment that adequate differentiation has occurred before moving to the integration phase of the agenda. However, as with all problem solving interventions, it is possible to recycle back for further diagnosis and stimulation when additional differentiation is required. For example, some proposed element of a solution might raise deeper fears that had not been acknowledged and that must be addressed before joint movement and closure is possible. At the same time, there is usually a turning point in a confrontation, whether a single session or a workshop, which signals the consultant that it is now desirable to move the agenda into the integration phase. This phase typically involves items such as the identification of activities to de-escalate the conflict, the joint creation of alternative solutions, and an examination of potential constraints and resistances to de-escalation and resolution. At this point, the facilitated escalation of the conflict has largely made its contribution, and the emphasis of the intervention shifts to de-escalation and peacemaking.

The implementation of the intervention

The actual carrying out of the intervention builds directly on the agenda, but requires a finer grained analysis of third party behaviour during the confrontation in order to see how conflict intensity is stimulated and controlled. The theorizing of Walton (1969) and Fisher (1972, 1976) identifies core strategies or functions which define the essence of the third party's contribution in behavioural terms. While Walton enumerates seven functions, Fisher synthesizes these into four: (1) inducing and maintaining mutual positive motivation, (2) improving communication, (3) diagnosing the conflict, and (4) regulating the interaction. He further suggests that the functions are operationalized primarily by specific behavioural tactics which the third party contributes to the on-going interaction. Each function and its related tactics have a contribution to make in terms of the controlled stimulation of the conflict.

Positive motivation to enter the confrontation and to seek mutually satisfactory outcomes is essential if the intervention is to be accepted by and useful to the parties. They must be willing to take risks, to discuss sensitive issues, to hear disturbing and aggravating comments from the other, and to persist in difficult interactions. The third party needs to judge that both parties have adequate initial motivation to engage each other in this manner and also must provide support throughout the process. Sometimes, for example, this can be done by stressing the continuing costs of not resolving the conflict, or the benefits of doing so. Indirectly, the third party's presence and attributes serve as the catalyst which allows the parties to interact in a direct and unique manner. Directly, the third party often helps maintain motivation when the going gets tough, e.g. by indicating how a sensitive issue links to an essential need of a frustrated party and therefore must be discussed and resolved. As Van de Vliert (1985) indicates, there are times when the frustration level of parties needs to be maintained or even increased so that they are motivated to search for ways out of their conflict.

Improving communication is perhaps the most pervasive function. It focuses on increasing both the openness and the accuracy of messages between the parties. Confrontations are designed to reduce the risk and threat the parties experience, and one result is the exchange of negative emotions, perceptions and attributions. Thus, an important consultant intervention is the prescribing of contentious behaviour, such as venting feelings or sharing negative perceptions (Van de Vliert, 1985). These forms of interparty communication escalate intensity within the differentiation phase, but also induce a clear picture of the reality that must be addressed. In the exchange process, the consultant works hard to clarify statements, to distinguish feelings, opinions and facts, and to ensure that the parties hear each other as intended. Van de Vliert (1985) draws on the work of Bach and Wyden (1969) to suggest that the consultant helps the antagonists to manage their conflict by teaching them to 'fight fairly'. Once a fuller mutual understanding has been achieved on the perspectives of the conflict, the parties are in part ready to move into the integration phase.

Further differentiation is provided by the third party function of diagnosing the conflict. Here, the consultant draws on his or her knowledge of conflict etiology and escalation in order to bring forward concepts, models and comparable cases that might provide some illumination for the parties in understanding their unique situation. In addition, diagnosis sometimes occurs when the third party points out how behaviour within the workshop parallels interaction in the wider relationship, such as the dominating and discounting treatment by a majority of a minority and the latter's resentful submission to this. These types of interventions can be particularly threatening to the parties, and usually escalate intensity considerably, since they both explain frustrating behaviour and emphasize the frustrating consequences of it (Van de Vliert, 1985). They also hold the potential for much learning, since the parties see before their eyes a segment of the real problem that exists. Thus, along with content interventions, process observations by the third party play an important role in the differentiation phase.

Given that one of the intentions of the third party is to stimulate and escalate conflict in a controlled manner, it is not surprising that a major function is to regulate the interaction within the confrontation. That is, the third party serves as the catalyst for the reaction, but must also work to contain the interaction within acceptable bounds. In general, the consultant works to facilitate productive, respectful confrontation between the parties, and to control, modify and if necessary terminate destructive interchanges. Adversarial debate, argumentation and attack designed to dominate or defeat the other party are proscribed by the agenda and ground rules, and are further constrained by direct intervention when necessary. Process interventions can be used to illuminate the negative effects of such behaviour on the other party and the interaction, and in so doing to demonstrate its ultimate futility. This is not to say that the rationale for positions and other information should not be shared, but that this should be done through dialogue, where one speaks to inform rather than convince and listens to understand rather than construct counterarguments. Thus, the third party is directive over process and at times over content in order to ensure that the constructive nature of controlled stimulation is maintained. In addition, regulation requires the consultant to facilitate the shift from differentiation to integration when appropriate.

This analysis indicates that a considerable amount of the third party's preparation and implementation work is geared towards creating an optimal level of conflict intensity within the confrontation. The extent to which conflict stimulation is required will depend on many factors, including the degree of conflict suppression or avoidance, the conflict behaviour of the parties, and the organizational norms relevant to conflict expression and management. The skilful consultant must read these kinds of factors and design and carry out the intervention in a manner that maintains the conflict interaction at a moderate and productive level of intensity.

Applications for optimizing performance

Van de Vliert and De Dreu (1994) argue that conflict stimulation is often necessary to optimize performance in organizational settings. Their thesis is that joint performance and outcomes can at times be better attained through limited escalation rather than by means of prevention or de-escalation. This usually means stimulating conflict intensity in the short term in order to obtain the benefits of enhanced productivity in the long term. The development of third party consultation provides a number of illustrations that support Van de Vliert and De Dreu's contentions. Mention has already been made of the pioneering efforts of Walton (1969) and Blake et al. (1964). Further illustrations will be briefly described:

Fisher (1983) reviews applications to intergroup conflict in both business/industrial and human service organizations. Golembiewski and Blumberg (1967), for example, describe a design for a three-day confrontation which they applied successfully to both interdepartmental and headquarters/field conflict. Within the context of a week-long training workshop for the organization, the design involved the development and sharing of inter-group images followed by the identification and resolution of core issues emerging from the image exchange. An evaluation using pre- and post-attitude questionnaires yielded mainly positive outcomes in areas such as motivation for collaboration and commitment to the organization. Burke (1974) developed a general approach to intergroup problem solving and applied it to interdepartmental conflict in a manufacturing plant. The two-day workshop was assessed with a post-questionnaire which indicated that the parties developed more positive perceptions of each other and improved their interdepartmental relations.

In the human service domain, Blumberg and Weiner (1971) served as con-sultants who facilitated a difficult merger between two subsystems of a national recreation association. Within a five-day workshop, they employed a confrontation design to diagnose barriers to the merger and to strengthen the norms for open communication. Members of one subsystem remained divided on their participation in the merger, but those who were in favour pre-ferred future collaboration and formed task forces with members of the other subsystem to develop joint recommendations. This input focused on partici-pative norms for the new organization and affected organizational decision making in ways that brought about a successful merger. Fisher (1976) reports on a series of consultation meetings between housing agency personnel and tenant representatives designed to improve a distrustful and antagonistic relationship, which stemmed partly from a traditional style of management and a lack of constructive tenant input to policy making. An exchange of per-ceptions brought to the surface tenant frustrations with management and a concern on the agency's part about the legitimacy of the tenant representa-tives. This led to the formation of a new tenant association, a survey of tenant concerns, and the implementation of regular meetings between agency per-sonnel and tenant representatives, all of which led to an improved relationship.

Brown (1983) presents a comprehensive approach for managing conflict at organizational interfaces, i.e. between departments, between levels, or between different cultures in the same organization. Brown proposes that there can be too little conflict in organizations as well as too much, and develops a range of interventions to deal with both situations. Too little con-flict generally involves suppression, in which critical differences requiring discussion are denied or submerged, or withdrawal, in which differences are recognized but not articulated or dealt with directly. In the former case, deci-sions are based on restricted information, while in the latter they are made by default or not at all. In both cases, organizational participation, commit-ment and productivity are in jeopardy. To manage conflict effectively, Brown delineates four general categories of interventions: (1) redirecting behaviour, (2) reallocating relevant resources, (3) reframing perspectives, and (4) realign-ing structural forces. It should be noted that the consultant as conflict manager usually has more control over 1 and 3, whereas 2 and 4 are usually more within the power of organizational decision makers.

Brown (1983) describes a variety of interventions to deal with too little conflict through redirecting behaviour and reframing perspectives. A number of these are similar to ones proposed by Van de Vliert (1985) and Robbins (1974), although in contrast to Robbins, Brown proposes interventions that are open and direct rather than deceptive and manipulative. For example, to address too little conflict through altering communications, the consultant can raise suppressed issues or encourage the discussion of potential problems at the interface. To stimulate conflict, the consultant can enlarge the issues by bringing in larger related problems or identifying the principles at stake. Under reframing perspectives, the consultant can reduce unrealistic stereotypes of similarity between the parties or can clarify the forces that are working to reduce conflict. Brown emphasizes that in working to achieve an optimal level of conflict, consultants must be sensitive to the specific circumstances of each situation and to their own values.

Brown (1983) presents a variety of situations where organizations failed to deal effectively with either too little or too much conflict, and paid a range of prices for their negligence. Detailed cases include interdepartmental conflict between production and maintenance in a chemicals company, a levels interface between workers and management at a city transit authority, and cultural conflict between blacks and whites in a hospital laboratory. In the first two cases, unique and complex interventions were implemented which addressed difficulties at the interface and resulted in more effective long-term relations with attendant benefits to the organizations. In the third case, the suppressed cultural conflict first escalated and then stalemated, eventually debilitating and fractionating the consultant team and requiring the involvement of the next level of management to achieve some positive outcomes. Brown concludes by discussing the advantages and disadvantages of the various types of interventions, and by offering some rules of thumb for intervenors who wish to deal with interface conflicts.

The professional field of organization development has grown significantly in the last thirty years and consists of a wide variety of interventions designed to improve organizational functioning. French and Bell (1995) provide a comprehensive survey of this field and include third party peacemaking and intergroup problem solving interventions in their coverage. This example demonstrates how conflict management is now regarded as an integral part of the wider practice of organization development. There are both advantages and disadvantages to this. On the one hand, it is useful that dealing with conflict is seen as an essential part of increasing organizational satisfaction and productivity. On the other hand, conflict management interventions are being taken for granted without a large body of rigorous research which demonstrates their efficacy (Fisher, 1983). In addition, the emphasis is typically on de-escalating destructive conflict and does not include the important theme of this book – that stimulating conflict is sometimes necessary in order to improve organizational functioning.

Conclusion and summary

In order to have conflict work for the organization rather than against it, consultants and/or managers must first decide whether there is too much or too little in any given situation. Brown (1983) provides a number of indicators to assist in such a diagnosis in terms of four critical dimensions: perceptions, communications, actions and outcomes. Too much conflict is signalled by good vs. bad perceptions, mistrust and hostility, and a lack of recognition of common interests. Communication is restricted and distorted, and coercive influence attempts are directed towards the other party. Dysfunctional outcomes include poor decision making, harmful effects on the parties, and a deterioration in future relations, especially in the capacity to manage conflict productively. On the other hand, too little conflict is indicated by the denial of critical differences between the parties and the suppression of controversial information. Disagreements are not brought to the surface, and decisions are thus based on inadequate information and analysis, and outmoded traditions and myths are perpetuated to the detriment of the organization. Nonetheless, Brown notes that there are no easy answers to the question of what level of conflict is just right, and that each situation is unique and has to be judged on its own merits.

In this regard, Van de Vliert and De Dreu (1994) argue that conflict stimulation is appropriate when dealing with task issues, but that when identity issues are involved, a conflict de-escalation intervention would be prescribed. However, in designing and implementing an intervention, consultants know that task and identity issues often become interfused in the same conflict. Thus, in situations of high intensity, the confrontation must deal with identity issues and move through them to the task issues, where mutual understanding and joint action are more likely to occur. This usually means stimulating conflict within the context of the intervention in order to diagnose and remedy the difficulties. In situations of low intensity, the intervention is geared directly to stimulation, so that the parties come to see the investment they actually have in the issues, usually task ones, and are motivated to manage the conflict directly. In either case, one goal of the intervention is to establish a moderate level of tension so that performance is enhanced both within and beyond the confrontation.

It is also assumed that many conflicts are mixed motive, i.e. they evidence both negative and positive goal interdependence. In conflict suppression, the parties may be ignoring or de-emphasizing the negative, conflicting goals, while in conflict escalation they typically do not see the positive, shared goals. Again, in conflict stimulation the consultant should assist the parties in acknowledging and dealing with the incompatible goals, while in conflict management the consultant works to bring to the surface common goals and build joint action towards achieving them. Thus, the third party must tailor the intervention to each unique situation.

To summarize, the field of conflict resolution typically prescribes strategies for collaboration, problem solving and integration for both managers and consultants. There exist, however, some exceptions calling for conflict stimulation to raise intensity to a productive level when so required. Third party consultation is a well-accepted method which first stimulates conflict as part of the differentiation phase of problem solving, and then moves to integration and closure. This approach is compatible with Van de Vliert's work on escalative interventions focused on the five core elements of conflict.

The model of third party consultation provides a base for understanding and describing the controlled stimulation of conflict to useful levels. First, a credible and impartial identity and a relationship of respect and trust with the parties is necessary for them to enter into the crucible of conflict interaction. Second, the design of the confrontation must provide a setting and an agenda which supports and sequences the controlled stimulation of intensity. The third party stipulates ground rules which invite open expression, and often adds items to the agenda which escalate conflict. The examination of underlying needs, fears and wants is a necessary part of the analysis before integration can proceed. Finally, each of the third party functions makes a contribution to the controlled stimulation of conflict through direct interventions.

The practice of third party consultation evidences a number of applications which illustrate the utility of conflict stimulation and escalation prior to resolution. Brown adds to this literature by describing a comprehensive model for dealing with both too little and too much conflict at organizational interfaces. In conclusion, third party consultation provides an approach for optimizing the constructive use of conflict in organizational settings, assuming that each programme is tailored to the unique aspects of the particular situation.

Note

The author would like to thank Martin Rempel for research assistance in the preparation of this chapter.

References

Bach, G.R. and Wyden, P. (1969). *The intimate enemy*. New York: Morrow.

Blake, R.R. and Mouton, J.S. (1961). Union–management relations: From conflict to collaboration. *Personnel, 38*, November/December, 38–51.

Blake, R.R., Mouton, J.S. and Sloma, R.L. (1965). The union–management intergroup laboratory. *Journal of Applied Behavioral Science, 1*, 25–57.

Blake, R.R., Shepard, H.A. and Mouton, J.S. (1964). *Managing intergroup conflict in industry*. Houston, TX: Gulf.

Blumberg, A. and Weiner, W. (1971). One from two: Facilitating an organizational merger. *Journal of Applied Behavioral Science, 7*, 87–102.

Brown, L.D. (1983). *Managing conflict at organizational interfaces*. Reading, MA: Addison-Wesley.

Burke, W.W. (1974). Managing conflict between groups, in J.D. Adams (ed.), *Theory and method in organization development: an evolutionary process*. Arlington, VA: NTL Institute, pp. 255–68.

Burton, J.W. (1969). *Conflict and communication: the use of controlled communication in international relations.* London: Macmillan.

Doob, L.W. (ed.) (1970). *Resolving conflict in Africa: the Fermeda workshop.* New Haven, CT: Yale University Press.

Fisher, R.J. (1972). Third party consultation: a method for the study and resolution of conflict. *Journal of Conflict Resolution, 16,* 67–94.

Fisher, R.J. (1976). Third party consultation: a skill for professional psychologists in community practice. *Professional Psychology, 7,* 344–51.

Fisher, R.J. (1983). Third party consultation as a method of intergroup conflict resolution: a review of studies. *Journal of Conflict Resolution, 27,* 301–34.

Fisher, R.J. and Keashly, L. (1990). Third party consultation as a method of intergroup and international conflict resolution, in R.J. Fisher, *The social psychology of intergroup and international conflict resolution.* New York: Springer-Verlag, pp. 211–38.

Follett, M.P. (1924). *Creative experience.* New York: Longmans, Green & Co.

French, W.L. and Bell, C.H. (1995). *Organization development: Behavioral science interventions for organization improvement* (5th edn). Englewood Cliffs, NJ: Prentice-Hall.

Golembiewski, R.T. and Blumberg, A. (1967). Confrontation as a training design in complex organizations: Attitudinal changes in a diversified population of managers. *Journal of Applied Behavioral Science, 3,* 525–47.

Metcalf, H.C. and Urwick, L. (eds) (1940). *Dynamic administration: the collected papers of Mary Parker Follett.* New York: Harper & Brothers.

Robbins, S.P. (1974). *Managing organizational conflict: a nontraditional approach.* Englewood Cliffs, NJ: Prentice-Hall.

Schmidt, W.H. and Tannenbaum, R. (1960). Management of differences. *Harvard Business Review, 38,* December, 107–15.

Van de Vliert, E. (1985). Escalative intervention in small-group conflicts. *Journal of Applied Behavioral Science, 21,* 19–36.

Van de Vliert, E. and De Dreu, C.K.W. (1994). Optimizing performance by conflict stimulation. *International Journal of Conflict Management, 5,* 211–22.

Walton, R.E. (1969). *Interpersonal peacemaking: Confrontations and third party consultation.* Reading, MA: Addison-Wesley.

Walton, R.E. (1987). *Managing conflict: Interpersonal dialogue and third party roles* (2nd edn). Reading, MA: Addison-Wesley.

14

Enhancing Performance by Conflict-Stimulating Intervention

Evert Van de Vliert

Conflict is both an enemy and a friend on our perpetual expedition to organizational efficiency and effectiveness. The authors in this book have painted
an impressive and intriguing kaleidoscopic portrait of conflict as a friend.
This is a one-sided picture. However, overstating the desirability and produc-
tiveness of conflict makes sense in view of the fact that, especially outside
scholarly circles, conflict is still predominantly viewed as undesirable and
unproductive. Consequently, as a rule, not only principal parties, but also
amateur third parties including bystanders, managers and constituents, do
not use conflict escalation as a vehicle for optimizing organizational performance. Even professional intervenors carrying conflict-stimulating strategies
in their 'tool chest' are few and far between. For example, Prein (1982) did not
find a single case of escalative intervention in his empirical study of sixty-nine
conflict intervention projects carried out by internal and external organization consultants (but see Laskewitz, Van de Vliert & De Dreu, 1994, for the
occurrence of escalative intervention by personnel managers).

Taking an intervention perspective, this final chapter focuses on forms of
deliberate induction and escalation of organizational conflict as one key to
higher performance. It summarizes and discusses what can be learned from
the previous chapters by attempting to answer the following questions. Why
is conflict-stimulating intervention so rare in the first place? What are appropriate objectives for intervenors who seek to enhance performance by conflict
stimulation? How can entry points of action for such strategic intervention be
mapped best? And, finally, which strategies of conflict-stimulating intervention are to be recommended in particular?

Why is conflict-stimulating intervention so rare?

In the context of this book, intervention refers to a systematic operation
through which an outsider seeks to enhance the overall efficiency or effectiveness of the behaviour of the participants in an organizational conflict. As
mentioned above, de-escalative intervention is the rule, and escalative intervention is the exception which proves the rule. This overexposure of
de-escalative intervention holds for both practitioners (e.g. Mastenbroek,

1987; Moore, 1986) and academic researchers (e.g. Carnevale, 1986; Conlon, Carnevale & Murnighan, 1994; Elangovan, 1995; Karambayya & Brett, 1994; Kolb, 1986; Pinkley, Brittain, Neale & Northcraft, 1995). How come? The role relationship between the intervenor and the conflicting parties suggests two more specific questions: Why don't the principal parties demand conflict stimulation? Why doesn't the intervenor apply conflict stimulation? Needless to say, there are no definitive answers to these queries, but some educated speculation may provide food for further theory development.

Almost by definition, conflict issues are accompanied by cognitive and affective strain. As evidenced in several preceding chapters, the short-term consequences of this aversive state include the experience of feelings of being obstructed or irritated by the other party (e.g. Baron, Chapter 12), the painful suppression of outward reactions to the conflict issue experienced (e.g. Turner & Pratkanis, Chapter 4), taking the trouble of losing, winning or solving the conflict (e.g. Carnevale & Probst, Chapter 9), and mutual misunderstanding and distrust (e.g. Van de Vliert, Nauta, Euwema & Janssen, Chapter 3). In short, the immediate consequences of conflict are often costly rather than beneficial for the principal parties. For that obvious reason, it is unlikely that the victims of the discord themselves will confront potential intervenors with the role expectation of triggering escalation. Sure, disputants often try to involve one or more outsiders in the conflict. But, depending on their own modes of conflict management, they enlist these outsiders to avoid, cover up, win or solve the issue, seldomly to deliberately intensify the conflict (Rubin & Sander, 1988; Van de Vliert, 1981), let alone to employ conflict stimulation as a means for improving joint performance.

Compared to the role of the physician, the role of the intervenor in organizational conflict is still in its infancy (cf. Kressel & Pruitt, 1989). Like the role of the physician in ancient times, the role of today's intervenor is to prevent and to cure organizational discord, and to care for principal and other aggrieved parties. Unlike today's physician, who is familiar with the idea that controlled induction of illness through vaccination improves physical functioning in the longer run, to date only few intervenors have internalized a similar insight about limited stimulation of conflict to improve organizational functioning in the longer run (see Robbins, 1974 for an early exception, and Van de Vliert, 1985 for a later elaboration). Indeed, there is no such thing as a role of conflict stimulator, although this book reflects some signs that intervenors in the role of go-between, mediator, arbitrator or decision making authority are beginning to recognize the value of controlled conflict stimulation.

Objectives of conflict stimulation

First and foremost, this chapter is dedicated to improved organizational efficiency and effectiveness as the ultimate goal of purposeful conflict induction and intensification. That is, conflict stimulation serves as an instrumental goal, as a stepping stone to the desired ultimate performance effects. The conflict can, however, act as an instrument in three different ways. The overall objective may be brought nearer along the prototypic routes of conflict as a direct or indirect determinant of improved organizational functioning, or as a necessary but insufficient condition for such improvement. Scattered throughout the book, the authors suggest at least nine objectives of conflict stimulation, which may easily be subsumed under the headings of striving for direct, indirect or conditional effects on organizational performance (see Table 14.1).

Table 14.1 *Objectives of conflict stimulation*

	Performance effects	
Direct	Indirect	Conditional
Decision quality	Intragroup cooperation	Group identity maintenance
Decision consensus	Learning to fight fairly	Differentiation before integration
Acceptance of team members	Optimal level of tension	Constructive controversy

Direct performance effects

Amason and Schweiger (Chapter 7; see also Amason, 1996) portray three end states of enhanced organizational performance that may be reached in a straightforward manner with the help of cognitive and affective conflict. The first, *decision quality*, refers to the effective achievement of a substantive goal. Cognitive conflict moves decision makers towards high quality production, whereas affective conflict moves them away from high quality production. A dual subgoal, therefore, is to search for, emphasize, magnify and intensify the cognitive aspects, and to avoid, de-emphasize, reduce and mitigate the affective aspects of organizational conflict (see also Jehn, Chapter 6).

Amason and Schweiger's other objectives, *decision consensus* and affective *acceptance of team members*, refer to the effective achievement of relational goals. Cognitive conflict is assumed to also move decision makers towards more common understanding, commitment and mutual acceptance; again, affective conflict is assumed to have opposite effects. If this is a valid pair of assumptions – and Amason (1996) makes a strong case that it is – much cognitive conflict and little affective conflict will produce much group consensus and unity, thus more chance of groupthink. Consequently, the otherwise attractive goals of group consensus and unity may sometimes degenerate into the goal of group identity maintenance that works out unproductively in the end (Turner & Pratkanis, Chapter 4). Perhaps the pursuit of moderate rather than high degrees of decision consensus and mutual acceptance is an even better pair of objectives. Clearly, on this point, the debate continues unabated.

Indirect performance effects

Thanks to the early experiments of Blake and Mouton (1961), and Sherif (1966), we have known for decades that, as a rule, the objective of *intragroup cooperation* and subsequent productivity can be achieved through intergroup competition. Bornstein and Erev (Chapter 8) and Carnevale and Probst (Chapter 9) now demonstrate that the intragroup performance can be accounted for at least in part by motivational, rather than structural, effects of the intergroup competition. In this context, too, the distinction between cognitive and affective issues may play a part. Doise and Lorenzi-Cioldi (1989) reviewed the connections between intergroup and intragroup relations, and showed that intergroup hostility can also generate intragroup competition, especially when the affective relations between the ingroup members are brought into focus (for an intervention case where the intergroup discord produced cooperation within the one group but competition within the other, see Van de Vliert, 1995).

As briefly mentioned by Fisher (Chapter 13), *learning to fight fairly* is yet another reason for strategic escalation of a conflict. Many family therapists primarily aim to teach married couples how to implement fair fights. Bach and Wyden (1969), for example, emphasize openness, honesty, equality and reciprocity as relevant criteria to differentiate between fair and unfair fights, and to keep fights fair. They contend that the ultimate goal should be to pursue a better relationship instead of a knockout. To that end, the intervenor must teach the parties not only to communicate better with one another, but also – and especially – to acquire skills in communicating about the rules that they themselves are developing for fair conflict management: no bluffing, generalizations or ultimatums; no underhandedness; no aiming for the opponent's Achilles' heel; no deliberate actions in either the presence or the absence of certain outsiders; and the like.

The next objective of conflict stimulation, an *optimal level of tension* (De Dreu, Chapter 1; Fisher, Chapter 13), has received considerable scholarly attention (e.g. Brown, 1983; Fisher, 1990; Levi, 1981; Rahim, 1992; Robbins, 1974; Van de Vliert, 1996; Walton, 1969). It is rooted in Yerkes and Dodson's (1908) classic demonstration of an inverted U-shaped relation between need level and task achievement, regardless of the complexity of the task. Sixty years later, Walton (1969) operationalized need level as level of tension, and task achievement as the productivity of a conflict interaction. On the basis of persuasive experimental and experiential evidence he postulated that an individual's capacity for complex and effective thinking is altered in a curvilinear fashion as the level of tension increases. Specifically, conflicts at a low level of tension lead to inactivity and avoidance, neglect of information and low joint performance as there is no sense of urgency and no necessity to act assertively. Because a group's maximum ability to compromise or to solve a conflict occurs at some moderate level of tension, low tension conflicts require limited stimulation to enhance performance and well-being.

As a case in point, De Dreu and De Vries (Chapter 5) discuss why and how conflict in the form of minority deviation from a majority position elicits divergent thinking. If the escalation is kept within bounds, such minority dissent produces greater creativity, better solutions to complex problems, and more adequate responses to a changing environment. Similarly, in her study of teachers' negotiations, Putnam (Chapter 10) observes that controlled conflict escalation helps in discovering problems and uncovering divergent opinions about a variety of affairs.

Conditional performance effects

According to Turner and Pratkanis (Chapter 4), widely accepted goals and procedures for stimulating intragroup conflict often fail to enhance performance in situations where social identity protection pressures are operative. In such situations, conflict-stimulating interventions will have performance-enhancing effects only if the condition of *group identity maintenance* is also met. Interventions, such as generating, evaluating and selecting action alternatives, should therefore be designed to facilitate the critical processing of ideas, assumptions and plans in ways that are supportive rather than threatening to group membership and group distinctiveness. The challenging dual objective is to sail between the Scylla of groupthink and the Charybdis of driving the group to the wall.

'Reformed sinner strategy' (Deutsch, 1973), 'black-hat/white-hat routine' (Hilty & Carnevale, 1993) and conglomerated conflict behaviour of 'forcing followed by problem solving' (Van de Vliert et al., Chapter 3) all refer to the phases that effective conflict intervention must necessarily go through. Following Walton (1969; Fisher, Chapter 13), the corresponding objective may be labelled *differentiation before integration*. The core idea is that conflict intensification through distributive behaviour has a beneficial effect on organizational performance only if it is designed as a prelude to conflict mitigation through integrative behaviour. It is most likely that it also helps when the conflicting parties are aware of and agree with the desirability of the behavioural sequence of differentiation before integration.

Tjosvold (Chapter 2) advocates *constructive controversy*, the open-minded discussion of opposing views, as the ideal goal of optimizing performance by conflict stimulation. In his view, however, constructive controversy is possible only in combination with promotive outcome interdependence between the parties to the conflict. Only in such a cooperative reward context (Amason & Schweiger, Chapter 7) is it in everyone's self-interest to promote each other's effectiveness, to freely speak their minds and to engage in conflictful discussions. In contrast, under competitive conditions efforts to implement constructive controversy take a destructive course as people are more likely to avoid conflict, try to win the fight or even dissolve the relationship.

Relativization?

Three marginal notes may put this overview in perspective. First, the list of objectives is intended to be neither exhaustive with respect to all possible goals of escalative conflict intervention nor necessarily mutually exclusive. For example, it neglects egocentric motives of intervenors who use conflict escalation as a vehicle for increasing their own influence and prestige (Van de Vliert, 1992). However, the list of objectives does seem to represent a relevant range and categorization of the kinds of goals that can be set in making the most of organizational conflict.

Second, the intervenor's choice to deliberately stimulate organizational conflict raises ethical issues. Can escalative objectives pass from a moral viewpoint? Specifically, given the fact that escalation has detrimental rather than beneficial short-term consequences for the principal parties, conflict intensification involves manipulation. This confronts the intervenor with a basic dilemma. On the one hand, manipulation inherently violates the conflicting parties' fundamental right to make free, informed choices. On the other hand, there exists no formula for so structuring an effective conflict intervention that such manipulation is totally absent (cf. Kelman, 1965). However, the two horns of the unavoidable dilemma hurt less if we make a clear distinction between (a) *free choice*: the extent to which each party can put its stamp on a decision, (b) *effective choice*: the extent to which a decision achieves the result desired by each of the parties, and (c) *good choice*: the extent to which a decision contributes to the overall efficacy of the parties' organization (Van de Vliert, 1977). In my opinion, a manipulative conflict-stimulating intervention is acceptable if it fosters good choices that enhance organizational performance rather than free choices that enhance personal effectiveness. Similarly, Buchanan and Boddy (1992) take the position that most manipulative interventions are acceptable and ethical in context, and that, in the pursuit of desirable organizational performance, they can be considered 'benign interventions'.

Third, none of the objectives of conflict stimulation is conceptually related to a certain type of conflict issue or to a specific technique of conflict intensification. It implies that the relations between the objectives and the intervention strategies are, in essence, assumed to be characterized by equifinality. According to this principle, intervenors can attain the same objective of conflict stimulation, although they may proceed from initially different organizational conflict situations and use a variety of intervention strategies.

Entry points for intervention

Only if intervenors start actively to pursue the above objectives of conflict stimulation will this help counterbalance the customary practice of thinking and intervening predominantly in terms of de-escalation. Logically, the next question reads: What elements of the conflict can an intervenor use for strategic action to realize escalation if desired? An integration of structural and process models of organizational conflict (Van de Vliert, in press a) high-lighted four salient conflict elements that may be used to establish entry points appropriate for conflict stimulation. I will proceed from the following propositions (cf. Van de Vliert, 1985):

A. The elements the parties in conflict use either consciously or subcon-sciously for altering their levels of perceived obstruction or felt irritation are antecedent conditions, conflict issues, conflict behaviours and conse-quences.
B. The conflicting parties may use these four elements both to lower (de-escalate) and to raise (escalate) their levels of perceived obstruction or felt irritation.
C. The four elements used by the conflicting parties themselves for lowering or raising their levels of perceived obstruction or felt irritation are also most suitable as entry points for de-escalative or escalative intervention by outsiders.

As I am concerned with stimulation rather than mitigation of conflict, I will at this point disregard strategic de-escalation. This is not to say that pur-poseful conflict mitigation is less important. On the contrary, de-escalative interventions are indispensable for successful conflict intensification because they counteract escalation and thus allow one to keep the risky escalative intervention under control. Perhaps for that reason, the alternation of conflict escalation and de-escalation might be a relatively effective strategy (Van de Vliert et al., Chapter 3).

Figure 14.1 presents the above propositions A to C, taking into account my focus on conflict stimulation. Because each entry point of action corresponds to various escalative interventions, the model has an ordering function. In fact, it represents a typology of four conflict-stimulating strategies, which I will elaborate upon below. Many commonalities among these types of escala-tive intervention are apparent, although I believe the differences between them are sufficiently significant to justify the distinction.

Strategies of conflict-stimulating intervention

As represented in Figure 14.1, the intervenor may concentrate on (I) manip-ulating antecedent conditions; (II) extending the conflict issues; (III) stimulating escalative behaviours; or (IV) developing escalative consequences. Partly because they occur so rarely, the strategies of conflict stimulation have not yet been fully developed and tested. This is a serious restriction that should inspire one to use caution in applying any escalative intervention at all. Moreover, for types I and II, the controllability of the resulting intensifi-cation is subject to additional restrictions, which will be discussed in a later, evaluative section.

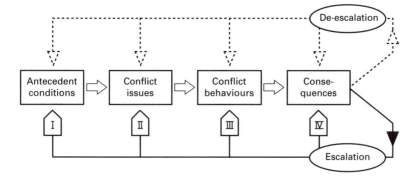

Figure 14.1   *Four types of conflict-stimulating intervention*

I. Manipulating antecedent conditions

Conflict issues are rooted in organization characteristics (e.g. joint means), group characteristics (e.g. ingroup/outgroup differentiation), relation characteristics (e.g. unfair inequality) or individual characteristics (e.g. dogmatism). It is therefore possible to apply operations intended to actuate an obstruction or irritation on the basis of those antecedent conditions. In this vein, Robbins (1974) recommended the implementation of conflict-prone contexts in the form of complex organizational structures, redistribution of resources, irreconcilable collective goals, changeable styles of leadership, unacceptable role prescriptions, carefully contrived transfers and the like. An intervenor may also reinforce some specific conflict-stimulating factor, such as disappointment, a somewhat overwrought reservation or distrust. Walton (1969, p. 76) stated: 'We refer to these stimuli as *triggering events*, and propose that they can have their effect either by increasing the magnitude or salience of the issues in the conflict or by lowering one of the barriers to action.' Barriers to be lowered include physical obstacles, lack of time, public image and the vulnerability of one party.

In this book, Bornstein and Erev, and Carnevale and Probst highlight the productivity of organizing intergroup competition; and Turner and Pratkanis recommend structured discussion principles as appropriate techniques for eliciting conflict through antecedent conditions. Furthermore, Amason and Schweiger, and Jehn emphasize the manipulation of who will work with whom in order to increase profitable heterogeneity and value diversity in task groups. However, these last authors view differences among employees as only one side of the coin. Members of work teams should also be assisted to develop norms of openness and tolerance of differing viewpoints, which encourage them to express their doubts, disagreements and demands (see De Dreu & De Vries, Chapter 5). Such norms are only one manifestation of regulating mechanisms that influence the form the conflict takes and the (de-)escalating course of the process.

Regulating mechanisms also include permissible 'weapons' and manoeuvres, such as the custom of face-to-face confrontation, procedures in cases of disagreement or grievance such as enlisting an ombudsman, and rights and duties such as the right to appeal. The intervenor who eliminates, suspends or takes less seriously some de-escalative regulating mechanism, or who implements or reactivates some escalative regulating mechanism, often takes up a double-edged sword. Donnellon and Kolb's chapter on disputes rooted in or complicated by social diversity provides an apt illustration. Nowadays a wide array of organizations has installed formal complaint systems to give employees voice in the expression of their grievances that have gender, racial or ethnic significance. On the one hand, these dispute resolution systems stimulate conflict by bringing to the surface hidden frustrations and magnifying trivialized issues. On the other hand, they tend to individualize problems, thus preventing organizations from recognizing and addressing the possible generality and institutional background and bedding of the conflict.

When a professional helper enters the stage, a particularly relevant set of regulating mechanisms is agreed upon in the intervention contract. Fisher (Chapter 13) discusses the following ground rules that may help build a productive discordant atmosphere: the approach to the conflict must be confidential rather than public, analytical rather than adversarial, and depersonalized rather than personalized. An additional ground rule reads that the problematization, confrontation and finalization of the conflict must remain in the principal parties' hands. Interestingly, this nondirective approach not only reduces the necessity of manipulation but also, according to Bush and Folger (1994), who propagated this ground rule, opens up the possibility of a new conception of intervenor neutrality. Neutrality may take the shape of the intervenor's commitment to use the inevitable influence of the escalative intervention only for the sake of keeping free, effective and good choices in the principal parties' hands.

II. Extending conflict issues

As indicated in De Dreu's introductory chapter, a variety of conflict issues exists including division of scarce resources, goal setting, procedural choice, role prescription, and threatened individual or group identity. These issues can be created, enlarged or sharpened through escalative intervention from the outside.

First of all, lifeless work dyads, teams or departments whose members 'dozed off' can be revived by creating or bringing to the surface mutual disagreement, and by giving the new issue substantive and social boundaries, and a clear label. Both Putnam and Fisher address this strategy in Chapters 10 and 13 respectively. More structured, well-known techniques for injecting controversy into decision making processes are dialectical inquiry and devil's advocacy (see for descriptions and references De Dreu & De Vries, Chapter 5, and Amason & Schweiger, Chapter 7). But Turner and Pratkanis (Chapter 4) argue that these and similar strategies may decrease rather than increase the number or comprehensiveness of conflict issues when social identity maintenance pressures exist. Instead, they recommend the use of the 'two column method' as a conflict-stimulating device by listing and rating the advantages and disadvantages of all aspects of the conflict situation and of all possible courses of action.

Additionally, an intervenor can enlarge the conflict by tying a disputed topic to previously conflict-free topics. The parties' tasks and relationship, loyalty, norms of fairness and appropriate behaviour, as well as broader goals and visions, can all be handy for this purpose (Lax & Sebenius, 1986). For example, on one occasion I linked an old trench fight between a school principal and a few teachers to the fresh topic of the next year's teaching schedule. The demanding way in which one of the teachers then treated the principal was subsequently turned into an extra issue that unfolded as a first step to ultimately overcoming the impasse. Note that this intervention demonstrates the use of the tendency for issues to proliferate from different positions, interests and emotions towards different evaluations of each other's conflict behaviour.

Among the most straightforward tactics of sharpening the issues (Fisher, Chapter 13) are raising the perceived stakes and emphasizing the importance of the matter. The conflict may be reformulated so that the parties come to see it more in an abstract way, as a matter of principle, in terms of either–or, and therefore as harder to solve. The intervenor may wash some dirty linen in public through whistle blowing, outlined by De Dreu and De Vries (Chapter 5). Also, cognitive conflict can be intensified in the direction of feelings of denial of one's own identity. Though the authors in this book agree on the rule of thumb that cognitive task-orientated issues should be promoted while affective identity-orientated issues should be avoided, it seems wise not to absolutize this advice. A temporary intensification of the parties' emotional involvement can be more fruitful than a too considerate and too cautious cognitive approach, which, unintentionally, often tends to obscure the real personalized aspects of the conflict.

III. Stimulating escalative behaviours

The main ways to elicit escalative reactions, other than through the seriousness of the issues, are that the intervenor prescribes, encourages or provokes contentious behaviour.

When the principal parties are dependent on the intervening third, this third party especially holds a position to steer the course of the conflict process by, for example, stipulating that one party should prove to the other that it is right, vent all its feelings or depict the opposite party as unreliable. Such a third party also has the power to establish procedures for protecting minority opinions to facilitate the critical evaluation of potential decisions (Turner & Pratkanis, Chapter 4; De Dreu & De Vries, Chapter 5), or for supporting collective action taken by a minority coalition (Donnellon & Kolb, Chapter 11). The context of the intervention plus possible additional rules of play ensure that the confrontations will have the character of a 'limited war' (Shepard, 1964).

The aforementioned objective of learning to fight fairly implies the gradual and joint development of a set of prescriptions that makes forcing actions predictable, acceptable and retaliatable, and the actors mutually accountable, forthright and frank (Amason & Schweiger, Chapter 7). Once an operationalization of fair fighting is agreed upon, no party may unilaterally change it. Perhaps most importantly, to fight fairly means that one must not only inflict fair blows but also receive them (Van de Vliert, 1985). Many people should learn to give their opponent an opportunity to strike back, just as many people should learn to receive and absorb blows in a more constructive manner. Some consider almost every confrontation a blow below the belt. They will have to change their limits for fair conflict management in order to make themselves accessible to healthy aggressive approaches by their conflict partners (Bach & Wyden, 1969). Others do not sufficiently realize that each blow received says something both about themselves and about the opposite party. Once the intervenor has made such disputants see and recognize this, they will find it less difficult to receive blows.

As yet another method of behavioural escalation, the intervenor may encourage the parties to form a coalition with others or try to influence specific groups or public opinion. Various reasons exist as to why the situation of outsiders taking sides results in escalation (Van de Vliert, 1981). Obviously, one potential coalition partner is the intervening party itself. Wall (1981), Ippolito and Pruitt (1990) and Laskewitz et al. (1994) indeed reported that organizational and other mediators provide information, advice and friendship to weaker conflict parties. Alternatively siding first with one party and then with the other seems to constitute an even more practicable form of escalative intervention. However, Prein (1982) found that organization consultants intervening in interpersonal or intergroup conflicts apply such a technique of alternating support on a rather small scale and to different degrees. I myself have made successful use of a tactic I call 'having them fight over you'. This entails presenting oneself to both parties as a potential ally. A relatively easy way to do this is to meet with each of the parties, asking them who is most to blame. Each party will start to blacken the other and to exculpate itself in order to win your support.

Controlled provocation of escalative behaviours may be realized by avoiding negotiations when a settlement is most obvious; providing reminders of a combative constituency; encouraging hitting back; taking lies, misunderstandings and distortions seriously; permitting everyone to turn a deaf ear, to laugh at the adversary, to interrupt, to speak disparagingly, to utter unfounded accusations, to threaten; and so forth.

IV. Developing escalative consequences

As the feedback loops in Figure 14.1 indicate, conflict behaviours have all kinds of consequences which change the organization, the group and the interpersonal relations, as well as the parties' opinions, emotions and further behavioural reactions. To raise the existing levels of perceived obstruction or felt irritation, an outsider can either create or stress particular consequences.

Escalative consequences are created, for example, by ascribing hostile intentions to relatively neutral or unintentional actions, and by explaining behaviours as signals of unrealistic desires, distrust or even injustice (Baron, Chapter 12; De Dreu et al., 1995b). One can also point to the possible boomerang effects of concealing frustrating issues on the one hand, or putting too much trust in unilateral openness or the unilateral introduction of superordinate goals on the other (Van de Vliert, in press a). Furthermore, a party will usually be sensitive to the intervenor's expectation that it will lose face if it does not stand up better for its own interests. This is a special case of providing a loss rather than gain perspective on the dispute, which generally promotes resistance to concession making and subsequent escalative behaviour in both self and opponent (De Dreu et al., 1995a).

In Chapters 1 (De Dreu), 2 (Tjosvold) and 9 (Carnevale & Probst), concern for one's own and for the other party's goals has been portrayed as a behavioural determinant. If we look at cycles of on-going conflict interactions, however, dual concern qualifies itself as a mediator between preceding and following behaviours. Thus, dual concern, being both consequence and cause, can be pre-eminently utilized to create an escalative conflict spiral. But should the intervenor push the parties in the direction of more concern for one's own goals, less concern for the other's goals, or both? Recently (Janssen & Van de Vliert, 1996; Van de Vliert, in press b) it has been theoretically and empirically shown that developing less concern for the other party's goals constitutes a better vehicle for conflict stimulation than developing more concern for the party's own goals.

Other easily available and applicable kinds of escalative intervention include stressing the intrapersonal conflicts elicited by the opponent's behaviours (Tjosvold, Chapter 2), highlighting feelings of disapproval and distaste and emphasizing visions of victory and defeat. For example, the hierarchical suppression of conflict and other forms of forceful exertion of power, as well as illegitimate steps, arouse negative experiences that can often be employed. Stereotypes as pictured by Baron (Chapter 12), and self-serving evaluations of conflict behaviour (De Dreu et al., 1995), may be used as well. Because of various intrapersonal processes, the parties come to consider themselves as good, reasonable, cooperative, and victimized, and the opposite party as bad, unreasonable, combative and instigative (Carnevale & Probst, Chapter 9; Van de Vliert, in press a). Such black-vs.-white mirror images form an excellent stimulus for new conflict issues and subsequent escalative behaviour, and may therefore be reinforced by an intervenor.

Comparative evaluation

No matter how badly an organization is in need of the above and similar interventions, stimulating conflict is playing with fire. One runs the risk of conjuring up spirits that refuse to be restrained, and the resulting changes may turn out differently from those intended. For this reason, competent third party intervention has to be preferred to implementation of escalation by principal parties themselves. Intervenors should have a sophisticated idea as to the hazards of their task when they select a conflict-stimulating intervention to match an overly harmonious or protest-repressive situation. The following considerations may come in useful:

In general, stimulating escalative behaviours and developing escalative consequences (type III and type IV interventions) are preferable to manipulating antecedent conditions and extending conflict issues (type I and type II interventions), for several reasons. First of all, compared to type I and type II interventions, type III and type IV interventions require less manipulation and have a less permanent nature because the intervenor stays within the boundaries of the principal parties' present definition of the conflict situation. Secondly, the third party's feedback lines to and fro the principal parties are shorter in the case of behaviours and their consequences than in the case of antecedent conditions and resulting conflict issues. In the third place, type III and type IV interventions allow more for escalation by degrees than type I and type II interventions do because they fan out less in unknown directions towards unknown conflict issues and unknown behavioural reactions. A fourth reason to prefer type III and type IV to type I and type II interventions lies in the fact that they allow better for the correction of over-escalation by means of de-escalative interventions. In short, as one moves from I to IV, higher ranked types of escalative intervention deserve preference because of their higher degrees of controllability.

Concluding propositions

This final chapter mapped and discussed objectives and strategies of conflict stimulation that intervening outsiders can use to enhance the organizational performance of conflicting individuals or groups. The most basic and most innovative contributions can be summarized in the following five propositions:

1. Conflict-stimulating intervention is an undervalued and underdeveloped vehicle for optimizing organizational performance (cf. illness-stimulating vaccination).
2. Objectives of conflict stimulation include direct, indirect and conditional performance effects.
3. Intervenors may use antecedent conditions, conflict issues, conflict behaviours and consequences as entry points for escalating the parties' levels of experienced obstruction or irritation.
4. Intervenors can attain each objective of conflict stimulation by means of each strategy of escalative intervention.
5. For reasons of controllability, stimulating escalative behaviours and developing escalative consequences are better suited to piecemeal escalation than manipulating antecedent conditions and extending conflict issues.

Note

Preparation of this chapter was sponsored by Grant 560-270-031 from the Netherlands Organization for Scientific Research (NWO), awarded to Evert Van de Vliert.

References

Amason, A.C. (1996). Distinguishing the effects of functional and dysfunctional conflict on strategic decision making: Resolving a paradox for top management teams. *Academy of Management Journal, 39*, 123–48.

Bach, G.R. and Wyden, P. (1969). *The intimate enemy*. New York: Morrow.

Blake, R.R. and Mouton, J.S. (1961). Reactions to intergroup competition under win–lose conditions. *Management Science, 7*, 420–35.

Brown, L.D. (1983). *Managing conflict at organizational interfaces*. Reading, MA: Addison-Wesley.

Buchanan, D. and Boddy, D. (1992). *The expertise of the change agent*. New York: Prentice-Hall.

Bush, R.A.B. and Folger, J.P. (1994). *The promise of mediation: Responding to conflict through empowerment and recognition*. San Francisco: Jossey-Bass.

Carnevale, P.J. (1986). Strategic choice in mediation. *Negotiation Journal, 2*, 41–56.

Conlon, D., Carnevale, P.J. and Murnighan, K. (1994). Intravention: Third-party intervention with clout. *Organizational Behavior and Human Decision Processes, 57*, 387–410.

De Dreu, C.K.W., Carnevale, P.J.D., Emans, B.J.M. and Van de Vliert, E. (1995a). Outcome frames in bilateral negotiation: Resistance to concession making and frame adoption, in W. Stroebe and M. Hewstone (eds), *European review of social psychology*. Chichester: John Wiley & Sons, Vol. 6, pp. 97–125.

De Dreu, C.K.W., Nauta, A. and Van de Vliert, E. (1995b). Self-serving evaluations of conflict behavior and escalation of the dispute. *Journal of Applied Social Psychology, 25*, 2049–66.

Deutsch, M. (1973). *The resolution of conflict: Constructive and destructive processes*. New Haven, CT: Yale University Press.

Doise, W. and Lorenzi-Cioldi, F. (1989). Patterns of differentiation within and between groups, in J.P. van Oudenhoven and T.M. Willemsen (eds), *Ethnic minorities: Social psychological perspectives*. Amsterdam/Lisse: Swets & Zeitlinger, pp. 43–57.

Elangovan, A.R. (1995). Managerial third-party dispute intervention: a prescriptive model of strategy selection. *Academy of Management Journal, 20*, 800–30.

Fisher, R.J. (1990). *The social psychology of intergroup and international conflict resolution*. Berlin: Springer-Verlag.

Hilty, J.A. and Carnevale, P.J. (1993). Black-hat/white-hat strategy in bilateral negotiation. *Organizational Behavior and Human Decision Processes, 55*, 444–69.

Ippolito, C.A. and Pruitt, D.G. (1990). Power balancing in mediation: Outcomes and implications of mediator intervention. *International Journal of Conflict Management, 1*, 341–55.

Janssen, O. and Van de Vliert, E. (1996). Concern for the other's goals: Key to (de-)escalation of conflict. *International Journal of Conflict Management, 7*, 99–120.

Karambayya, R. and Brett, J.M. (1994). Managerial third parties: Intervention strategies, process, and consequences, in J. Folger & T. Jones (eds), *New directions in mediation: Communication research and perspectives*. Thousand Oaks, CA: Sage, pp. 175–92.

Kelman, H.C. (1965). Manipulation of human behavior: an ethical dilemma for the social scientist. *Journal of Social Issues, 21*, 31–46.

Kolb, D. (1986). Who are organizational third parties and what do they do? in R.J. Lewicki, B.H. Sheppard and M.H. Bazerman (eds), *Research on negotiation in organizations*. Greenwich, CT: JAI Press, Vol. 1, pp. 207–28.

Kressel, K. and Pruitt, D.G. (1989). Conclusion: a research perspective on the mediation of social conflict, in K. Kressel and D.G. Pruitt (eds), *Mediation research: the process and effectiveness of third-party intervention*. San Francisco: Jossey-Bass, pp. 394–435.

Laskewitz, P., Van de Vliert, E. and De Dreu, C.K.W. (1994). Organizational mediators siding with or against the powerful party? *Journal of Applied Social Psychology, 24*, 176–88.

Lax, D.A. and Sebenius, J.K. (1986). *The manager as negotiator: Bargaining for cooperation and competitive gain.* New York: Free Press.

Levi, L. (1981). *Preventing work stress.* Reading, MA: Addison-Wesley.

Mastenbroek, W.F.G. (1987). *Conflict management and organization development.* Chichester: John Wiley & Sons.

Moore, C.W. (1986). *The mediation process: Practical strategies for resolving conflict.* San Francisco: Jossey-Bass.

Pinkley, R.L., Brittain, J., Neale, M.A. and Northcraft, G.B. (1995). Managerial third-party dispute intervention: an inductive analysis of intervenor strategy selection. *Journal of Applied Psychology, 80*, 386–402.

Prein, H.C.M. (1982). *Conflicthantering door een derde partij* (Conflict management by a third party). Lisse: Swets & Zeitlinger.

Rahim, M.A. (1992). *Managing conflict in organizations* (2nd edn). Westport, CT: Praeger.

Robbins, S.P. (1974). *Managing organizational conflict: a nontraditional approach.* Englewood Cliffs, NJ: Prentice-Hall.

Rubin, J.Z. and Sander, F.E.A. (1988). When should we use agents? Direct vs. representative negotiation. *Negotiation Journal, 4*, 395–401.

Shepard, H.A. (1964). Responses to situations of competition and conflict, in R.L. Kahn and E. Boulding (eds), *Power and conflict in organizations.* London: Tavistock, pp. 127–35.

Sherif, M. (1966). *In common predicament.* Boston, MA: Houghton-Mifflin.

Van de Vliert, E. (1977). Inconsistencies in the Argyris intervention theory. *Journal of Applied Behavioral Science, 13*, 557–64.

Van de Vliert, E. (1981). Siding and other reactions to a conflict: a theory of escalation toward outsiders. *Journal of Conflict Resolution, 25*, 495–520.

Van de Vliert, E. (1985). Escalative intervention in small-group conflicts. *Journal of Applied Behavioral Science, 21*, 19–36.

Van de Vliert, E. (1992). Questions about the strategic choice model of mediation. *Negotiation Journal, 8*, 379–86.

Van de Vliert, E. (1995). Helpless helpers: An intergroup conflict intervention. *International Journal of Conflict Management, 6*, 91–100.

Van de Vliert, E. (1996). Interventions in conflicts, in M.J. Schabracq, J.A.M. Winnubst and C.L. Cooper (eds), *Handbook of work and health psychology.* Chichester: John Wiley & Sons, pp. 405–25.

Van de Vliert, E. (in press a). Conflict and conflict management, in H. Thierry, P.J.D. Drenth and C.J. de Wolff (eds), *A new handbook of work and organisational psychology.* Hove: Erlbaum (UK) Taylor & Francis.

Van de Vliert, E. (in press b). *Theoretical frontiers of complex interpersonal conflict behaviour.* Hove: Erlbaum (UK) Taylor & Francis.

Wall, J.A. (1981). Mediation: an analysis, review, and proposed research. *Journal of Conflict Resolution, 25*, 157–80.

Walton, R.E. (1969). *Interpersonal peacemaking: Confrontations and third party consultation.* Reading, MA: Addison-Wesley.

Yerkes, R.M. and Dodson, J.D. (1908). The relation of strength of stimulus to rapidity of habit formation. *Journal of Comparative Neurological Psychology, 18*, 459–82.

Subject index

Author index

DATE DUE